MAKING MEN

A bust thought to be of Polemo, found in the Olympieion of Athens and now in the National Archaeological Museum of Athens, inv. no. 427.

MAKING MEN

SOPHISTS AND SELF-PRESENTATION IN ANCIENT ROME

MAUD W. GLEASON

PRINCETON UNIVERSITY PRESS

PRINCETON, NEW JERSEY

Copyright © 1995 by Princeton University Press
Published by Princeton University Press, 41 William Street,
Princeton, New Jersey 08540
In the United Kingdom: Princeton University Press, Chichester, West Sussex

Library of Congress Cataloging-in-Publication Data

Gleason, Maud W., 1954–
Making men : sophists and self-presentation in ancient Rome / Maud Gleason.
p.   cm.
Includes bibliographical references and indexes.
ISBN 0-691-04800-2
1. Greek literature, Hellenistic—Rome—History and criticism.   2. Speeches, addresses,
etc., Greek—Rome—History and criticism.   3. Greek literature, Hellenistic—
Appreciation—Rome.   4. Rome—Civilization—Greek influences.   5. Sophists (Greek
philosophy).   6. Civilization, Greco-Roman.   7. Self in literature.   8. Rhetoric,
Ancient.   I. Title.

PA3083.G58   1994   885'.0109—dc20   94-9443

This book has been composed in Bembo

Princeton University Press books are printed
on acid-free paper and meet the guidelines for
permanence and durability of the Committee on
Production Guidelines for Book Longevity
of the Council on Library Resources

Printed in the United States of America

10 9 8 7 6 5 4 3 2 1

TO THE MEMORY OF TESSIE,

Theresa Ross

MY FOURTH-GRADE TEACHER,

WHO TAUGHT US HERODOTUS, THE

PYGMIES, AND THE PENTATEUCH

AND KNEW WHAT THE NILE LOOKS LIKE

FROM THE AIR

Ex visu cognoscitur vir,
Et ab occursu faciei cognoscitur sensatus.
Amictus corporis, et risus dentium,
Et ingressus hominis, enuntiant de illo.
Ecclesiasticus

Tell me of the man who lives in wisdom,
Ever aware of the Self, O Krishna;
How does he talk, how sit, how move about?
Bhagavad Gita

If you are to be a gentleman,
As I suppose you'll be,
You'll neither laugh nor smile
For a tickling of the knee.
Mother Goose

CONTENTS

PREFACE

LIKE INVESTIGATORS arriving at the scene of a crime, readers encountering a new work of scholarship want to know whether it was committed under the influence. Of course the answer is yes, so I will give a brief account of my movements and associates. A fondness for the spectacle of Greeks defending themselves in embarrassing situations led me from Julian's *Misopogon* to Favorinus' *Corinthian Oration*, by way of E. A. Judge's article on the "boasting" of St. Paul.[1] At that point I read Stephen Greenblatt's study of Renaissance self-fashioning[2] and Erving Goffman's *The Presentation of Self in Everyday Life*[3] and decided that second-century rhetorical texts, despite their thoroughgoing lack of introspective material, might nonetheless serve to illuminate the performance conditions of selfhood in that period. It was only after a lot of reading in medical texts that I crossed paths with Michel Foucault, whose *The Care of the Self*[4] has put on the scholarly map a whole archipelago of concerns about the self, the body, and sexuality that were either invisible before, or but little visited by persons of repute.

I found out about Antyllus' treatise on the voice from Rousselle;[5] my understanding of the sociology of verbal competitiveness among the lettered elite of the Roman world owes a lot to Robert Kaster's unpublished essays on Gellius. While feminist scholarship has helped us to see gender as a social construct in general, work on the social construction of manhood has lagged behind work on women. Michael Herzfeld's wonderful study, *The Poetics of Manhood: Contest and Identity in a Cretan Mountain Village*,[6] is a bittersweet read for classicists, forever denied participant observer status in the ancient culture they long to know firsthand. David Gilmore's *Manhood in the Making: Cultural Concepts of Masculinity*,[7] shows how far we have yet to go in developing a theoretically sophisticated account of these matters. Whatever conceptual clarity I have been able to muster about them myself goes back to stimulating conversations with David Halperin. It was

[1] "Paul's Boasting in Relation to Contemporary Professional Practice," *Australian Biblical Review* 16 (1968), 37–50.
[2] *Renaissance Self-Fashioning* (Chicago, 1980).
[3] Garden City, New York, 1959.
[4] Vol. 3 of *The History of Sexuality*, trans. R. Hurley (New York, 1986) = M. Foucault, *Le Souci de soi* (Paris, 1984).
[5] Aline Rousselle, "Parole et inspiration: Le Travail de la voix dans le monde Romain," *History and Philosophy of the Life Sciences* (Pubblicazioni della Stazione Zoologica di Napoli, Section 2) 5 (1983), 129–57.
[6] Princeton, 1985.
[7] New Haven, 1990.

my privilege to know the late Jack Winkler, and I thank him particularly for the awareness that public discourse about gender roles in ancient Greece was itself a form of bluffing performance. Whenever I felt over-whelmed by the coercive stereotypes of masculine deportment that are the focus of this study, it was refreshing to remember his observation that "Mediterranean anthropocentrism is both an unquestioned truth and a universal fib: each man acknowledges its force, nodding sagely and si-lently, with his fingers crossed behind his back."[8]

In general, semiotics has provided this study with a way of looking at gesture and habitual behavior as units of conventionalized signification analogous to language and has encouraged me to look beyond individual historical figures and individual texts to the culture that suspends them in its web of interconnected signs. Pierre Bourdieu told the scholarly world what every mother knows: that training in correct deportment "extorts the essential while seeming to demand the insignificant."[9] His concepts of the *habitus* and of symbolic capital have been immensely helpful to me. The recent and still controversial *rapprochement* of history and anthropol-ogy has provided inspiration, particularly as exemplified in the work of Peter Brown, who taught me to read Mary Douglas, Victor Turner, and Clifford Geertz, and who shares my interest in the body as a theater in which to observe the performance of ideological dramas.

Beyond and beneath intellectual influences lies the *habitus* of the individ-ual author—the point of intersection of culture and the flesh. My interest in deportment developed in the wake of an unusual experience: learning to walk for the second time as a self-conscious adult. My interest in the sociology of elite education developed in response to a demoralizing para-dox of my own education: how can the elite university manage to incorpo-rate itself as a meritocracy while excluding women from power?

Since some readers may wish to pick and choose their way through the subjects covered in this book, here follows a sketch of its contents: Chapter One, "Favorinus and His Statue," introduces Favorinus and discusses his self-presentation in the *Corinthian Oration*. It is a case study in wounded sophistic dignity and the means whereby it might be recouped. The Co-rinthians have responded to Favorinus' fall from imperial favor by taking *down* the statue that they had set up in happier times to honor his achieve-ments. Sensitive to the constraints of sophistic performance culture, which relished self-assertion but condemned crude self-praise, Favorinus resorts to a thought experiment. He asks the audience to imagine that his

[8] *The Constraints of Desire: The Anthropology of Sex and Gender in Ancient Greece* (New York and London, 1990), 5.
[9] *Outline of a Theory of Practice* (Cambridge, 1977), 95.

statue is on trial, and adopts the persona of his statue's advocate—and sometimes of the statue itself—to avoid the appearance of praising himself. Having adroitly combined the activities of apology and invective without appearing to take responsibility for either, Favorinus ends his oration by claiming to levitate the statue before our very eyes by the power of words alone.

Chapter Two, "Portrait of Polemo: The Deportment of the Public Self," introduces Polemo as a public figure and as a physiognomist. It discusses his self-presentation as an imperiously successful sophist and, within the example narratives of his own treatise, as an inscrutable master of a system of signification that he used to decode the self-presentation of others.

In Chapter Three, "Deportment as Language: Physiognomy and the Semiotics of Gender," Polemo's *Physiognomy* serves as a source for the "body language" of his cultural milieu, particularly for the coercive way images of male deviance functioned in the semiotics of gender. Because gender categories were invoked as ordering principles for physiognomic data, the treatises of Polemo and his predecessors offer a unique source of insight into the way sex and gender categories could be used to sort human differences into readily comprehensible hierarchies and oppositions. For Polemo and his contemporaries, gender categories did not constitute a clear-cut binary taxonomy, but a complex language that the body had to learn to speak. The language that a man's body spoke through its deportment was a language that his contemporaries could read, even against his will.

Chapter Four, "Aerating the Flesh: Voice Training and the Calisthenics of Gender," explores vocal exercise in the context of second-century "care of the self." The voice was of central concern to the discipline of self-fashioning because it functioned as a point of contact between a man's private self and his public role. A man's voice served to assert and to defend his status, revealing (or concealing) his birthplace, social origins, and education. Yet it also served as a focus of his self-control and thus became an index of his self-mastery in the areas of exercise, education, food, and sex. Rhetorical training was perceived to be a discipline with hygienic consequences: those who declaimed in deep tones (women and eunuchs are hence excluded) could incorporate more *pneuma* into their physical constitutions, becoming drier, lighter, and warmer, all attributes of the ideally masculine body.

Romans were ambivalent about vocal exercise. The first part of Chapter Five, "Voice and Virility in Rhetorical Writers," explores what the anonymous *Ad Herennium,* Cicero, Quintilian, and the two Senecas had to say about the use and abuse of the voice and its effect on manly dignity. The chapter then explores the stereotypes of hyper-masculine and effeminate rhetoric as they appear in two Greek writers of the imperial period, Aristides and Lucian.

The last chapter, "Manliness Achieved through Speech: A Eunuch-Philosopher's Self-Fashioning," returns to Favorinus to assess what others made of him, the paradoxically eloquent philosopher-sophist who was not physically a "real man." After examining the hostile presentation of Lucian and the reverential portrait of Gellius, the book will conclude with Favorinus' presentation of himself as exile: a wild beast caged in a Persian garden.

This book aspires to a variety of audiences. It is of course addressed to classicists, both those who study the Second Sophistic and those who wonder why it is worth studying. It should also be useful to those who study the history of education and the history of rhetoric. It is a contribution to the study of sex and gender that could be of interest to feminists and to those who are developing Lesbian and Gay studies as a discipline. It is also an essay in symbolic anthropology by an unlicensed practitioner, proper fieldwork being impossible until the author gets to Hades.

All translations, unless otherwise noted, are my own. I hope readers will understand that the absence of gender-neutral phraseology in this book reflects the worldview of the subjects rather than of its author. Where I use the generic masculine, I do so by design. This is a book about men, and the ancient world was not a gender-neutral place.

This manuscript bears the invisible imprint of the many kind hands that have helped it toward completion. Robert Kaster, Donald Russell, Averil Cameron, Carolyn Dewald, Elaine Fantham, David Potter, Chris Faraone, David Halperin, and Kenneth Dover read and improved various chapters at various stages. Anne Fadiman read it all. It should go without saying that I have not always been able to implement their suggestions to best advantage. Ted Courtney, Mike Wigodsky, Susan Treggiari, and Mike Jameson graciously fielded urgent telephone inquiries about odd subjects at odd times. I am grateful to Susan Stephens for her readiness to see something interesting in non-canonical texts. Margaret Malamud helped me generously by checking the Arabic text of Polemo when I could stand uncertainty no longer. I also thank Livia Tenzer, Kathy Veit, and Sarah Jones for their enthusiastic bibliographical assistance. My editor at the Press, Marta Steele, has also been very helpful. My colleagues at Stanford's Institute for Research on Women and Gender shared their work and improved mine in many stimulating seminars. Ron Stroud, Erich Gruen, and Mark Griffith courteously supervised the dissertation from which this book evolved. The Danforth Foundation financed my graduate education, and the Rotary Foundation made possible my studies in England where, as a traveling sophist, I gave epideictic displays to the notables of local towns under Rotarian auspices.

My deepest debt is to my parents for the education they gave to all of us—a large, lively, and histrionic family—in the polycultural laboratory of New York City. I first discovered the pure joy of academic work in the classroom of the remarkable Belgian woman to whom this book is dedicated. Whatever wit or zest it may possess is the product of a passionate refusal to let that joy be separated from learning. It has not always been easy. I wish to thank Joan Burton, Gary Holland, and Tom Walsh for providing the intellectual companionship that sustained me during graduate school. My husband, Frederick Holley, and Peter Brown have always helped me to keep faith in my work, especially when poor health made it difficult. Helen Murray, Judy Caverley, Pina Della Casa, and Ann and Bob Holley provided the loving childcare without which none of this would have been written.

It is traditional in this space to devote a few words to the interplay of work and family.

> The brothers said to Abba Poimen, "Let's get out of here. The crowds here trouble us and we are losing our souls. See: even the crying children do not let us have interior peace."

> And Abba Poimen said to them, "Is it because of the voices of the angels that you wish to go away from here?"[10]

[10] *Apophthegmata Patrum*, Migne *PG* 65, 360.

INTRODUCTION

A S A STUDENT in Athens, I ridiculed the crudity of Roman walls and affected regret that the barbarian hordes had not wrecked every brick. A similar condescension has conditioned the response of mature scholars to the literary remains of Hellenic culture under the Roman Empire. Its efflorescence during the second century, commonly known as the Second Sophistic, has been evenhandedly reviled for derivative literature and moral decay. Gibbon saw the prosperity of the Antonine age as a prelude to disintegration. Just as in ancient biography the fair face of the youthful emperor, because it was followed by the depravity of later years, must be but the false front of *dissimulatio*, so Gibbon thought that the public felicity of the second century, soon to be followed by the chaos of the third, not only concealed, but actually introduced, "a slow and secret poison into the vitals of the empire."[1] While the material conditions of life seemed safe and solid enough, the rot showed itself in literature. To Gibbon, the immersion of second-century rhetoricians in the models of the past—those "bold ancients" who had expressed their "genuine feelings in their native tongue"—produced only "cold and servile imitations." "The name of Poet was almost forgotten; that of Orator was usurped by sophists. A cloud of critics, of compilers, of commentators, darkened the face of learning, and the decline of genius was soon followed by the corruption of taste." This "genius" Gibbon associates with freedom, and, more subtly, with manhood itself. He quotes with approval Longinus' comparison of the minds of his contemporaries, "fettered by . . . a just servitude," to children stunted by excessive swaddling. While criticizing Longinus in a footnote for lack of "manly boldness," Gibbon extends his metaphor to characterize the bodies of the citizenry as a whole: "The Roman world was indeed a race of pygmies." He sees this defect as something to be remedied by insemination: "The fierce giants of the north broke in and mended the puny breed." Though Gibbon concludes by emphasizing the intangible benefits of the giants' violent re-virilization of the Roman world ("They restored a manly spirit of freedom"), we are left with the impression that defects in literature and learning somehow reflect deficiencies in manliness that are susceptible to eugenic improvement.

For the greatest Hellenist of modern times, the body politic of the second century was not merely defective but diseased. Writing in the

---

[1] *The Decline and Fall of the Roman Empire*, (first published in 6 vols., London, 1776–88), chap. 2, end.

nineteenth century, when the hygiene of the national body had become a matter of state concern, Ulrich von Wilamowitz-Moellendorff adduced, as evidence for "an age whose god was grown effete," the physical weakness of the second century's leading literary figures: Aristides on the Greek side, laid low by epilepsy; Fronto on the Latin side, at death's door with gout; and last, born without testicles, "that Gaul, highly learned in both languages, whose appearance his enemy Polemo thus described in his *Physiognomy*: 'forehead taut, cheeks soft, mouth relaxed, skinny neck, fat calves, fleshy feet, a feminine voice, women's words, all limbs and joints without vigor, lax and loose.'" To Wilamowitz, Favorinus was "an exemplar of his times. . . . A solecistic Atticizer, a rhetor-philosopher, a courtier vaunting his liberty, a eunuch itching with desire . . . a man (pardon the expression!) of that sort suits the age, an age glowing with pleasingly variegated color, the color of a corpse on the brink of putrefaction."[2] In other words we are invited to physiognomize the age, drawing inferences from the visible imperfections of the body (sometimes themselves deceptive, as in the "pleasing color" of the putrid corpse) to the rot within. Even G. W. Bowersock, who has done so much to elucidate the social context of sophistic activity in the Antonine age, occasionally succumbs to the metaphor of invisible disease: "In the midst of that glorious era there *was* a real illness, but Galen could do nothing about it. Unknowingly, he too suffered from it."[3]

Metaphors of unrecognized disease convey a dissonance between apparent and actual health, between the way we judge the practitioners of second-century high culture and the way they saw themselves. Some recent work on the Second Sophistic challenges the disease metaphor by suggesting that what makes us uncomfortable about Gellius or Philostratus is that they are too much like ourselves.[4] But to admit that the lecturers, compilers, and polymaths of the Second Sophistic are a bit donnish does not advance our understanding of their culture very far.

Historically it has been difficult for critics who admire the Greek literary giants for their originality to appreciate that originality *per se* was not considered a virtue by the Greeks themselves. It has been difficult for critics attracted to the moral seriousness of Roman writers to appreciate that "sincerity" may not be precisely the right criterion to use in evaluating the self-presentation of a Roman elegist or orator. The archaizing style of many second-century authors, both Greek and Latin, simply accentuates

---

[2] This quotation comes from an open letter to E. Maass, who, in a dissertation prepared under Wilamowitz's direction, had dared to claim that Favorinus was the principal source of Diogenes Laertius (*Philologische Untersuchungen* 3 [1880], 146). Heaven forbid that our knowledge of Greek philosophical tradition come through such a tainted source!

[3] *Greek Sophists in the Roman Empire* (Oxford, 1969), 75.

[4] For example: B. Baldwin, *Studies in Lucian* (Toronto, 1973), 49; G. Anderson, *Philostratus* (London, 1986), 10, 286–88 (sophists as "media dons").

these problems. We are invited to condemn an "essentially weak literature," where "neither originality of thought nor sincerity of feeling was
pursued or expected."[5] As to the rhetoric of this period, attempts to pin
down the notorious Asianism-Atticism controversy have absorbed a dis-
proportionate amount of scholarly energy with somewhat disappointing
results.[6] Developing an aesthetic taste for archaizing improvisation in a
traditional medium has proved extremely difficult, although increasing
acceptance of the large role that tradition played in the Homeric process of
composition may eventually help. French appreciation of declamation as a
form of controlled improvisation akin to a baroque fugue or twentieth-
century jazz,[7] commendably unpatronizing, has not inspired sustained
analysis in English.[8] When discussing declamation, critics tend to adopt a
somewhat defensive or apologetic posture, as if expecting at any minute to
be censured for the essential triviality of their subject, which they feel they
cannot quite defend as literature.

This book aims to cut the cross-cultural knot of literary evaluation by
addressing itself to rhetoric not as product but as process. By developing a

[5] B. A. Van Groningen, "General Literary Tendencies in the Second Century A.D.,"
Mnemosyne 18 (1965), 41–56. E. L. Bowie aims to establish a wider cultural context for
linguistic archaism in the constraints on the political freedom of Greek aristocrats imposed by
Roman rule ("The Greeks and Their Past in the Second Sophistic," *Past and Present* 46 (1970),
3–41). To see educated Greeks as seeking consolation in the past for their political impotence
in the Roman present, however, does not quite do justice to the vitality with which they
experienced their continuity with tradition.

[6] This "magnifique querelle" was set in motion by W. Schmid in the late nineteenth
century and involved most of the big names in German classical scholarship. For an assessment and bibliography, see B. Reardon, *Courants littéraires grecs des IIᵉ et IIIᵉ siècles après J.-C.*
(Paris, 1971), 81ff., esp. 90. An essential ancient text is Dionysius of Halicarnassus' preface to
his *Lives of the Ancient Orators*, which contains the notorious comparison of the Asiatic harlot
and the chaste Attic wife. On this see E. Gabba, "The Classicistic Revival in the Augustan
Age," *CA* 1 (1981), 43–65.

[7] J. Bompaire, *Lucien écrivain: Imitation et création* (Paris, 1958), 113; H.-I. Marrou, *A
History of Education in Antiquity* (Madison, 1982), 204–5. See the index of the sixth French
edition s. v. *jazz, hot.* Anderson compares sophists to concert pianists in the days when they
could only be heard live: "It is difficult for readers inured to broadcasting to come to terms
with the impact of extempore spoken words which acted in effect as the living embodiment
of a universally acknowledged culture" *Philostratus,* 289n.10.

[8] Notable appreciations in French: A. Boulanger, *Aelius Aristide* (Paris, 1923); B. Reardon
(above n.6). Sympathetic studies of second-century authors have been appearing in English:
C. P. Jones, *The Roman World of Dio Chrysostom* (Cambridge, Mass., 1978), *Plutarch and Rome*
(Oxford, 1971), and *Culture and Society in Lucian* (Cambridge, Mass., 1986); J. L. Moles, "The
Career and Conversion of Dio Chrysostom," *JHS* 98 (1978), 79–100; D. A. Russell, *Plutarch*
(London, 1972); R. B. Branham, *Unruly Eloquence: Lucian and the Comedy of Traditions* (Cam-
bridge, Mass., 1989); L. Holford-Strevens, *Aulus Gellius* (Chapel Hill, 1988). See also S. F.
Bonner, *Roman Declamation* (Liverpool, 1949); M. Winterbottom, *Roman Declamation* (Bris-
tol, 1980); D. A. Russell, *Greek Declamation* (Cambridge, 1983). Readers may now consult
G. Anderson, *The Second Sophistic* (London and New York, 1993), which I did not obtain in
time to use.

model of why rhetorical performance was so intensely exciting for contemporaries, it hopes also to correct somewhat the focus of the conventionally gloomy picture of this period, suggesting how negative judgments on the moral fiber of the era often derive from a misreading of the function of the censorious comments of the ancients themselves, and from a misunderstanding of the notorious preoccupation with the body exhibited by these gentlemen, all too easy to despise as neurotic. Indeed, the preoccupation of contemporary scholars with the body (which may one day prove equally notorious) invites this reassessment. In general, I hope to refocus our attention on the social dynamics of rhetoric as an instrument of self-presentation, and in the process refine our appreciation of the functional aesthetics of a profoundly traditional performance genre.

RHETORIC AS PROCESS

Because as twentieth-century readers our experience of ancient rhetoric is entirely an armchair affair, we find it easy to forget its physical aspects: the sheer sweat of exertion involved in projecting an unamplified voice before a large outdoor audience, the demands of managing the heavy folds of the cloak or toga, the exhilarating risk of stumbles and solecisms lying in wait for a moment's loss of nerve, the vibrant immediacy of a collaborative live audience, ready to explode with jeers or applause. We must imagine the intoxicating sense of power that surged through the performer as he mastered the crowd, overwhelming skeptics and hecklers with the hypnotic charm of a beautifully controlled voice in full spate. We must also try to remember the terror of defeat and public humiliation, the courage required to risk both. Indeed, the repetitive verbal exercises that were a prominent part of rhetorical training but seem so thin as they survive on paper, derive their chief value not from their stereotyped content, but from their function as incantations against failure. To put it more positively, they served as a form of conditioning to give the speaker that ironclad expectation of success that extempore performance required.

One reason that these performances were so riveting was that the encounter between orator and audience was in many cases the anvil upon which the self-presentation of ambitious upper-class men was forged. Like military officers (who now came increasingly from outside the ranks of the traditional elite), rhetorical performers were repeatedly called upon to vindicate their competence in public.[9] Great sophists and declaimers,

[9] K. Hopkins makes this observation of upwardly mobile litterateurs but fails to do justice to the vast amount of effort expended by aristocrats on developing their rhetorical skill precisely in order to be "good without seeming to try." "Elite Mobility in the Roman Empire" in *Studies in Ancient Society*, ed. M. I. Finley (London, 1974), 110.

however, were only the tip of the iceberg: all aristocrats had to be able to perform as public speakers, if only to do their duty at wedding banquets, defend their property in litigation, and participate as an educated equal in self-consciously learned discussions at the baths.

Paideia, for both Greek and Roman gentlemen, was a form of symbolic capital. Its development required time, money, effort, and social position (as Lucian saw clearly);[10] eloquence was the essential precondition of its display. The tradition of euergetism in the ancient city provides an analogy. Wealthy citizens were expected to provide many urban amenities at their private expense: fuel to heat the baths, oil for the gymnasium, porticos for the marketplace, and public entertainment for the holidays. Thus the elite established with their fellow-citizens a relationship that was asymmetrical, but not without reciprocity: what the benefactor bestowed in material gifts to his fellow-citizens was returned to him in symbolic form as deference or gratitude. This is an example of what Pierre Bourdieu would call the conversion of economic capital into symbolic capital, producing "relations of dependence that have an economic basis but are disguised under a veil of moral relations." This transformation works only by grace of a kind of collective disavowal of what is really going on; the exchange of munificence for deference must appear on both sides to be voluntary, or the game is spoiled. Essentially, the voluntariness of the exchange transforms arbitrary social relations into legitimate relations, generating as a sort of "symbolic surplus value" the legitimation of the euergetist's political power.[11] Thus the structured display of material generosity served as a strategy of political legitimation for the liturgical class, defining it vis-à-vis other groups in society and providing a stylized and structured context in which the wealthy could compete with one another without damage to their class interests.

The display of *paideia* in public speaking served a similar function. All well-born males were trained in adolescence, by competing with their peers, to display the "cultural capital" that distinguished authentic members of the elite from other members of society who might quite literally speak a different language. The star performers who attracted large audiences valorized *paideia* by making it appear to be the prize of a bruising competition for status dominance. By this kind of dramatization, enhanced by all the charms of symbolic violence, the gap between the educated and the uneducated came to seem in no way arbitrary, but the result of a nearly biological superiority.

[10] *The Dream* 1: παιδεία μὲν καὶ πόνου καὶ χρόνου μακροῦ καὶ δαπάνης οὐ μικρᾶς καὶ τύχης δεῖσθαι λαμπρᾶς: "Education requires effort, a great deal of time and no small expense, as well as a distinguished social position."

[11] See Pierre Bourdieu, *The Logic of Practice* (Stanford, 1990), 118–25, and *Outline of a Theory of Practice* (Cambridge, 1977), 183–97.

The discipline involved in acquiring paideia extended beyond the teen-age years. For many aristocratic gentlemen, declamation (both practice speeches and solitary vocal exercise) served as a mechanism for maintaining mental fitness through disciplined effort, in the teeth of the endless opportunities for inertia, self-indulgence, and excess afforded by their wealth. Modern critics may be offended by the spectacle of adults indulging in declamation ("overgrown schoolboys"), but in this period school exercises were not what separated the men from the boys, but what made boys into men. And since, in accordance with the way gender roles were constituted in their society, manhood was not a state to be definitively and irrefutably achieved, but something always under construction and constantly open to scrutiny, adults needed to keep practicing the arts that made them men. Rhetoric was a calisthenics of manhood. This is easier for us to grasp if we remember that the art of self-presentation through rhetoric entailed much more than mastery of words: physical control of one's voice, carriage, facial expression, and gesture, control of one's emotions under conditions of competitive stress—in a word, all the arts of deportment necessary in a face-to-face society where one's adequacy as a man was always under suspicion and one's performance was constantly being judged.

The large element of role-playing in the surviving declamations has elicited some scholarly disdain, as if play-acting were an inherently trivial activity, but it is necessary to consider how important role-playing and stylized behavior actually must have been in the social life of an ancient city. To play the part of host, ambassador, or patron, to present oneself effectively as a bestower or seeker of favors, to enforce by the weight of one's very presence the submission of those beneath one in the social hierarchy, and to command respect from one's reluctant peers, all these— the tasks of everyday living for aristocrats in an underpoliced society— required fluency in a stereotyped repertoire of gestures as well as words. In the catalog of great sophists, we read of Antipater, who performed outstandingly as an imperial secretary because in his letter-writing he resembled "a brilliant tragic actor . . , whose utterances were always in keeping with the imperial role."[12] Few men would ever have the opportunity to impersonate the emperor in affairs of state, but it was important that everybody (who was anybody) be able to do so. All the lesser lights who studied rhetoric without earning a place in the historical record were by no means wasting their time. To *be* Demosthenes, to *convince* as the outraged father who disinherits his son, was to earn status in the eyes of one's contemporaries by presenting oneself as a man capable of putting forward *his* definition of a situation in a way that commands belief. The next

---

[12] ὥσπερ τραγῳδίας λαμπρὸν ὑποκριτὴν . . . ἐπάξια τοῦ βασιλείου προσώπου φθέγ-ξασθαι: Philostratus, *Lives* 607.

chapter will offer, as a case in point, the self-presentation of an aggrieved sophist, whose defense of his dismantled statue transforms a moment of apologia into a moment of triumph. Indeed, Favorinus' entire career can be read as a successful effort to "carry off" a masculine identity on the strength of *paideia*, nerve, and eloquence, despite the lack of some of the physical attributes of maleness.

For those who listened to such a performance, part of the attraction would be seeing whether the speaker could carry it off. Thus the audience itself played a critical role, as arbiter of a suspenseful process. When the moment of crisis was passed, and suspense resolved itself into scorn or approbation, those who were listening would collectively affirm their connection to the very values they had tested. Spectatorship provided an affective education, through which the individual became attuned to a collective dramatization of status relationships.[13] To Plutarch, the role of listener was an active one: "He is a participant in the discourse and a collaborator with the speaker." The ensemble, he says, is like a game of ball, where thrower and catcher adapt their movements to each other.[14] Plutarch describes the momentum of a successful performance in a way that highlights the nonverbal aspects of the orator's self-presentation and the emotional intensity of the audience's response: "The speaker's grey hair, his figure, his facial expression, his air of self-assertion, and especially the shouts and excitement of the crowd as they leap to their feet, combine to sweep the inexperienced young listener away on the current."[15] For one man to triumph, the members of his audience had to allow themselves to be swept away—and this in a society where an intensely competitive ethos made it difficult to grant another man success. The relationship between performers was definitely a zero-sum game.[16] For one man to triumph, all his rivals had to lose. The emperor Caligula, with characteristic sadism, was only making this explicit when he required the losers in his rhetorical competition at Lyons personally to present the prizes to the winners and then perform an encomium for them on the spot.[17] This is not to say that competitiveness was something forced by the institutions of society upon unwilling participants. Favorinus himself put it this way: "For there is no other way for us to attain first rank than by competing with those who are first."[18]

Two factors specific to ancient education intensified a general cultural

[13] Compare the Balinese cockfights of C. Geertz, *The Interpretation of Cultures* (New York, 1973), 449–51.

[14] "On Listening to Lectures," *Mor.* 45E.

[15] Ibid., *Mor.* 41C.

[16] A. Gouldner, elaborating on Nietzsche's idea of Greek society as a contest system, introduced this term in *Enter Plato: Classical Greece and the Origins of Social Theory* (New York, 1965).

[17] Suetonius, *Gaius Caligula* 20; Juvenal, *Satires* 1.44.

[18] [Dio] 64.17.

tendency toward one-on-one competition. Ancient education was innocent of the sort of objectification effected by degrees and credentials that
renders all holders of the same credential formally interchangeable. Degrees and degree-granting institutions in a formalized educational system
tend to be sorted by social consensus into a status hierarchy, so that the
individual components of the system have a rough idea of where they
stand relative to one another before a face-to-face relationship is ever
established. In the absence of such standardization, as was certainly the
case in the ancient world, cultural capital tends to be incorporated in
particular individuals, who must compete directly with each other to
establish relationships of dominance and authority.[19] Ancient education
still preserved some of the features of an oral culture. Those who pursued
paideia may have acquired their linguistic competence in literary dialect
initially by reading, but they had to display it by speaking. Though educated men displayed their wealth by commissioning or collecting plastic
art, they did not display their level of culture by owning books, or even by
having read books owned by others, but only by having absorbed books
so completely that they could exhale them as speech. What we have in the
second century is a mixed culture of literacy and orality in which the
master rhetorician and his pupils preserved and transmitted the cultural
capital of the elite.

The rhetorical performer embodied his civilization's ideal of cultivated
manliness. The young men who consciously studied his rhetorical exempla unconsciously imitated the gestalt of his self-presentation. The result
was, for many generations, the smooth-flowing cultural reproduction of
the patterns of speech, thought, and movement appropriate to a gentleman. This is not to deny that evolution in these practices may have taken
place over time; what counts is that they were *perceived* to be unchanging.

Deportment matters. It is a shorthand that encodes, and replicates, the
complex realities of social structure, in a magnificent economy of voice
and gesture. It is no accident that a late-twentieth-century sociologist like
Pierre Bourdieu should reach back to Greek and Latin to dub the aggregate
of these patterns the *hexis* or *habitus*.[20] Demeanor expresses—or extorts—
deference, an awareness of one's place in relation to others.[21] In a relatively
static society, individuals can learn behaviors by observation and then
reproduce them without ever bringing "the rules" to the level of consciousness and discourse, just as the traditional poet learns to improvise in

[19] P. Bourdieu, *The Logic of Practice* (Stanford, 1990), 132.

[20] "Bodily *hexis* is political mythology realized, *em-bodied*, turned into a permanent disposition, a durable manner of standing, speaking, and thereby of *feeling and thinking.*" P.
Bourdieu, *Outline of a Theory of Practice* (Cambridge, 1977), 93–94. On the *habitus* see 72–95.

[21] On deference and demeanor, see E. Goffman, *Interaction Ritual* (Garden City, N.Y.,
1967), 47–95.

meter without consciously memorizing "formulae."[22] Such was the ideal Athens that Socrates' accuser had in mind when he claimed that "any decent Athenian gentleman" could make young Meno a good man just by personal association. When Socrates asks whether the virtue of such gentlemen is self-taught, the impatient traditionalist responds, "They learned it from their ancestors, I assume, who were gentlemen themselves."[23]

What we seem to have in the second century, however, is a heightened level of conscious awareness about deportment training. The physiognomical treatises, moral essays, medical advice manuals, and rhetorical handbooks that appear to proliferate in this period are perhaps a sign that the wordless replication of the elite *habitus* could no longer be counted on to function automatically. The age-old system of acculturation through association with cultivated gentlemen that we glimpse in the scene-setting of both Ciceronian and Platonic dialogue did not perhaps adequately prepare its young apprentices for social and political dealing outside the circle of their fathers' friends, yet that was precisely what public life in an increasingly centralized imperial government would require. Hence efforts to articulate and formalize an empire-wide code of elite deportment might be welcomed by provincial aristocrats who suddenly found themselves faced with a wider world.

Foucault has suggested that the second century's growing concern with manly deportment fits with other historical developments. In the imperial period, the direct competition of aristocrats for status in an overtly agonistic political environment gave way to a system of "revokable offices which depended . . . on the pleasure of the prince." The relationship between status and function, between power over oneself and power over others, became more problematic. There was an intensification of interest in those "behaviors by which one affirms oneself in the superiority one manifests over others." During this period

> there is an accentuation of everything that allows the individual to define his identity in accordance with his status. . . . One seeks to make oneself as adequate as possible to one's own status by means of a set of signs and marks pertaining to physical bearing, clothing . . . gestures of generosity and munificence. . . . But at the opposite extreme one finds the attitude that consists, on the contrary, in defining what one is purely in relation to oneself . . . through a relation that depends as little as possible on status and its external forms, for this relation is fulfilled in the sovereignty that one exercises over oneself.[24]

Of the two rhetoricians who form the focus of this book, one will be seen to expound the sign-system of status in his treatise on physiognomy, while

---

[22] P. Bourdieu, *Outline*, 87–88.
[23] Plato, *Meno* 92e–93a.
[24] M. Foucault, *The Care of the Self* (New York, 1986), 85.

the other will assert the primacy of self-definition in terms of self-sovereignty in his philosophical discourse.

EMBODYING THE RHETORIC OF MANHOOD

Looking at rhetoric as part of the process of male socialization enables us to explore rhetorical *praxis* and gender identity as parts of an interconnected whole, rather than as entirely separate fields of inquiry. The interconnected whole is the complex business of self-presentation, in which conscious choices interact with instinctive responses to traditional paradigms to produce a carefully modulated public identity. In a study like this, it is important not to reify rhetorical (or behavioral) conventions as "laws" or "traditions" that have an autonomous existence, somehow ontologically prior to the individuals who gave them life. Neither a system of objective laws nor one of subjective intentions is adequate to explain the consistency of individual actions and improvisations within a culture and the persistence of such behavior patterns over time.[25] Similarly, gender identity is not a transhistorical constant but a social construct, a series of choices, of stressed and unstressed possibilities, of subterfuges perpetually in the making.

This book proceeds from the assumption that, whatever their biological basis or evolutionary utility, sexual differences and gender roles function symbolically as an interrelated system. Humans are a weakly dimorphic species; unlike, for example, birds, the color of our plumage does not immediately reveal our sex. Instead, human societies tend to organize gender differences into kinesthetic systems for communication and display. One has to learn to move like a gendered human body.[26] Hence the importance of the so-called tertiary sexual characteristics: the tilt of the pelvis, the gestures of the hand, even certain movements of the eyes—all these function as a conventional language through which gender identity may be claimed and decoded. The same may be said for differences of social class: these are made visible through the minutiae of body language, not just through the external language of dress. As the psychologists put it, "Nonverbal behavior encodes power well."[27] We can study both the formal aspects of such systems in the abstract and their influence on the lives and choices of individuals, whose perceptions of nature, of society,

---

[25] This point is central to Bourdieu's critique of anthropology *The Logic of Practice* (Stanford, 1990), 25–51.

[26] R. L. Birdwhistell, "Masculinity and Femininity as Display," in *Kinesics and Context* (Philadelphia, 1970), 39–46.

[27] C. Mayo and N. Henley, *Gender and Nonverbal Behavior* (New York, 1981), 8.

and of the self are conditioned by their culture. Indeed, if we regard cultures as systems of euphemism that disguise the arbitrariness of asymmetrical social relations by presenting them as grounded in nature, then the paradox emerges that it is precisely when our sources assert the superiority of masculine physiognomical signs over feminine, of "dry" flesh over "wet," or privilege certain sexual acts (natural) over others (unnatural),[28] or characterize certain persons and their modes of deportment and speech as "well-born" or "not worthy of a free man," that we should most intensely suspect the invisible hand of convention at work; nature, as a category, is the creation of culture.

Although our most accessible source for these conventions may be written materials of a prescriptive nature (the medical, physiognomical, and rhetorical handbooks mentioned above), we must remember that most accessible to their contemporaries were the embodied paradigms themselves: the sophists and teachers of rhetoric who traversed the empire on lecture tours and diplomatic missions and attracted elite youths from capital or hinterland to absorb high culture at their feet.

This study is built around two star performers of the Second Sophistic, Favorinus of Arles and Polemo of Laodicea. In taking as a starting point the life and works of these paradigmatic figures, my aim is to tease out the larger issues that were at stake in their rivalry, and in so doing to evoke in the reader a clearer sense of the constraints and possibilities that governed the game of self-presentation within the highly competitive elite society in which they moved.

Favorinus described himself as the incarnation of three paradoxes: "a Gaul who spoke Greek, a eunuch who was prosecuted for adultery, and a man who had quarreled with the emperor and was still alive," while Polemo "conversed with cities as his inferiors, with Emperors as if they were not his superiors, and with gods as his equals."[29] The opposition between Favorinus and Polemo developed on many levels. As cultural assets and tokens of municipal pride, they were drawn into the long-simmering rivalry between Ephesus and Smyrna. They were also participants in a high-stakes competition for imperial favor—a game in which Polemo gained immense wealth and influence while Favorinus, for a time at least, apparently lost his liberty. But there was also another sort of competition going on: Favorinus and Polemo represented opposing paradigms of masculinity. Polemo's formulation of this difference (in the zestful poison-pen portrait of his effeminate rival quoted by Wilamowitz)

[28] J. Winkler, *The Constraints of Desire* (New York/London 1990), 17–18.
[29] Philostratus, *Lives* 489, 535.

invites generalization because it was presented as part of a physiognomical treatise; we will examine how Polemo's notions of gender identity depend on polarized distinctions (smooth/hirsute, high voice/low voice, panther-like/leonine etc.) that purport to characterize the gulf between men and women but actually serve to divide the male sex into legitimate and illegitimate players.

Both gentlemen composed invectives against each other which do not (most regrettably) survive.[30] Hence Favorinus' formulation of the difference between himself and his rival cannot now be recovered. We can look instead at the way he chose to represent himself: the paradoxes that he used to define his identity are notable for the way they emphasize his power to transcend the limitations of his birth (whether provincial origins or anatomical deficiencies). He used his rhetorical virtuosity, combined with a remarkably fluent manipulation of personae in narration, to redefine his political setbacks as moral victories. He boldly exploited the aesthetic possibilities of his high-pitched voice and appears to have claimed that his physical condition, far from being a handicap, was actually the gift of Providence. The "singing style" that he practiced was wildly popular with second-century audiences and widely criticized by moralists as a sign of effeminacy and decadence. Favorinus undoubtedly appealed to popular taste. It must have added to his appeal, in ways that we cannot quite assess, that he somehow managed to combine the charm of a certain feminine softness with the articulate dignity of a man. His claim to the status of philosopher was an important part of his social identity, and, at least in some circles, this was the role he succeeded in carrying off, appearing in the memoirs of Gellius as a dignified sage capable, when necessary, of skewering his opponents with an effortless verbal thrust.

Favorinus is particularly useful for a study of this sort because, as a biological anomaly, he *required* interpretation on the part of his contemporaries—or, at the very least, he required a highly elaborated self-presentation on his own part to condition the perceptions of his contemporaries. Polemo's value, on the other hand, lies in his very conventionality and in the intensely normative character of physiognomical thinking.

Obviously, not everyone was as hyper-masculine in his self-presentation as Polemo, or as a physiognomist and social critic he would never have found so many crypto-catamites to unmask. So I think of Favorinus and Polemo as opposite poles of possibility in masculine deportment. In an attempt to get at the full range of possibilities, I devote part of this study to discussing how the voice and the body served as variables in upper-class self-presentation. Using the evidence preserved in technical

[30] Ibid. 491, 536.

works (physiognomical, medical, and rhetorical), I explore how these variables influenced both the face that men presented to the world and the way that face was interpreted. I hope to show how people believed that the voice, by the way it is used, may affect the constitution of the body just as the body, by the way it is used in one's deportment, may quite literally speak.

ABBREVIATIONS

Adam.	Adamantius
Aesch.	Aeschines
AJP	American Journal of Philology
Anon. Lat.	Anonymi de Physiognomonia liber Latinus
Anth. Pal.	Palatine Anthology
apud/ap.	"quoted in," "cited in"
BICS	Bulletin of the Institute of Classical Studies of the University of London
CA	Classical Antiquity
CAF	Comicorum Atticorum Fragmenta, 3 vols. (ed. T. Kock; Leipzig, 1880-88)
CIG	Corpus Inscriptionum Graecarum (ed. A. Boeckh; Berlin, 1828-77)
CIL	Corpus Inscriptionum Latinarum (Berlin, 1862)
CMG	Corpus Medicorum Graecorum (Leipzig and Berlin, 1908 –; Berlin, 1947 –)
Const. Ath.	(Aristotle) The Constitution of Athens
Contr.	(Seneca the Elder) Controversiae
CP	Classical Philology
Decl.	(Libanius) Declamationes
Dem.	Demosthenes
Dio Chrys.	Dio Chrysostom
Diss.	(Arrian) Discourses of Epictetus
Ep.	Epistles
Eth. Nic.	(Aristotle) Nicomachean Ethics
fr.	fragment
Gen. An.	(Aristotle) On the Generation of Animals
GRBS	Greek, Roman and Byzantine Studies
Gyn.	Soranus, Gynecology
H.E.	(Eusebius, Theodoret) Historia Ecclesiastica
Hist. Anim.	(Aristotle) Historia Animalium
On Hyg. Decl.	(Antyllus) On Hygienic Declamation
IG	Inscriptiones Graecae (1873-)
IGR	Inscriptiones Graecae ad res Romanas pertinentes (ed. R. Cagnat et al., 1906–27)
Incerta	Oribasius, Collectiones Medicae (libri incerti)
Inst.	(Quintilian) Institutiones Oratoriae
K	(in Galen citations) C. G. Kühn, Claudii Galeni Opera Omnia, 20 vols. (1821; reprint Hildesheim, 1964)

Lives	(Philostratus) *Lives of the Sophists*
Mor.	(Plutarch) *Moralia*
ms(s).	manuscript(s)
Od.	(Homer) *Odyssey*
Or.	(Aristides, Demosthenes, Dio Chrysostom, Libanius) *Orations*
Paus.	Pausanias
PDM	*Papyri Demoticae Magicae*, as cited in H. D. Betz, *The Greek Magical Papyri in Translation* (Chicago, 1986)
PG	*Patrologiae cursus completus, series Graeca* (ed. J. P. Migne, 162 vols.; Paris, 1857–66)
PGM	*Papyri Graecae Magicae* (2nd ed. K. Preisendanz and A. Henrichs, 2 vols., 1973–74)
Phys.	(Polemo) *De physiognomonia*
[Phys.]	(Ps.-Aristotle) *[Physiognomonica]*
RE	*Paulys Real-Encyclopädie der classischen Altertumswissenschaft* (ed. G. Wissowa, E. Kroll, et al., 1893–)
REA	*Revue des Études anciennes*
REG	*Revue des Études grecques*
Rep.	(Plato) *Republic*
Rh. Mus.	*Rheinisches Museum für Philologie*
Rhet. ad Her.	*Rhetorica ad Herennium*
Teacher	(Lucian) *Teacher of Rhetoric*
Thuc.	Thucydides
s.v.	"under the word/heading"
VH	(Aelian) *Varia historia*
YCS	*Yale Classical Studies*
ZPE	*Zeitschrift für Papyrologie und Epigraphik*

MAKING MEN

Chapter One

FAVORINUS AND HIS STATUE

> He used to speak in oracular riddles about the three
> paradoxes of his life: he was a Gaul who spoke Greek, a
> eunuch who was prosecuted for adultery, a man who had
> quarreled with the emperor and was still alive.

IN THE LAST YEARS of the first century, in a well-to-do family in
southern France, there took place an unusual birth. The infant in question could have been exposed as a *monstrum*,[1] since it apparently possessed a penis but no testicles,[2] but for reasons lost to history the family
decided to rear it as a male. They gave him an auspicious name, Latin in
flavor but not commonly used: Favorinus. The Rhone valley had been
settled by Greeks long before the Romans arrived,[3] so there is no way to
know how much Greek, how much Latin, and how much Celtic dialect
was spoken in his family's household. Favorinus may have enjoyed as an
infant the well-known educational advantage of a Greek-speaking wet
nurse.[4] His bilingual proficiency as an adult suggests that his formal education included training with Greek and Latin teachers of grammar and
rhetoric—first at Arles, his native city, and then at Marseilles, where a
wider selection of teachers would be found.

This child proved to be a prodigy in more ways than one. He applied
himself to rhetorical training with the zeal of the future professional and

Epigraph in the original: ὅθεν ὡς παράδοξα ἐπεχρησμῴδει τῷ ἑαυτοῦ βίῳ τρία ταῦτα·
Γαλάτης ὢν ἑλληνίζειν, εὐνοῦχος ὢν μοιχείας κρίνεσθαι, βασιλεῖ διαφέρεσθαι καὶ ζῆν.
(Philostratus *Lives* 489)

[1] Malformed infants had counted as signs of ill omen (*prodigia*) among the Romans from
the earliest times, as the custom of consulting Etruscan experts about them shows. Evidence
of a second-century interest in sexually ambiguous births and miraculous changes of gender
may be seen in the *Mirabilia* collected by Favorinus' contemporary, Phlegon of Tralles. See
Paradoxographi Graeci, ed. A. Westermann (1839; rpt. Amsterdam: Hakkert, 1953), pp. 116–
42, esp. sections 2, 6, 10 (births of ambiguous sex), 6–9 (sudden transformations of females
into males), and 26 (a *cinaedus*, supposedly a deviant male, gives birth).

[2] Perhaps this was an ancient case of Reifenstein's syndrome, in which an endocrine
disorder leads to incomplete virilization of a genetic male, often with undescended testicles.
H. Mason, "Favorinus' Disorder: Reifenstein's Syndrome in Antiquity?" *Janus* 66 (1979), 1–
13.

[3] Arles (Arelate), originally a Greek settlement, was refounded as a Roman legionary
colony in 46 B.C.E. (Suetonius, *Tiberius* 4.1).

[4] Soranus, *Gyn.* 2.19.15.

developed a mastery of Greek that enabled him to leave his native region far behind. Yet the province of Narbonensian Gaul had a long tradition of urban life and was by no means a cultural backwater. Tacitus' father-in-law, the exemplary Agricola, received his education in Marseilles, which provided a happy combination of Greek refinement and provincial simplicity.[5] The orator Votienus Montanus came from Narbo; he was sufficiently distinguished to be tried for treason in Rome.[6] Gaul was also the birthplace of Marcus Aper, whose forensic talent earned him a Roman praetorship and a leading role in Tacitus' dialogue on oratory.[7] In Narbonensis the atmosphere among the cultivated was bilingual: Agroitas, a provincial native, declaimed in Greek but appeared to Seneca to have learned more from the Romans; the assumption is that he had access to both Greek- and Latin-speaking teachers.[8] Lyons hosted a rhetorical competition where prizes were offered for both Greek and Latin eloquence by imperial decree.[9] Certainly it was not necessary to go to Rome, Athens, or Ephesus to learn the moves of rhetorical one-upmanship. The famous orator Moschus, in exile from Pergamum,[10] might find his style parodied by a local rhetorician one morning in Marseilles; he in turn might impugn the masculinity of a Roman rival by making a bilingual joke of his name.[11] Greek performers toured in Gaul: Lucian made a great deal of money there in his days as a traveling sophist, and one of Plutarch's friends went to Gaul on a lecture tour—never to return, the victim of a tragicomic accident and his own professional pride.[12] Although the elite of Narbonensis obviously supported Greek rhetoric as a spectator sport, it had no forensic application in the west, and those who contemplated a political career usually put their time into Latin. Thus Favorinus' decision to concentrate on Greek was unusual. Unless the initial plan was that he should himself open a local school, we may assume that as a very young man he had made another decision: not to spend his life as landowner and liturgist in the service of his

---

[5] Tacitus, *Agricola* 4.

[6] Tacitus, *Annals* 4.42. Montanus, like Favorinus, did not apparently maintain good relations with his native city (Seneca *Contr.* 7.5.12).

[7] Aper may have been from a small town in Narbonensis or from backwoods Gaul (*Tres Galliae*): R. Syme, *Tacitus* (New York: 1980), appendix 91; on oratory in Gaul, see also pp. 459, 623n.5, 799–800.

[8] Seneca *Contr.* 2.6.12.

[9] Suetonius *Gaius Caligula* 20; Juvenal 1.44.

[10] Convicted of poisoning despite the forensic efforts of Asinius Pollio, Moschus set up shop as a rhetorical teacher in Marseilles and gratefully bequeathed his wealth to his adopted city (Tacitus *Annals* 4.43; Seneca *Contr.* 2.5.13; Horace *Ep.* 5.9 with scholia).

[11] The butt of this joke was Passienus, temptingly close in sound to πάσχειν: *Ille Passieno prima eius syllaba in Graecum mutata obscenum nomen imposuit*: Seneca *Contr.* 10, preface 10–11.

[12] He swallowed a fishbone but, because another foreign sophist was performing in town, insisted on declaiming despite the danger of infection lest he appear to have conceded the match: Plutarch *Mor.* 131A. On Lucian's trips to Gaul: *Twice Accused* 27; *Apology* 15. For rhetorical competitions in Gaul, see Suetonius *Gaius Caligula* 20; Juvenal 1.44.

hometown, but to pursue a riskier though potentially more glamorous course as an itinerant intellectual.

To glance back for a moment at the road not taken: Arles, the town Favorinus found too small for his genius, had all the amenities of sophisticated urban life. It could boast of twenty-five miles of Roman aqueducts, a forum with cool cryptoporticos to shelter strolling citizens from the Mistral, baths, temples, a theater, a circus, and an enormous amphitheater in two stories with sixty arcades.[13] As a member of the local aristocracy,[14] Favorinus would have been expected to maintain those aqueducts, heat the baths, sacrifice in the temples, and fill the amphitheater with beasts and gladiators on festive occasions, in exchange for front-row seats. For some men it was enough to lead processions as the town priest of Augustus, to serve on the Treasury Board, review the Night Watchmen, and receive the congratulations of the Pontoon Bargemakers' Association as patron of their guild.[15] From among these the most wealthy and distinguished would rise to a provincial priesthood.[16] The chief priest of the imperial cult in southern Gaul enjoyed (in exchange for substantial but unspecified benefactions) the dignity of lictors on state occasions, the privilege of purple garments for his wife, and, at the end of his year of office, the opportunity to donate a statue of himself to the temple of Augustus.[17]

This was not enough for Favorinus. There were other ways to earn a statue. He went abroad, studied philosophy for a while with Dio Chrysostom, performed as a public lecturer in the major cities of Greece and Asia, establishing himself on terms of intellectual and social intimacy with Plutarch and Herodes Atticus, and settled eventually in Rome. Narbonensis did not forget him, however. A fortune of at least four hundred thousand *sestertii*[18] must not be allowed to bypass opportunities for public service. So Favorinus found himself elected to the provincial priesthood in absentia.[19] An appeal to the emperor brought no relief—indeed, may have brought him out of favor—[20] and, much against his will, the eunuch sophist from Arles became high priest of Augustus in the province he left behind.

[13] For documentation see A. Rivet, *Gallia Narbonensis* (London, 1988), chap. 14.

[14] His family was of equestrian rank: [Dio Chrysostom] *Or.* 37.25.

[15] *CIL* 12 contains numerous examples of local careers (e.g.: 700, 704, 672, 692).

[16] Examples of the careers of Narbonensian provincial priests may be found in *CIL* 12, 392, 3183, 3184, 3212, 3213, 3274, 3275.

[17] The law establishing the flaminate (*CIL* 12, 864), surviving in a fragmentary state, enumerates privileges but not duties. Support of provincial games must have been required, as well as other amenities. We know of one provincial priest who improved the road between Arles and Marseilles by building a bridge that still stands today (*CIL* 12, 647; Rivet, *Gallia Narbonensis*, 205, with plate 35).

[18] The *minimum* property qualification for equestrian rank; it would feed eight hundred families at subsistence level for a year.

[19] Philostratus, *Lives* 490.

[20] On Favorinus' exile and his troubles with Hadrian, see below, Chapter Six.

Congenital eunuchs are a rare phenomenon, and eunuchs of any kind were probably not a daily sight in the provincial cities of the western empire at this time, or even in the east, where self-castrated priests were traditionally associated with certain religious cults.[21] Castrated slaves were not as commonly seen as they were in later centuries, although grisly how-to instructions were available in medical texts.[22] We may assume that at this time eunuchs with social position were practically unknown.[23]

Exceptional specimen that he was, Favorinus did not fail to make an impact on his contemporaries, and, embalmed in a mythology that was partly his own creation, he was remembered by later generations for his unusual appearance as well as his professional attainments.

> Favorinus, like Dio, was a philosopher whose verbal facility proclaimed him a sophist. He came from the Gauls of the west, from the city of Arles on the river Rhone. He was born double-sexed, both male and female, as his appearance made plain: his face remained beardless even into old age. His voice revealed the same ambiguity, for it was penetrating, shrill, and high-pitched, the way nature tunes the voices of eunuchs. Yet he was so hot-blooded when it comes to sex that he was actually charged with adultery by a man of consular rank. He had some differences with the emperor Hadrian but came to no harm. Thus he used to speak in oracular riddles about the three paradoxes of his life.[24]

Favorinus boasted of himself as anomalous; evidently he thought of himself as unique. He seems to have generated his identity from contradictions. As a philosopher, he stressed the instability of human knowledge. He defended the Academic practice of arguing both sides of the same question and attacked the Stoics' claims for the reliability of sense-perception.[25] A similar refusal to buy into any monolithic construction of

---

[21] On the eunuch attendants of Atargatis at Hieropolis, see Lucian, *On the Syrian Goddess* 51–52. On eunuch slaves and freedmen, see P. Guyot, *Eunuchen als Sklaven und Freigelassene in der griechisch-römischen Antike*, Stuttgarter Beiträge zur Geschichte und Politik 14 (Stuttgart, 1980).

[22] Paul of Aegina 6.68, which derives from the first-century Heliodoros via Oribasius.

[23] The closest parallel that I have been able to find is Dorotheus, a late-third-century presbyter of Antioch, who, like Favorinus, was born a eunuch. Like Favorinus, he was known for his mastery of literary studies—in this case, Hebrew scripture as well as the liberal arts of traditional Greek education; and like Favorinus, he performed in public with words: Eusebius heard him expounding the scriptures in church "very intelligently" (*H.E.* 7.32.2). He too enjoyed the patronage of an emperor (Diocletian appointed him manager of the imperial dye-works at Tyre), and he too may have fallen from imperial favor—to die, as a Christian, a martyr's death. (Eusebius *H.E.* 8.6; see T. D. Barnes, *Constantine and Eusebius* [Cambridge, Mass., 1981], 192 with nn.).

[24] Philostratus, *Lives* 489.

[25] Galen, *On the Best Teaching* (K 1.40ff. = Barigazzi fr. 28); on Favorinus as a skeptical Academic, see J. Glucker, *Antiochus and the Late Academy* (Göttingen, 1978) = *Hypomnemata* 56, 280–95.

reality lent a shimmer of phenomenological playfulness to his rhetorical works, in whose remains, as we shall see below, we can still detect a taste for self-dramatization through constantly shifting personae.

His arch rival in the performance culture of the Second Sophistic found both Favorinus' indeterminate gender and the ambiguities of his self-presentation highly suspect. M. Antonius Polemo was a physiognomist as well as a sophist, and in his casebook of physiognomical examples he did not scruple to infer moral depravity from Favorinus' physical anomalies (note the backhanded way in which he concedes his rival's mastery of Greek):[26]

He was libidinous and dissolute beyond all bounds. . . . He had a bulbous brow,[27] flabby cheeks, wide mouth, a gangling scraggly neck, fat calves, and fleshy feet. His voice was like a woman's, and likewise his extremities and other bodily parts were uniformly soft; nor did he walk with an upright posture: his joints and limbs were lax. He took great care of his abundant tresses, rubbed ointments on his body, and cultivated everything that excites the desire for coitus and lust. . . . Endowed with that sort of appearance, he indulged in insulting jokes and used to do whatever came into his head. He was thoroughly schooled in the Greek language and idiom and used to make great use of them; he was even called a sophist.

He used to go about cities and marketplaces, gathering crowds in order to display his wickedness and indulge his taste for sexual debauchery. On top of this he was a charlatan in the magic arts. He induced people to believe that he could confer life and death, and because of this enticed men and women to gather round him in crowds. He made men believe that he could compel women to pursue men the way men pursue women, using a hidden voice to make himself credible. He was a master of evil doing, and made a practice of collecting lethal poisons which he secretly offered for sale.[28]

[26] Polemo, De physiognomia, in Förster, Scriptores Physiognomonici Graeci, vol. 1, 160–64. This edition gives an Arabic text based on only one of the five extant Arabic manuscripts (with a Latin translation by G. Hoffmann). My English translation was originally produced from Hoffmann's Latin and checked against the Arabic by Margaret Malamud. In the passage quoted, Polemo does not actually mention Favorinus by name, but since he describes his subject as a eunuch from the land of the Celts, born without testicles, we can be pretty sure whom he means. Cf. Anonymi de Physiognomonia liber 40 (Förster, vol. 2, 58).

[27] Hoffmann's apparatus indicates that there is a problem in the text here. See L. Holford-Strevens, who offers a paraphrase in his Aulus Gellius (Chapel Hill, 1988), 73, and points out that there is little to be gained from speculation about the text until all the Arabic mss. have been collated.

[28] Polemo considers eunuchs like Favorinus, born without testicles, to be more uncanny, more "perfect in evil" than eunuchs who were produced of normal males by castration. Mary Douglas discusses such anomalies as a source of danger in Purity and Danger: An Analysis of the Concepts of Pollution and Taboo (London, 1966).

Some of the physical traits noted here appear even in Philostratus' more sympathetic portrait: effeminate appearance, high-pitched voice, unexpected libido. In the complex symbolic system within which ancient aristocrats constructed male identities, peculiarities of physical appearance, deportment, and voice (rather than libido) were the major signifiers. Subsequent chapters of this book explore their symbolic value to contemporaries. Polemo's charges of black magic should not be taken literally: they merely serve as an index of his rival's professional success.[29]

Successful he was: even in Rome, where many knew no Greek, Favorinus' performances left his audiences spellbound.[30] In Asia Minor Polemo was all the rage at Smyrna, but Favorinus was the darling of Ephesus. In Greece he dazzled the Corinthians; they voted him a public statue.[31] It would seem that Favorinus had achieved everything that he left Gaul to attain. But then the Corinthians took his statue down again, for reasons still obscure. The speech that purports to be the sophist's reply to this insult reveals him at work as an elaborate artificer of self-presentation— indeed as a prestidigitator worthy of Polemo's worst fears.[32]

SELF-PRESENTATION IN THE CORINTHIAN ORATION

Like every great sophist, Favorinus lived his life in fierce pursuit of international recognition and immortal fame. An honorific statue like those awarded him in Corinth and at Athens[33] was an enduring symbol of his ability to reenact countless transient triumphs. The destruction of such a statue was a defamation that demanded a response. Invective alone might

---

[29] The rhetorician Apuleius, for example, was actually accused in court of practicing erotic magic by the jealous relatives of a wealthy older woman whom he had persuaded to marry him (Apuleius, *Apology*).

[30] Philostratus, *Lives* 490–91, who uses the word *enchanted* (ἔθελγε) twice. Favorinus' style has been examined by A. Barigazzi, *Favorino di Arelate Opere* (Florence, 1966), and his prose rhythm by M. Goggin, "Rhythm in the Prose of Favorinus," *YCS* 12 (1951), 149–201.

[31] Compare for example the statue of the sophist Lollianus at Athens, paid for by his grateful students (Kaibel, *Epigrammata Graeca* 877; Philostratus, *Lives* 527). Apuleius *Florida* 16 mentions statues of sophists in the forum of Carthage.

[32] This is the thirty-seventh oration in the corpus of Dio Chrysostom, now generally attributed to Favorinus. It will be cited in the text by paragraph numbers in parentheses. We cannot know whether this speech was actually delivered, though it is perhaps unlikely that a virtuoso performer like Favorinus would have allowed a speech with such dramatic possibilities to languish in manuscript. We also cannot know the identity of the actual audience, which need not have been Corinthian. The only exegesis of this speech known to me is in Adelmo Barigazzi's commentary *Favorino di Arelate Opere* (Florence, 1966).

[33] *Lives* 490. The Athenians also destroyed a statue of Favorinus when he fell out of favor with the emperor, but he was able to pass off the insult with a philosophical remark that implicitly compared himself to Socrates. Compare Demonax's refusal of a statue on the grounds that Socrates and Diogenes had no statues either (Lucian *Demonax* 58).

not suffice: some form of praise or eulogy of the injured party was required, yet there were limits to the extent one could play Pindar to one's
own achievements. Favorinus' friend Plutarch devoted an entire treatise to
the touchy subject of self-praise. He writes as one intimately acquainted
with the psychology of competition in his culture:

> First, when others are being praised, our love of honor causes the urge for self-
> praise to break out [like boils]; it is seized by a lust or urge for glory that stings
> and tingles like an almost unendurable itch, especially if a person is being praised
> for something in which he is our equal or inferior. For just as those who are
> starving find that the sight of other people eating food intensifies and aggravates
> their hunger, so the praise of near-equals inflames the rivalry of those who
> cannot control their appetite for fame.[34]

Thus praising oneself, according to Plutarch, is a poor strategy, since it
renders others deaf to one's merits by making them yearn to trumpet their
own. Besides, there is the sheer vulgarity of it all. Would Favorinus really
want to rank himself with "soldiers and nouveaux-riches, reciting their
pompous purple-bordered tales" or with "sophists, philosophers, and
generals, swollen with their own importance and accustomed to dilate on
that theme"?[35] In this respect his diminished status as bereaved "owner" of
a deposed statue brings with it a rhetorical advantage: self-praise, Plutarch
says, is less offensive if you are answering an accusation or defending
yourself from slander.[36] To make the most of the rhetorical opportunities
presented by his embarrassing situation, Favorinus must exploit the possibilities of his defensive posture without allowing himself to appear pitiable
or pathetic in any way. He must also find a way to censure the Corinthians
without totally alienating his audience. In effect, he has to combine the
activities of apology and invective without appearing to perform either.
He does this by burying ironic mockery of Corinth inside historical and
literary allusions, and by adopting the identity of imaginary personae in
order to cover his tracks when he is actually praising himself. Sometimes
he pretends that his statue is on trial and plays the role of its advocate; at
other times he impersonates the statue itself. By speaking in multiple
personae, he offsets the dramatic limitations of the monologue, expanding
the cast of characters involved.

This is how he begins: "When first I visited your city, about ten years
ago, and displayed my eloquence to your citizens and magistrates, I
seemed to be on even more intimate terms with you than Arion of
Methymne—for you did not have a statue made of *him*."
Favorinus' own statue thus makes its first appearance in a rather ghostly

[34] "On Inoffensive Self-Praise," *Mor.* 546C.
[35] Ibid. 547E.
[36] Ibid. 540C.

way, as the unexpressed antithesis of the statue that a mythical poet never received. The story continues: as Arion was traveling back to Corinth after a successful tour, his wealth proved an irresistible temptation to the sailors on his ship. When they ordered him to jump into the sea, he begged leave to give one last performance. His voice so charmed the dolphins that one carried him safely to shore, where, having exacted vengeance from the sailors, he set up a statue of himself astride a dolphin. By comparing himself to Arion, Favorinus implies that his own voice has magical power. The legendary artiste, granted one last chance to sing before the unmusical villains who are about to throw him overboard, is an appropriate analogue for Favorinus, permitted to give one last speech before judges who have, in effect, thrown his statue overboard already. Favorinus' audience also might remember that Arion's wicked mariners were, in fact, Corinthians.[37]

Favorinus scores his points subtly: how can he be blamed for making his audience remember a fact that he has not explicitly mentioned? It was traditional for a visiting sophist to praise the city of his hosts with a farrago of historical and literary allusions. Favorinus manages to conform to custom while deliberately intruding a few false notes.[38] This section of his *Praise of Corinth*[39] is on one level just a catalog of famous visitors to the city. He mentions Solon, who was not honored with a statue, and Herodotus, who, when denied payment by the Corinthians for his services as an itinerant lecturer, achieved a lasting revenge in his writing (6–7). Here the pattern of analogical thought that runs through the entire catalog suggests that by spurning Favorinus' just claims to fame the Corinthians have laid themselves open to a similar revenge.

When Favorinus came to Corinth a second time, he says, the city actually tried to persuade him to stay, but since that was not possible they had "an image of his body" (*eikōn tou sōmatos*) set up "in a front row seat" in the library to inspire young men to diligence in literary pursuits (8). This honor constitutes the climax of the catalog of literary visitors, and the peripeteia of Favorinus' fortunes. He must now explicitly confront the accident that has befallen his statue. To suggest the poignant impermanence of such tokens of worldly glory, he appropriates a line from Homer, "But honor, like a dream, takes wing and flies away."[40] He has, however, changed one word, substituting "honor" (*timē*) for Homer's "soul" (*psuchē*). This substitution introduces a number of themes that will be

[37] Herodotus 1.24.2.

[38] Compare the remarks of Erving Goffman on what might now be called "preserving deniability," in *The Presentation of Self in Everyday Life* (Garden City, New York, 1959), 190–91.

[39] The ms. title is Κορινθιακός (sc. Λόγος), which would usually mean an encomium.

[40] [Dio] 37.9, cf. *Od.* 11.222.

important later on. A statue is precisely a form of *honor* without *soul*. One
would like to claim that both one's honor and one's soul are immortal, but
one's statue clearly is not. In the Homeric context, these words are spoken
by the ghost of Odysseus' mother. Odysseus tries to embrace her, but her
shade evades his arms. Odysseus asks in anguish whether she is nothing
but an image (*eidōlon*) sent by Persephone to torment him. She denies that
she is an illusion and explains how after death the body is burned but the
soul "takes wing and flies away." This famous Homeric scene resonates
with some of the central themes of Favorinus' oration, which plays with
questions of identity and explores the ambiguous relationship of soul and
statue, self and image.

Faced with the loss of his statue, Favorinus wonders aloud, "Did I not
see what I saw? Was it all a dream . . . the enthusiasm of the populace, the
vote of the council? Or was the statue an invention of Daedalus that ran off
of its own accord?" (9). He is taking temporary refuge from insult in the
world of illusion: either the statue was never set up, or it was set up but
disappeared without being taken down. In either case there was no damage
to honor.

But even if the statue were the work of Daedalus, Favorinus asks, why
would it ever leave Corinth? Thus he makes for himself an opportunity to
display the sort of erudite praise of the city's past that is appropriate to a
"straight" encomium (11–15). As Favorinus reasons, the conclusion is
inevitable: since neither Daedalus nor my statue would ever leave such a
city of their own accord, it must have been the Corinthians themselves
who banished it without trial. Yet who would believe this of the Corinthians, whose forefathers were so renowned for justice? . . . (16) Here follows more traditional praise of Corinth, into which Favorinus slips a
backhanded allusion to Corinthian cowardice at the Battle of Salamis. He
concludes this historical excursus with the Corinthians' liberation of Syracuse from her tyrants, which provides a transition to the next topic: the
Trial of the Statues at Syracuse (20–21).[41]

It was not enough to allude to the shortcomings of the Corinthians'
past. Without appearing to eulogize himself, Favorinus must show that
they were wrong to slight his worth. So he invites his audience to participate in a thought experiment. The citizens of Syracuse once ran out of
money and voted to recycle the bronze statues of their tyrants. They held a
trial to determine which statues deserved to be spared. Favorinus asks us to
imagine that such a trial is happening right now, and sets up the imaginary
scenario within which the remainder of his oration will take place: suppose
there were such a law in Corinth and my statue were on trial; permit me to
speak on the statue's behalf (22).

[41] The story is found in Plutarch's *Timoleon* 23.4.

Fictional devices of a similar kind were popular among the training exercises of Greek rhetorical education.[42] Students in their *progymnasmata* would debate the implications of imaginary laws, and sophists in their public declamations would tax their ingenuity with complicated hypothetical problems. Sometimes the technique was exploited less for its paradoxical possibilities than as a framework for a polemical treatise or a dramatic monologue. Galen would have us imagine the medical sects squaring off, "And now let the Dogmatist speak first, as if before the judge in a court of law, ridiculing the arguments of the Empiricist, his opponent."[43] Libanius' showpiece, "Self-Accusation of the Grouch Who Has Married a Talkative Wife,"[44] is built on the legal fiction that hemlock was available in Athens for a would-be suicide who could prove his case to the Council. In Lucian, the imaginary trial gambit becomes obscene. While attacking a fellow sophist, he adopts the persona of his opponent's *tongue*—which promptly indicts its owner for mouth abuse![45]

An oration in praise of Fortune that is nowadays attributed to Favorinus[46] shows how he might deploy in another context some of the same rhetorical devices that he uses to defend his statue to the Corinthians. He arranges this oration also as a mock trial, where it becomes his duty to defend Fortune from her detractors (5).[47] His general line of defense is that people tend to blame Fortune for their own faults. One example he uses is particularly telling because its tragic conflicts of gender identity and self-presentation crystalize in a most unusual statue.

"Once upon a time, even some women were famous."[48] We are in the realm of historical fiction. Demonassa ("Woman Ruler of the People") was known on Cyprus as a politician and a legislator. Her success as a public figure, however, blighted her achievement as a mother. She gave the people of Cyprus three strict laws, but in fairy-tale fashion each of her

---

[42] A full discussion may be found in D. A. Russell, *Greek Declamation* (Cambridge, 1983), 35–37, 91.

[43] *Galen On Medical Experience*, translated from the Arabic in the edition of R. Walzer (Oxford, 1944), 87.

[44] *Decl.* 26, which provided Ben Jonson with inspiration for his *Epicene*.

[45] *False Critic* 25–26.

[46] [Dio Chrysostom] 64. For the attribution to Favorinus, see Barigazzi, 245, with references, and the stylistic analysis of M. Goggin, "Rhythm in the Prose of Favorinus," *YCS* 12 (1951),151,191–92.

[47] This oration is a *jeu d'esprit*, a form of paradoxical encomium in which the orator demonstrates his inventiveness by lavishing praise on something generally disliked. For a discussion of the genre, see A. Ste. Pease, "Things Without Honor," *CP* 21(1926), 27–42. Other efforts of Favorinus in this genre are known to us only by title: "In Praise of Thersites," "In Praise of Quartan Fever" (Gellius, *Attic Nights* 17.12.1).

[48] ἤνεγκεν ὁ παλαιὸς βίος καὶ ἐνδόξους γυναῖκας (2).

three children eventually ran afoul of one of her laws and was ruined by the penalty. "For a while, she toughed it out, as both a childless woman and a law-giver,"[49] but at last, when she encountered a cow mourning for her dying calf, she could no longer evade the tragic paradox of her own maternity. "She recognized her own fate in another." Impelled by this revelation to self-destruct, she melted a huge vat of bronze and leaped into it headlong. She disappeared, but the molten metal that congealed around her vanished form remained. The bronze she left behind was both her statue (*andrianta chalkeon*), by the lost wax process, as it were, and a mimesis of her story (*mimēma tou diēgēmatos*). Thus Favorinus expresses the paradox of a woman's immortalizing fame: it is a self-canceling impossibility, a shape that nobody can see. To twentieth-century readers, Demonassa's statue is also iconic in the way it represents the implosion of identity awaiting those who transgress gender boundaries and the psychic costs of the whole self-presentation crucible in which the "hard" public exterior is to be achieved at the cost of evacuating the "soft," "feminine" interior.

In order to establish an imaginary trial scenario for his own statue in the *Corinthian Oration*, Favorinus begins with a conditional, "If there should be a measure like this passed in Corinth too," but changes his grammatical footing immediately to an absolute construction that takes for granted the existence of the legal practice postulated at the beginning of the sentence, "Or rather, if you please, this measure has already passed and a trial has been instituted." At the risk of some grammatical awkwardness, these absolutes remove us from the realm of the conditional both syntactically and rhetorically and permit Favorinus to establish his hypothesis as if it were real. The hypothetical element that loomed so large at the beginning of the sentence has shrunk to an insignificant "if you please." The absolute constructions, detached from the syntax of the conditional sentence in which they are embedded, provide a sort of neutral spot in the gear box that facilitates the sentence's upcoming shift into the imperative mood: "Permit me, permit me to speak on the statue's behalf as if in court" (22).[50] The effect of the repeated imperative is to obscure the hypothetical nature of the scene and pull the audience abruptly into the fantasy.

Editors have emended "Permit me to speak on the statue's behalf" to "Permit me to speak on my own behalf."[51] This emendation is unnecessary because Favorinus is referring to the statue in the masculine (*ho andrias*) and it suits his purposes to build the illusion that the "defendant" in this trial is a person other than himself. To avoid the spectacle of self praising self *in*

---

[49] ἡ δὲ τέως μὲν ἐκαρτέρει καὶ ἄπαις οὖσα καὶ νομοθετοῦσα.
[50] δότε μοι, δότε τοὺς λόγους ὑπὲρ αὐτοῦ πρὸς ὑμᾶς οἷον ἐν δικαστηρίῳ ποιήσασθαι.
[51] See Crosby's Loeb edition (cited in n.77) 22–23.

propria persona, the orator has constructed an imaginary stage on which he can appear to be the advocate not of himself but of his statue. At other times, instead of playing the statue's advocate, Favorinus actually impersonates the statue itself. It was a well-known technique in Greco-Roman rhetoric to add extra voices to a monologue by anticipating the objections of opponents and even putting words right into their mouths. But Favorinus' rhetorical strategy—both his simulation of a trial at which his statue is a defendant and his ploy of making his statue speak for itself—depends upon gracefully sustaining the illusion of the personification of an inanimate object. Several features of Greek language and culture favored this trope and prepared his audience to accept the fruits of his imagination: the practice of making objects of daily life, like drinking cups, announce themselves with first-person inscriptions ("I belong to Miltiades"); first-person funerary epigrams; and the ancient legal custom of making objects (including statues) that had caused a person's death stand trial for murder.[52] In the traditions of Greek story-telling, statues sometimes played an active role. Everybody knew that after the death of Theagenes of Thasos an old enemy paid nightly visits to his statue and scourged it with a whip. The statue fell over and killed him; the victim's relatives brought suit for murder. The statue was condemned and tossed into the sea, but the Thasians suffered from famine until they restored the statue in accordance with oracular advice.[53] Favorinus was surely familiar with this story: it was retold by Dio Chrysostom in *his* oration about maltreated statues.[54] Of course it would have appealed to Favorinus' antiquarian instincts that poetic justice exacted by statues was a topos in Greek literature. Aristotle in his discussion of plot commends the aptness with which a statue of a dead man fell upon his murderer.[55] A poem attributed to Theocritus tells the story of a heartless lover killed by a statue of Eros,[56] an epigram in the *Palatine Anthology* records the fate of a boy killed by the toppling stele of his wicked stepmother,[57] and Lucian tells of a household statue that got down off its pedestal to flog the slave who had been filching its offerings.[58]

In the supernatural realm, statues certainly did talk. We have details from Christian exposés: at Alexandria some temples had "talking statues"

---

[52] Dem. 23.76; Aesch. 3.244; Antiphon, *Second Tetralogy*; Aristotle, *Const. Ath.* 57. 4. Cf. Plato, *Laws* 9.873e–874a. At Athens the knife that killed the bull at the *Bouphonia* was tried for murder: Paus. 1.28.10; Aelian *VH* 8.3; Porphyry *De abstinentia* 2.30.

[53] Paus. 6.11.2–9.

[54] *Or.* 31.95–97. Favorinus was said to have been Dio's pupil: Philostratus, *Lives* 490.

[55] *Poetics* 1552a7ff. See also Plutarch, *Mor.* 553D.

[56] *Idyll* 23.59–60. The victim is, in a sense, a murderer himself since he has caused his rejected suitor to commit suicide.

[57] *Anth. Pal.* 9.67.

[58] *Lover of Lies* 18–20.

whose hollow insides were manned by pagan priests with secret access from the room next door,[59] and polemicists claimed that the talking heads used in craniomancy were actually fitted out with speaking tubes.[60] Favorinus was not averse to exuding an aura of mystery, but whether his hocus-pocus was intended to have any disquieting effect on his audience (was he just perhaps animating his statue *against them?*) we can only surmise.[61]

Another source of precedents for speaking statues would be funerary epigrams. In logical, if not historical, progression, they move from impersonal statements of fact ("Here lies . . ."), to verses in which the tomb speaks *qua* tombstone ("I am the tomb of . . . " or "I hold . . . "), to verses in which a statue of something else talks about the deceased,[62] to cases in which the deceased seems to speak in the first person. Certainly in some of those cases, we are being asked to imagine that the speaker is the deceased's statue or portrait standing on the tomb.[63] In short, Favorinus' decision to animate his statue brought to his speech the charm of novelty without the shock of the totally unexpected.

To erode the audience's sense of certainty as to the precise identity of his own narrating voice, Favorinus cultivates grammatical ambiguity around the word *statue*. By avoiding the feminine noun *eikōn*,[64] and using instead the masculine alternative *andrias*, Favorinus manages to sprinkle his speech with masculine pronouns whose antecedents are ambiguous. When we are told, "This one here (*houtos*) is in danger of being put up (*tethēnai*) as the best of the Hellenes and being thrown out (*ekpesein*) as the worst, all in a short space of time"(22), it is by no means clear whether "this" refers to the statue or to the sophist. If it refers to the sophist, then who is speaking now? Actually, the ambiguity may be deliberate. In one sense, *houtos* does refer to the statue and can be understood to come from the mouth of Favorinus' first persona, The Advocate of the Statue, conjured up two sentences before. In another sense, *houtos* refers to Favorinus himself and comes from the mouth of his second persona, the speaking statue.

[59] These were finally revealed to the light of day by the statue-smashing bishop Theophilus during the reign of Theodosius: Theodoret *H.E.* 5.22. Compare Lucian's exposé of the oracular serpent-god Glycon, *Alexander the False Prophet* 26.

[60] Hippolytus, *Refutatio omnium haeresium* 4.41; cf. F. Poulsen, "Talking, Weeping and Bleeding Sculptures: A Chapter in the History of Religious Fraud," *Acta Archeologica*, 16 (1945),178–95.

[61] The rhetorician-cum-philosopher Apuleius was alleged to have used his portable statue of Hermes for nefarious purposes (Apuleius *Apology* 63).

[62] For example, a statue of a satyr on Sophocles' tomb, *Anth. Pal.* 7.37; a dog guarding Diogenes, ibid. 64, cf. 161.

[63] Dialogues that begin, "Tell me, O stele, who . . ." (as in *Anth. Pal.* 140, 165, 470, 503), are like the captions of imaginary pictures. Cf. F. E. Consolino, "L'appello al lettore nell' epitaffio della tarda latinità" *Maia* 28 (1976), 129–43.

[64] The term preferred by Dio in his speech about statues, *Or.* 31.

By the next sentence, the statue has definitely assumed the first person, saying, "Now I shall demonstrate at length . . . that I was rightly and justly set up (*estathēn*),[65] but first I want to tell you about an incident that took place in that same Syracuse" (23). The substance of this digression is that a Lucanian ambassador once so impressed the Syracusans with his masterful command of Doric Greek that they gave him a talent and set up a statue of him (24). Favorinus immediately draws the moral of the tale as it applies to himself:

> If someone who is not a Lucanian, but a Roman, and not one of the masses, but an Equestrian, who has emulated not only the language, but also the thought and habits and costume of the Greeks, and has done it so masterfully and conspicuously that of all Romans before him and all Greeks of his own time *not one*, let it be said, has done the equivalent (for while Greek aristocrats incline toward Roman ways, he inclines toward Greek ways, and for their sake has let go his property, his political standing, and absolutely everything else, aiming at all cost not to seem Greek but to be Greek too)—then ought not that man stand among you in bronze? (25).[66]

The effect of this comparison is to camouflage self-praise by embedding it within the ostensibly impersonal structure of an *a fortiori* argument. Indeed, the speaker concludes, there should be statues of Favorinus everywhere! (26) The gods have equipped him for this very purpose: "to show the Greeks of Hellas that education can produce the same results as birth, to show the Romans, so freighted with their own dignity, not to neglect its enhancement by education, and to show the Celts that not even barbarians need despair of Hellenic culture when they look at his example."[67] "So I was erected," the statue continues, "for reasons like these (not to expose myself to hostility by saying any more)" (28).

Favorinus' conception of himself as a universal cultural paradigm with a message for Greeks, Romans, and barbarians invites comparison with the polyvalence of another sophist who had once addressed the Corinthians thus: "To the Jews I became as a Jew, in order to win Jews; to those under the law I became as one under the law . . . that I might win those under the law. To those outside the law I became as one outside the law . . . that I might win those outside the law. . . . I have become all things to all men,

---

[65] The first person ἐστάθην should not be emended to the third person here or in section 27, as some editors suggest.

[66] The combination of an intransitive verb (like the second perfect ἑστάναι) with a predicate adjective (like χαλκοῦν) seems to be a special locution particularly suitable for semi-personified things like statues or stelai. For parallels to Favorinus, compare Herodotus 2.141.6, ὁ βασιλεὺς ἕστηκε . . . λίθινος, and Lucian, *Parasite* 48, ἕστηκε χαλκοῦς.

[67] Note how the statue refers to Favorinus in the third person (βλέπων εἰς τοῦτον).

that I might by all means save some."[68] The kind of self-transformation that the apostle Paul describes is only temporary, a means to an end. He indulges in it only in order to become enough like others that he can transform them into what he, underneath all transformations, really is: a person "under the law of Christ."

For Favorinus, however, the transformation he embodies is in itself his accomplishment. Born in Gaul, a freak of nature, he has become an international celebrity in the Roman Empire as a virtuoso exponent of Greek culture. Implicit in the vision of Greek culture that he represents is the assumption that self-transformation is possible through rhetorical training, that diligent practice in the art of improvisation in a very traditional medium will result in the alteration of one's *habitus*. Favorinus is himself both his medium and his message. This helps to explain why he was even able to fascinate audiences who did not understand Greek.[69]

Favorinus presses the claim that statues, once dedicated, should never be taken down, least of all because of slander (33). Only now do we find out that our speaker has been the victim of unjustified attacks. He presents them as the inevitable inconvenience of those who lead a life of renown. Furthermore, he asserts that the slander against him has its origin in the seductive charm of his rhetoric (*epaphrodisia*)—the very charm that the Corinthians, with their wives and children, have endorsed. Since the slander Favorinus refers to seems to have been some sort of morals charge (perhaps his notorious affair with the consular's wife?), his choice of *epaphrodisia* to describe his eloquence is definitely tongue-in-cheek. We are reminded of Polemo's claim that Favorinus was actually an erotic magician, whose spells could compel sexual desire at will. This eunuch's sexuality is his rhetoric. If the Corinthians had willingly exposed their wives and children to the latter, how can they fairly criticize him for the former? Especially since Corinth is of all cities the most favored of Aphrodite: *epaphroditotatē* (34). Favorinus is slyly calling the kettle black.

Chapters 34–36 combine evasion and allusion to produce a very murky picture of The Incident (whatever it was). He implies, but does not actually state, that the emperor gave the informers a hearing but rendered no judgment against him. Our ignorance and the lapse of time, however,

---

[68] I Corinthians 9.20–22. On Paul as a sophist, see E. Judge, "The early Christians as a Scholastic Community: Part II," *Journal of Religious History* 2 (Sydney, 1961), 125–37, and "Paul's Boasting in Relation to Contemporary Professional Practice," *Australian Biblical Review* 16 (1968), 37–50.

[69] "When he gave lectures in Rome, there was enthusiasm everywhere, and even those who knew no Greek heard him with pleasure. He charmed them with the resonance of his voice, with the significative power of his gaze, and with the rhythm of his speech" : Philostratus, *Lives* 491.

prevent us from sharing with the original audience an aesthetic appreciation of Favorinus' skill at coloring the truth without actually telling lies.[70]

Still speaking of himself in the third person, Favorinus makes the disin-
genuous claim that everything he has said so far has been aimed at preserving the good name of *Corinth*, lest she incur disgrace for maltreating a man
so widely honored among the Greeks. "But on behalf of myself and my
statue," he continues, barely catching breath to change into *propria persona*, "I'll quote the words of Anaxagoras when he lost his son: 'I knew I
had begotten a mortal.'" Just beneath the text lies the implication: I am like
Anaxagoras (falsely indicted by Athenians hostile to his friendship with
Pericles, he continued his career elsewhere with great success), and my
statue is like my son: my creation, not yours.

Every statue is set up as if it were going to last forever, but, Favorinus
admits, they all do perish through one agency or another, most commonly
and most appropriately through time. Midas' tomb had an epitaph that
began, "I am a bronze maiden. I am set up on Midas' tomb" (38). The
verses survive, but neither tomb nor statue can be found. The orator
apostrophizes the statue ("O Self-Announcing Maiden")[71] at the very
moment he tells us that she does not exist, thus conjuring her up to
undercut what he is saying. The poet who wrote the epitaph was wrong: it
is not the statue but his own words that are immortal. Similarly with the
next example: no one now knows who Hippaemon was, let alone what has
become of his statue, but we can still quote his epitaph (*Anth. Pal.* 7.304).
Verbal artifacts last forever.

Here Favorinus describes the desecration suffered by all sorts of statues
of the great, both gods and men (40–42). Agesilaus the Spartan king never
permitted statues of himself to be made because he realized that one should
not try to prolong one's fated span with a statue whose materials can be
destroyed (43). Favorinus continues to build on the tension we have already seen between statue and animating principle. "Would that we could
even be free of our bodies!" he exclaims. The danger of using statues as
stand-ins for ourselves is that, instead of immortalizing us, they may
merely extend our vulnerability to physical decay.

"Farewell to Daedalus and his mimetic inventions; enough of Prome-
theus, enough of clay! . . . For the soul is not present nor does it worry
when the body is worn out" (44). The tyrant Cambyses did not batter the
real king of Egypt, but merely his corpse, "a shape without a soul." And
while the philosopher Anaxarchus was being ground up in a mortar by an

---

[70] There seems to be a reference to Hadrian in Favorinus' comment about the Master of the
Games listening to informers (35). For a discussion of Favorinus' political troubles, see
Chapter Six.

[71] ὦ παρθένε αὐτάγγελε (39).

evil satrap, he taunted his tormenter with the claim that it was not Anaxarchus but only his outer covering that was being ground. Then *a fortiori* should not I allow my statue to be smelted, Favorinus asks, even if it did have sensation? (46).

The orator has almost painted himself into a corner here. Having gone to great lengths to distinguish the mortal husk from its animating principle, he has almost proved that statues don't matter. To resolve this paradox, he animates his statue. "Anaxarchus may have had mastery over his sensations, but I, like Laodameia, 'would not desert what's near and dear even though it lacks a soul.'"[72] Then Favorinus announces, "I wish therefore to address him as if he were a sensate being. 'O silent image of my eloquence, are you not plain to see?'" The sonorous cadences of the Greek must have had a sensational incantatory effect in performance: *O logōn emōn sigēlon eidōlon, ou phainē?* Then, continuing to address his statue, Favorinus compares him to the mythical poet Aristeas. By introducing an episode in which Aristeas' statue is stolen away by his enemies, our speaker has either muddled the details of Herodotus to fit his current preoccupations or is using a different version of the story.[73] But it is easy to see how the tale of a poet whose immortality survived interim disappearances of self and statue appealed to him. "But Aristeas lives! Then, now, and for all time."

Favorinus builds toward his peroration with quotations from Sappho and Hesiod that assert the immortality of fame.[74] Then, in a passage full of the singsong sound effects for which he was notorious,[75] Favorinus vows:

> I myself will raise you up by the goddess, where no one will take you down: not earthquake, not wind, not snow, not rain, not envy, not enemy—but even now I find you standing in place! Oblivion (*latha*) has previously tripped and cheated others, but intelligent judgment (*gnōmē*) has never caused good men to fall, and it is by such judgment that you stand upright for me like a man" (47).

---

[72] οὐκ ἂν προδοίην καίπερ ἄψυχον φίλον (46).

[73] According to Herodotus (4.13–15), Aristeas was a poet whose corpse disappeared from a locked fuller's shop like Jesus' body from the tomb. Some people claimed to have met and talked with him on the road to Cyzicus, and seven years later he showed up again and wrote an epic on the one-eyed Skythians. Many generations after that, he appeared in Metapontum and commanded the citizens to erect a statue of him near an altar of Apollo.

[74] Sappho fr. 147 Lobel-Page; Hesiod, *Works and Days* 763–64.

[75] "He charmed those who knew no Greek with the finale of his speeches, which they used to call the 'ode,' but which I call showing off, since he sang it after the argument was completed": ἔθελγε δὲ αὐτοὺς (sc. ὅσοι τῆς Ἑλλήνων φωνῆς ἀξύνετοι ἦσαν) τοῦ λόγου καὶ τὸ ἐπὶ πᾶσιν, ὃ ἐκεῖνοι μὲν ᾠδὴν ἐκάλουν, ἐγὼ δὲ φιλοτιμίαν, ἐπειδὴ τοῖς ἀποδεδειγμένοις ἐφυμνεῖται. Philostratus, *Lives* 492. See M. Goggin, "Rhythm in the Prose of Favorinus," *YCS* 12 (1951), 149–201, esp. 153–55.

What kind of theurgy is going on here? In words scented with the immutable sublimity of Mount Olympus,[76] Favorinus invokes his statue as if it were rising again before our very eyes. We need not postulate a second unveiling.[77] Just as Arion erected his statue without the help of Periander (4), so Favorinus can resurrect his statue without any assistance from the Corinthians. He has conjured it up by the power of words alone. True fame is immortal; the sophist's statue represents his fame: therefore his statue is immortal too. Praise bestowed by the self on itself has no value— it is indeed self-canceling. But praise that like a juggler's ball never touches the hands is a self-constructing artifact: truly Homeric "imperishable fame."

Such was that *monstrum* from Gaul, now full-grown and in more ways than one a self-made man, battling with the forces of slander and oblivion like every Greek poet and hero before him. His performance is a tour de force. We can watch him construct his identity as a multivalent paradigm of *paideia*, adopting by turns the personae of advocate, self, and statue; imposing *his* vision through rhetoric and imagination to transform defeat into triumph. What Favorinus has been doing in a particularly florid way—constructing an identity for himself in performance—reveals by exaggeration some of the basic dynamics of the process of self-presentation for aristocratic males in his culture. In the next chapter we turn to watch the self-presentation of Polemo, his mortal enemy, whose special art was the deconstruction of the personae presented by others, in the lecture hall, at the dinner table, and in the public square.

[76] Cf. *Od.* 6.43–44.

[77] As suggested by H. L. Crosby in his Loeb edition of Dio Chrysostom (Cambridge and London: Harvard University Press, 1946), vol. 4, p. 2.

Chapter Two

PORTRAIT OF POLEMO: THE DEPORTMENT OF

THE PUBLIC SELF

"Le Monstre Lui-Même"

NOT FAR OUTSIDE of Smyrna, in a small temple by the sea, a statue of Favorinus' great rival, M. Antonius Polemo, was still standing years after his death.[1] He was posed for immortality in ceremonial regalia, just as he used to stand upon the sacred ship of Dionysus which was carried triumphantly to the city center in an annual religious parade.[2] Smyrna had awarded this privilege to him and his posterity in gratitude for his services, although he was not a native of the place. The descendant of the Hellenistic kings of Pontus, Polemo was born in Laodicea.[3] The splendor and opulence of his domestic establishment, "like magnificent public monuments," added luster to his adopted city, wealthy and cultivated as it was, and Polemo had received from its citizens every honor that was theirs to bestow.[4] Polemo must have managed his dual citizenship very smoothly, for we never hear of disputes about liturgical immunity such as clouded the careers of Favorinus, Aelius Aristides, and, in the fourth century, Libanius. Polemo's great-grandson, a youth who inherited both his eloquence and his arrogance, was able to reject gifts offered him by the emperor on the grounds that they would be redundant: "My great-grandfather bequeathed to us crowns, immunities, meals at public expense, purple, and priesthoods—and why should I ask you today for what I already possess from a man like him?"[5] In addition to the priesthood that entitled him to officiate upon the sacred ship, Smyrna had awarded to Polemo and his descendants the right to preside ceremonially

[1] On the name, see C. P. Jones, "Prosopographical Notes on the Second Sophistic," *GRBS* 21 (1981), 374–77. On the statue: Philostratus, *Lives* 530, 543.

[2] *Lives* 530, 543; cf. Aristides *Or*.17.6.

[3] For the early history of Polemo's distinguished family, see G. W. Bowersock, *Augustus and the Greek World* (Oxford, 1965), 51–53; 143–44.

[4] *Lives* 530, 532.

[5] Ibid. 611. The immunities in question may be no more than free travel (the *libera legatio*); there is no evidence that Polemo enjoyed or sought liturgical immunity. On the rarity of such immunities for wealthy sophists in this period, see G. W. Bowersock, *Greek Sophists in the Roman Empire* (Oxford, 1968), chap. 3.

over Hadrian's newly founded Olympic games.[6] In this office he could
display himself as a prominent defender of Hellenic high culture: he expelled from the contest a tragic actor who had pointed earthward while he
cried, "O Zeus" and thus "committed a solecism with his hand."[7] He also
would have had the power to expel unworthy contestants for bribery, such
as the unfortunate musician who dreamed just before competing at
Smyrna that he went to the baths but found them dry.[8]

Polemo combined his duties as cultural arbiter with political activity as a
liaison to the ruling power, and this combination answered to a deep social
need. After all the second century was a time when "the benefits of Roman
rule were never so obvious, [and] the vulnerability of Hellenic culture—
the danger that bad culture might drive out good—was never more clearly
perceived."[9] Because Polemo's eloquence and deportment embodied the
essence of Hellenism (as it was then understood), the citizens of Smyrna
chose him to represent them in their dealings with a philhellenic emperor,
who found it politic to present Rome's political domination as cultural
patronage. Through Polemo's intercessions, Smyrna scored a major victory in its longstanding rivalry with Ephesus. Polemo secured permission
for the city to build a second temple for the imperial cult and to host a
provincial festival. Indeed, he obtained more than permission: he secured
funds. Thus Smyrna gained the prestige of a second neocorate and Polemo
gained the presidency of the Hadrianic games.[10] In addition to titles and
festivals, a city looked to its public buildings as a source of pride and
prestige. An inscription from Smyrna enumerates "what we obtained
from the Emperor Hadrian through the influence of Antonius Polemo": a
second imperial temple, sacred games, immunity from tribute, *theologoi*
(imperial encomiasts), hymnodists (who produced hymns for the imperial
cult),[11] 1,500,000 drachmas, and a specified number of marble and porphyry pillars for the anointing room of the senate house. Local officials

[6] He would have been ἀγωνοθέτης, director of the competitions, rather than παν-
ηγυριάρχης, director of the holiday market associated with the festival (see L. Robert,
"Samothrace 2.1: Frazer, the Inscriptions on Stone," *Gnomon* 35 [1963], 69).

[7] *Lives* 541. An actor whom Polemo had expelled applied to the emperor for satisfaction,
but Antoninus dismissed the suit with a witty allusion to his own experience of Polemo's
arrogance (*Lives* 534–35). This incident raises the interesting question of how a successful
show of independence to a person in power, if brought off with impunity, could confer a kind
of immunity from lesser threats.

[8] This dream portended the failure of his plan to buy off the judges at the *Hadrianea
Olympia*: Artemidorus 1.64.

[9] Peter Garnsey and Richard Saller, *The Roman Empire: Economy, Society, Culture* (Lon-
don/Berkeley, 1987), 183.

[10] For the neocorate in this period as a mark of civic prestige, see S. Price, *Rituals and Power*
(Cambridge, 1984), 64–65 with n. 47.

[11] On these terms for officials in the imperial cult, see L. Robert, "Recherches épigra-
phiques 6, Inscription d'Athènes," *REA* 62 (1960), 321 with nn. 6 and 7.

were expected to rise to the challenge of imperial munificence: one of the presidents of the Council agreed to gild the roof of the anointing room, and the Asiarch, as high priest of the imperial cult, contributed a solarium.[12] But no one could outspend the emperor. He gave Smyrna ten million drachmas to build a new grain market, a new gymnasium, "the most magnificent of all those in Asia," as well as the new temple on the headlands over the sea.[13] It appears to have been of the same immense dimensions as the Olympieion at Athens, which was likewise jointly dedicated to Hadrian and Zeus.[14] In a world where a city might acquire all this by a single nod of imperial favor, a sophist who could command the emperor's attention was in a position to earn his honorary degrees.[15] The goodwill of such a person might prove invaluable in times of crisis: when an earthquake destroyed the buildings that Hadrian, through Polemo's influence, had bestowed on Smyrna, it was Polemo's old student Aristides whose eloquence moved Marcus Aurelius to put them up again.[16]

The establishment of Smyrna's second imperial temple would have opened up a second imperial priesthood in that city. Various facts indicate that this was the priesthood awarded to Polemo. The coins that he issued as chief magistrate all have imperial portraits, and their legends suggest that he erected statues in sponsorship of the imperial cult—including a statue of Hadrian's lover Antinoos (although we may wonder how Polemo reconciled his enthusiasm for the cult of Antinoos with his professed contempt for effeminacy).[17] Unlike Favorinus, there is no evidence that Polemo ever tried to evade the expensive honors that came with his social position. Of

---

[12] *IGR* 4.1431 = *CIG* 3148.

[13] Philostratus, *Lives* 531. On these buildings see Aelius Aristides *Or.* 17.11, 18.6, 19.3; and C. J. Cadoux, *Ancient Smyrna* (Oxford, 1938), 181, 202.

[14] S. Price, *Rituals and Power* (Cambridge, 1984), p. 258, #46.

[15] The classic study of this phenomenon is G. W. Bowersock's *Greek Sophists in the Roman Empire* (above, n. 5), especially chaps. 2–4. See also E. L. Bowie, "The Importance of Sophists," *YCS* 27 (1982), 29–59, who emphasizes the high social status of the families from which most successful sophists came.

[16] Thanks to a relationship established some years before and sealed by an impressive display of eloquence at an "invitational" declamation, Aristides' intervention was successful (Aristides *Or.* 19; Philostratus, *Lives* 582–83).

[17] In Smyrna, at least, individual magistrates took the lead in adding imperial images to the city's coins and took individual credit for it: "So-and-so on behalf of the Smyrnaians." Polemo's legends follow this pattern: ΠΟΛΕΜΩΝ· ΑΝΕΘΗΚΕ· ΣΜΥΡ. or ΠΟΛΕΜΩΝ· ΣΤΡΑΤΗΓΩΝ· ΑΝΕΘΗΚΕ. (See British Museum, *A Catalogue of Greek Coins in the British Museum*, vol. 14, *Ionia* (Bologna, 1963–65), pp. 277–78; and R. Münsterberg, "Die Münzender der Sophisten," *Numismatische Zeitung* 48 (1915), pp. 119–24). Similarly, the large bronze coins Polemo issued to commemorate Antinoos emphasize his role as dedicator. Some fifteen different coin types survive in this series: G. Blum, "Numismatique d'Antinoos," *Journal International d'Archéologie Numismatique* 16 (1914), 39–41. Perhaps Polemo was the local notable who commissioned and dedicated (ἀνέθηκε) a cult statue of Antinoos at Smyrna (cf. C. J. Howgego, *Greek Imperial Countermarks* (London, 1985), 86–87).

course, unlike Favorinus, Polemo had descendants to bequeath them to. His high-spirited great-grandson Hermocrates, who claimed to have inherited from him "the right to wear purple and officiate as priest," was the imperial high priest of Asia,[18] and a third-century descendant was imperial priest in Smyrna.[19] If, therefore, as seems likely, an imperial priesthood gave Polemo the right to embark upon the sacred ship of Dionysus, then he was wearing a magnificent gold crown laden with imperial busts when he posed for his portrait statue in that small temple by the sea.[20]

Through political office and personal influence, Polemo exerted some measure of control over political affairs at Smyrna. He served as one of the "generals" who administered the city's civil affairs.[21] According to Philostratus he was instrumental in bringing about a reconciliation between the hostile factions of the upper and lower city and quelled insolence and folly in the city's corporate behavior with public rebukes.[22] Public figures of Polemo's stature who could carry off such rebukes were particularly valuable because in this period a Greek city that could not settle its internal disputes faced the unsavory alternative of having them settled by the Roman governor.[23] Presumably he delivered sermons "On Concord" to the opposing parties, in which patriotic exhortations were mingled with sarcastic criticism. Examples of this homiletic type of sophistic activity survive in the corpus of Aelius Aristides and Dio Chrysostom. In some ways, a preeminent sophist, in his combined role of prominent educator, public moralist, civic spokesman, and tourist attraction, was a prototype of the Christian bishop, disposing of the fiscal, political, and social crises of his adopted city while feuding energetically with his rivals.

[18] Philostratus, Lives 611; C. Habicht, Altertümer von Pergamon 8. 3, #34.

[19] Polemo the temple-warden, whom we find rounding up Christians in the martyr-acts of Pionios: H. Musurillo, The Acts of the Christian Martyrs (Oxford, 1972), 136ff.; C. J. Cadoux, Ancient Smyrna (Oxford, 1938), 380–99. The directorship of the imperial games, which Polemo exercised so imperiously, often went along with a priesthood in the imperial cult. Other famous sophists had held such posts: Herodes was an imperial priest (IGR 4.1410), and Scopelian, whom Polemo was appointed to succeed as imperial ambassador, was high priest of the imperial cult in Asia (Philostratus, Lives 521, 515).

[20] On these crowns see J. Inan and E. Rosenbaum, Römische und frühbyzantinische Porträtplastik aus der Türkie. Neue Funde. (Mainz am Rhein, 1979), 124–25. Made of gold: Acts of SS. Paul and Thecla 26–39 (Syriac), as cited by S. Price, Rituals and Power (Cambridge, 1984), 170.

[21] For the generals at Smyrna, see C. J. Cadoux, Ancient Smyrna (Oxford, 1938), 194–95. Polemo may have been unusually influential in his combined role of sophist and strategos, but he was by no means unique: cf. British Museum, Catalogue of Greek Coins (Ionia) (above, n. 17), pp. 261; 279#247–48, 351; 283#367–68; 301; Philostratus, Lives 596, 613.

[22] Philostratus, Lives 531–32.

[23] Compare the incident described in the New Testament, Acts 19, 23–41, where the secretary of the Ephesian city council quiets a furious crowd ("For we are in danger of being charged with rioting today"), and Plutarch's advice that the civic politician should always remember the shoes of the Roman governor poised above his head (Mor. 813).

Although Polemo urged his fellow citizens to settle civil suits among themselves so that disputes about money did not escalate to a point that required the intervention of the Roman authorities, his own venality inspired epigrams.[24] Indeed Polemo suffered the embarrassment of being accused of embezzlement before the emperor by his ungrateful fellow-citizens. It appears that some of the building funds that he obtained for the city from Hadrian went to support his own operating expenses.[25] Polemo's ties with the emperor outweighed the claims of the city, however, and the indignant citizens of Smyrna were unable to proceed. Polemo made up for his financial irregularities with zealous attacks on other forms of immorality. He made a distinction between offenses involving money and those that, if neglected, brought pollution. Accordingly he urged that adulterers, murderers, and temple violators should be "driven out of the city" (turned over to the Romans) "since they needed a judge with a sword in his hand."[26] This concern with moral offenses that characterized his political activities resurfaces in his physiognomical writing as a preoccupation with the detection of hidden vice.

Polemo's privileged access to special sources of power extended beyond his intimacy with Hadrian. He also received advice from Demosthenes in his dreams.[27] The commemorative inscription that he erected to Demosthenes in the healing shrine of Asclepius at Pergamum constituted a public claim of privileged access to the fountainhead of linguistic authority. To claim too directly in rhetorical contexts that one spoke with such authority (or, conversely, to claim that one's diction had no need of authority at all)[28] would be offensive self-assertion. Aristides, at least, although he received detailed rhetorical advice from Asclepius in his dreams, did not boast of these intimacies in his speeches.[29] When inaugurating the temple of Olympian Zeus at Athens, for example, Polemo was careful to use periphrasis to claim that he spoke "not without divine

---

[24] Ammianus of Smyrna, *Greek Anthology* 11.180–81.

[25] *Lives* 533. Philostratus excuses, but does not conceal, his guilt. For peculation in public building projects in the second century, see C. P. Jones, *The Roman World Of Dio Chrysostom* (Cambridge, 1978), 113–14.

[26] Philostratus, *Lives* 532.

[27] Phrynichus says that Polemo set up a bronze statue of Demosthenes in the sanctuary of Asclepius at Pergamum, which bore the inscription "Polemo dedicated this to Demosthenes the Paianian because of a dream" (Δημοσθένη Παιανιέα Πολέμων κατ' ὄναρ: Phrynichus ed. Rutherford [London, 1881], fr. 395, p. 494). The inscription has survived, but not the statue (C. Habicht, *Altertümer von Pergamon*, 8.3: *Die Inschriften des Asklepieions*, 1969 #33). He impersonated Demosthenes in several of his most famous declamations (Philostratus, *Lives* 542–43).

[28] The sophist Philagrus, known for his shocking manners, when challenged on a point of usage, claimed as his authority himself (Philostratus, *Lives* 578–79).

[29] See, for example, *Or.* 50.20, 97. Encomia of the gods were another matter: Ibid. 40.22.

impulse" on that occasion.[30] Yet it is still possible to discern in the medical dedication a touch of Polemo's notorious arrogance. It was Polemo, after all, who "conversed with the gods as his equals" and, while sleeping in this very precinct, rejected Asclepius' advice to abstain from cold drinks as a remedy for his painful joints. "Good Sir," he retorted to the divine apparition standing over him, "and what if you were treating a cow?"[31] Some of Polemo's contemporaries found his pretensions galling, as we may judge from the response of Phrynichus, who, though he could not directly challenge the validity of his fellow-sophist's dreams, could still, as a hyper-Atticist, impugn the linguistic purity of the inscription that commemorated them. "It was most incorrect of him to use the phrase *kat' onar*," this sophist tartly observes, suggesting a few pedantic alternatives. "For that is what correct diction demands—an area in which even the greatest of the Hellenes may be seen to stumble."[32]

Polemo was very conscious of his physical appearance and traveled in style on an exotic chariot. Trajan had awarded him the *libera legatio*, transport and lodging at public expense, a privilege that, considering Polemo's retinue of slaves, pack-animals, and specialized hunting dogs, must have been worth a good sum. His house was the most splendid in Smyrna, and when, returning after an absence, he found the Roman proconsul lodging there, he did not hesitate to throw him out.[33] That his table was lavish we may infer from his criticism of a fellow-sophist whom he caught in the act of buying sausages and sardines for supper: "My good man, it simply is not possible to impersonate convincingly the arrogance of Darius and Xerxes on *that* kind of food."[34] Nothing could illustrate more clearly the interdependence of verbal virtuosity, wealth, and social dominance that characterized the Second Sophistic than this impromptu comment from the "Stanislavsky school of declamation."

The costume and gestures that Polemo employed in rhetorical delivery earned him the wholehearted admiration of the wealthy and discriminating Herodes Atticus.[35] His voice was clear, intense, and marvelously reso-

---

[30] Philostratus, *Lives* 533.

[31] Ibid. 535, 543. Polemo's extremities were probably afflicted with saturnine gout, as one might guess from his extravagant life-style.

[32] Phrynichus, ed. Rutherford (1881), fr. 395 p. 494. We may gauge the spirit of this criticism from this last remark, and from the fact that κατ' ὄναρ is absolutely ubiquitous in dedicatory inscriptions. See F. T. van Stratten, "Daikrates' Dream," *Bulletin Antieke Beschaving* 51 (1976), 12 with appendix.

[33] The proconsul in question was the future emperor Antoninus Pius (Philostratus, *Lives* 534). Polemo's traveling style: ibid. 532.

[34] Ibid. 541.

[35] Ibid. 537–38. Our only eyewitness account, that of Marcus Aurelius (*Letters to Marcus* 2.5), which describes Polemo in action as a "hardworking farmer" (*agricola strenuus*), seems to be criticism of style rather than of delivery. Marcus describes Polemo as a shrewd farmer who has planted out all his territory in grain and vines but has left no room for ornamental plants or shade trees: *omnia ad usum magis quam ad voluptatem.*

nant as it rang out of his mouth.[36] But the declamations that survive are a pale shadow of the original performance:

> It is a rolling fire of wordplays, paranomasias, anaphoras, chiasmi, apostrophes, prosopopoeias. . . . If these classroom speeches scarcely seem to justify the reputation of the rhetor from Smyrna, we must not forget that he owed his immense success above all to distinctions that were completely external to his eloquence. It was "the prodigy himself" (le monstre lui-même) that one had to hear, his fervent delivery, his passionate impersonations. These declamations, edited and corrected for reading . . . are for us like the librettos of cantatas whose music has been lost.[37]

This was a man whose eloquence went beyond words, whose facial muscles simply did not know how to express apprehension. The relaxed and confident expression with which he began his declamations drew the admiration of posterity.[38] He would paw the ground as he approached a climax like a mettlesome horse and smile when he rounded off an elaborate period to show how effortless it was.

This was the man whose statue outlasted Favorinus' ill-fated effigy. Ever conscious of the dignity of his own appearance, he regarded effeminate physical characteristics with extreme distaste. The rivalry of these two star performers became a notorious dispute about gender correctness for two reasons: first, in a culture where accusations of gender deviance were a traditional component of invective, Favorinus' effeminate appearance invited comment;[39] and second, their contest for supremacy, on behalf of themselves and the cities they represented, was a struggle for power, and gender, as we now are well aware, readily becomes a language for signifying relationships of power.

What Polemo may have written privately to Hadrian to secure for himself such plums as the inaugural speech at the Athenian temple of Zeus, and what he might have said to ease his rival out of favor, we will never know. What gained currency were public witticisms, barbs designed to sting again with every repetition. Those that appealed to the taste of a Philostratus or an Aulus Gellius have been preserved, like flies in amber, as fossilized bits of spite. When Polemo's old teacher, the Cynic Timocrates, remarked, "What a talkative creature that Favorinus has become!" Polemo

---

[36] Philostratus, Lives 537.

[37] A. Boulanger, Aelius Aristide (Paris, 1923), 93–94; Polemo was rated by Norden as a moderate Asianist (Die Attic Kunstprosa [Stuttgart, 1958], 389); H. Jüttner, De Polemonis Rhetoris Vita Operibus Arte (Breslau, 1898), discusses his avoidance of hiatus and other matters. Polemo's two surviving declamations were edited by H. Hink (Leipzig, 1873).

[38] It was the sort of look that, according to Plutarch, demonstrated the cheerful courage of Alexander the Great: διακεχυμένον πρόσωπον (Philostratus, Lives 537; Plutarch, Alexander 19).

[39] Whereas nowadays it might be considered unacceptably rude to highlight the physical deformities of an opponent, the ancient world knew no such inhibitions.

was quick to jibe, "Just like every other old crone."[40] Remarks like this would spread far and wide, reinforcing the public relations impact of Polemo's personal appearance and ostentatious baggage train. Favorinus fought back with epigrams and speeches of his own, delivered, we may imagine, with ever more outrageous ululations of his bewitching high-pitched voice. Philostratus condemns both of them for composing speeches full of personal abuse but concedes that some of what they said was true.[41] For a rhetorician who aspired to preeminence, professional quarrels were not a luxury but a necessary medium for self-advertisement. Feuding sophists found indignation an unfailing stimulus to wit and a useful catalyst in the construction of a public personality. If they had had no rivals, they would have created them to define themselves.

Polemo was not a master sophist only; he presented himself also as a master physiognomist, whose gaze could peel back the carefully constructed integument of another man's self-presentation to penetrate the inner recesses of his private thoughts. Physiognomy was a merciless discipline because it acknowledged no exceptions to its rules and provided no shade under which certain privileged signs of human frailty or idiosyncrasy could shelter. Polemo was not a physiognomist by accident or caprice.[42] Rather, physiognomy as an elaborated science was a crystalline precipitate of certain habits of thought and social interaction that, in solution, pervaded his culture: the competitive face-to-face world of educated upper-class males. Polemo was perfectly adapted to this environment. The principles of physiognomic science were but the implicit prejudices that had molded his own education, made explicit as a system of universal rules. As an adroit manipulator of this system of signification, Polemo could use it for personal ends: to enhance his own reputation for dignity and omniscience, to define to his advantage the terms of his professional rivalry with Favorinus, and to claim for himself some of the freedom to censure the behavior of others that was traditionally accorded to philosophers.

The remainder of this chapter assesses Polemo as a physiognomist, first examining him as a phenomenon in the history of Greek (pseudo-) science. Readers who are quite sure they have no technical interest in physiognomy may proceed to the next section, which discusses Polemo's treatise as a vehicle of his own self-presentation. Finally, in Chapter Three, we look at

---

[40] Philostratus, *Lives* 541.

[41] Ibid. 491. What Favorinus found to say about Polemo has unfortunately not been preserved.

[42] Other sophist-physiognomists include Megistias of Smyrna (Philostratus, *Lives* 618); Eusthenes, whose epitaph is preserved in the *Palatine Anthology* (7.661); and, of course, Adamantius the epitomator of Polemo.

Polemo's work sociologically, as a prism that refracts the sex and gender stereotypes of his society into unusually distinct spectra.[43]

THE PHYSIOGNOMICAL CORPUS AND POLEMO'S *PHYSIOGNOMY*

The physiognomical tradition in Greek goes back at least to the fourth century before the common era. Polemo used two earlier physiognomical treatises that have survived in the corpus of Aristotle. Although they are not now considered to be the work of Aristotle himself, they echo the Aristotelian view that physical resemblances between men and animals determine personality types.[44] The first pseudo-Aristotelian physiognomy briefly describes the three approaches taken by previous physiognomists: one based on types of animals, another based on the geographical and ethnic differences between the human races, and a third based on general sketches of the physical manifestations of various temperaments.[45] We might call these the zoological, ethnographic, and dispositional schools of physiognomy. In the Aristotelian presentation—in marked contrast to Polemo's—disagreeable and sinister types do not noticeably predominate over more neutral or desirable ones. The argument of the whole depends on the premise that there exists a certain *sympathy* between the soul and the body: "It seems to me that the soul and the body react on each other. An altered trait in the soul will produce an altered shape in the body, while an altered form of the body will produce a corresponding change in the soul."[46]

The second pseudo-Aristotelian fragment focuses on animal signs, with particular attention to the alleged masculinity or femininity of each. In every class, females have nastier dispositions, smaller heads, and softer, moister flesh than do males, while males, as a class, have stronger sinews and braver, more equitable dispositions. Treating physical characteristics as signs of behavioral characteristics and vice versa has led to an erosion of any logical distinction between the two. The physiognomist is not primarily interested in sex differences within species, but in differences in overall "maleness" and "femaleness" between species. Among brave animals, for example, the lion represents the perfect male type, and the panther, with its narrow, ill-proportioned body and wily ways, is more female in shape

---

[43] Cf. J. Hahn, *Der Philosoph und die Gesellschaft* (Stuttgart, 1989), 6, on the philosopher as prism through which to view the social life of the high empire.

[44] See, for example, *Hist. Anim.* 1.1.488b. For a general discussion of evidence for Aristotle's interest in physiognomy, see E. C. Evans, "Physiognomics in the Ancient World," *Transactions of the American Philosophical Society* 59 (1969), 7–10, 22–24.

[45] [Aristotle], [*Phys.*] 805a.

[46] Ibid. 808b.

(excepting, of course, its powerful and efficient legs, which are masculine).[47] In this source there follows a long catalog of physical traits, according to which a person's character is to be categorized as strong and masculine or weak and feminine.[48] Other traits are mentioned too: anger, servility, gentleness, and gluttony may all be known by physical marks. This treatise ends with a recommendation to evaluate all individual signs in the light of both their gender affinities and their general appearance (*epiprepeia*). The best place to look for signs, we are told, is in the eyes, the forehead, and face.[49]

The physiognomical writings of Polemo's other source, Loxus, have not survived. He appears to have been a Hellenistic physician who was, at least for his ventures in physiognomy, most aptly named "he who looks sideways." A later Latin source preserves the essence of his discussion of animals and his catalog of eye signs, much briefer than Polemo's.[50] From that we learn that Loxus, as well as Polemo, used physiognomy to predict the future.[51]

Surviving Versions of Polemo's Physiognomy

Even without the complete text of Polemo's predecessors, we can tell that Polemo, by elaborating the semiology of the eye signs to a pitch of dizzying complexity, and by using *ad hominem* examples in an unprecedented way, impressed the traditional material with a distinctive stamp of his own. His treatise survives in an Arabic translation, a Greek epitome, and in an anonymous fourth-century Latin treatise that made extensive use of the Greek original. The Arabic translation was made in Damascus in 1356 A.D. One of the five surviving Arabic manuscripts was translated into Latin for the convenience of scholars by G. Hoffmann in the nineteenth century.[52] The result of this double process of translation is a text that lacks nuance: the connectives that would have guided the reader through the original Greek have disappeared, and the syntax that remains is almost completely

---

[47] Ibid. 809b–810a.
[48] εὔρωστοι τὰς ψυχάς or μαλακοὶ τὰς ψυχάς.
[49] [Aristotle], [*Phys.*] 814b.
[50] *Anon. Lat.* 81–82, 117ff., Förster vol. 2, 108–11, 137–44, hereafter cited in the form *Anon. Lat.* 2.108–11F.
[51] *Anon. Lat.* 133, 2.144F. In Suetonius, a "forehead reader" (μετωποσκόπος) predicts the future of Britannicus (*Titus* 2). Artemidorus mentions physiognomists and "body readers" (μορφοσκόποι) in a catalog of charlatans who claim to predict the future (2.69).
[52] See Förster, introduction to vol. 1, lxxxff. When quoting from Polemo, I have used Hoffmann's Latin version, supplemented by the Greek epitome and the fourth-century Latin treatise when possible. Margaret Malamud has checked my English versions against Hoffmann's Arabic in all places where I thought that a serious ambiguity was possible. In spite of these precautions, I must warn the reader that some undetected errors may remain.

devoid of subordination. In places where the Arabic text is corrupt or incomplete, a full collation of all the surviving manuscripts may eventually reduce confusion; the Greek paraphrase and the Latin treatise occasionally supply bits that are missing in the Arabic.[53]

Sometimes it is clear that the Arabic translator did not understand the Greek of his original, and we must seek help from other versions. The Greek paraphrase of Polemo's text is the work of "Adamantius the Sophist."[54] He describes physiognomy in his introduction as "something of great usefulness for posterity" that should be preserved in writing "the way a holy image is fenced in by a sacred enclosure."[55] He is quoted by Julian's physician Oribasius and so cannot be later than the first part of the fourth century A.D., but it is unlikely that the "Constantius" whom he addresses informally in his preface was the emperor of that name.[56] Adamantius needs to be read in tandem with the Arabic version to clarify details. We might well wonder why the sober deportment described in chapter fifty-eight of the Arabic should be attributed to *dandies*—if we could not see from Adamantius that the perfectly proper "orderly man" (*anēr kosmios*) of the Greek original was transformed by the Arabic translator into a man fond of cosmetics![57]

The anonymous Latin treatise on physiognomy, which may also belong to the fourth century,[58] used Aristotle, Loxus, and Polemo, but chiefly Polemo, citing the others where they disagreed with his main source.[59] This treatise sometimes preserves a fuller version of Polemo than does the Arabic; without it we might never learn how to recognize a criminally stupid man (*mōroblaptēs*). Where the Arabic text is fragmentary, the Latin preserves for us Polemo's colorful example of a contemporary who epitomized this otherwise unattested type.[60] Generally, neither Adamantius nor the anonymous Latin author transmits Polemo's individual example-sketches. Despite their entertainment value and skillful elaboration of detail, they constitute a catalog of irreproducible results that serve only to advertise Polemo's personal skill and as such did not appear to his successors sufficiently useful or universal to be worth copying. The "criminally stupid man" is the exception that proves this rule, because he

[53] Förster vol. 1, intro., cvi–cvii. Any future editor should consider producing a synoptic edition of all three treatises or at the very least supply a system of cross-references.
[54] See the *ms* title, 1.297F. For discussion of the treatise, see Förster vol. 1, intro., c–cix.
[55] 1.1, 1.297F. By this Adamantius would seem to be a pagan.
[56] Förster vol. 1, intro., ciii.
[57] Compare *Phys.* 58, 1.274F with Adam. 2.48, 1.413F.
[58] Förster vol. 1, intro., cxli ff.
[59] *Anon. Lat.* 80, 2.108F.
[60] Compare *Phys.* 65, 1.280F with *Anon. Lat.* 104–5, 2.126–30F and Adam. 2.58, 1.420–22F.

represented a category that was unfamiliar to later writers and appeared to require illustration.

The Plan of Polemo's Work

Polemo's physiognomy begins with the claim that the signs to be observed in the eyes are the most critical of all. Fully one-third of his treatise, amounting to some thirty Teubner pages out of ninety in the surviving Arabic text, documents how various features of the eye's external appearance—a droop in the eyelid here, a restless pupil there, and in particular certain subtle variations in the way an eye is colored and refracts light—reveal the hidden proclivities of the inward man. The novelty of his treatment lies in its sheer bulk, in the complexity of its categories, and in the pungency of the narrative examples used to illustrate them.[61] After the eyes comes a section on zoological physiognomy,[62] of a kind familiar from the Aristotelian treatise. The character traits of some ninety-two animals are passed in review, but unlike the zoological sections of the Aristotelian physiognomy, the physical traits in humans that are supposed to effect a physiognomic correspondence with the animal world are not spelled out. (How, for example, are we to distinguish the human counterpart of an ass from the human counterpart of a mule?) The chief value of animal correspondences for Polemo seems to lie in the way they may enable us to detect prevailing masculine (leonine) or feminine (panther-like) characteristics in the persons subject to our scrutiny. There follows a section on the signs of the various parts of the body, in which Polemo proceeds systematically from the fingernails, fingers, and feet, back up through the body to the neck, head, and features of the face.[63]

The final third of the treatise begins with a discussion of ethnographic physiognomy,[64] including skin color and eye color,[65] and moves from there to a discussion of the physiognomic significance of hair on head and body.[66] Polemo continues with a discussion of body movement, and the

[61] It appears that the extensive treatment of the eyes in Polemo is his original contribution. The Aristotelian treatise did not elaborate the eye signs in any detail. Loxus discussed eye signs, but since the anonymous Latin redactor summarizes his remarks in one chapter, devoting twenty-four chapters to Polemo's, it seems fair to conclude that Polemo's treatment was much more detailed. (*Anon. Lat.* 20–43, 2.31–61F on Polemo's eye signs, 81, 2.108–10F on Loxus'). The passages cited in Förster vol. 1, intro., lxxviiff. merely show that Heraclitus, Cicero, and the elder Pliny also thought that the eyes were the mirror of the soul, not that Polemo had any predecessors in his elaborately ramified working-out of this theory.

[62] *Phys.* 2, 1.170–98F.

[63] Ibid. 2–30, 1.198–236F.

[64] Ibid. 31–35, 1.236–44F.

[65] Ibid. 36–39, 1.244–48F.

[66] Ibid. 40–48, 1.248–56F.

signs, sometimes deceptive, of gait, gesture, and voice.[67] The concluding
section of the treatise deals with dispositional physiognomy, enumerating
the signs by which you may detect various types, such as the brave, effeminate, or ambitious man.[68] The last three of these "types" are really highly
specific examples designed, as we shall see later, to display the almost
supernatural power of Polemo's physiognomic insight.

Polemo's Methodology: Some Observations

The value of Polemo's treatise as a source for social prejudice lies precisely in
the places where it fails as a science to provide an objective record of social
conditions. Take for example his brief discussion of ethnographic physiognomy. The Aristotelian treatise shows that this approach was standard
fare.[69] Polemo prefaces his own rendition of the material with the observation that in this day and age, when one finds Syrians in Italy and Libyans in
Thrace, hair and skin color are hardly determinate in physiognomy
anymore—indeed, it is sometimes difficult to determine who belongs to
what race![70] Nonetheless, in Polemo's presentation, Greek scientific tradition wins out over Roman empirical realities to put the purebred vestiges
of the Hellenic race firmly in place as the central reference point for the
physiognomist's racial typology. This is very easily done: define Greece
and Ionia as the geographical center of the earth, partition off north from
south and east from west, define moral and physical excellence as the mean
between extremes, and—presto—the "pure Greek" becomes the ideal.
Hellenes even have eyes that are superior to those of other races![71] The
Aristotelian tradition displays a similar ethnocentricity, but this last remark about the eyes surely reflects Polemo's own preoccupations. Polemo
is also likely to have contributed the gratuitously insulting "example"
illustrating the concept of racial degeneration: "You will find, for example,
that the knowledge of the Egyptians does not match their reputation,
while among the Macedonians, by contrast, intelligence is widespread."[72]

The farther any diagnostic science is removed from genuinely inductive
reasoning, the more room there is for its practitioner to be guided by his

[67] Ibid. 49–52, 1.256–68F.
[68] Ibid. 53–70, 1.268–92F.
[69] [Arist.], [Phys.] 805a.
[70] Adam. 2.31,1.382–83F. The absence of this observation in the Arabic version is a useful
reminder that the Arabic is itself, to an indeterminable extent, a condensation of the original
Greek.
[71] εὐοφθαλμότατον γὰρ πάντων τῶν ἐθνῶν τὸ Ἑλληνικόν: Adam. 2.32,1.386F. Compare the Hippocratic Airs, Waters, Places 12–24.
[72] Phys. 31,1.236F. Perhaps, after Hadrian made him a member, Polemo found his colleagues at the Museum in Alexandria insufficiently impressed by his talents (Philostratus
Lives 532).

intuitive prejudices. In physiognomy the problem of inconsistent data is particularly acute and, as Polemo's treatise clearly shows, physiognomical theory adjusted itself to accommodate this problem by creating the concept of *epiprepeia*,[73] or "overall impression," in the light of which the physiognomist is permitted to overlook or disallow certain facts.

At the end of his precisionistic disquisition on the eyes, Polemo warns that we should not rely on one sign only but consider others as well. While the eyes may be of primary importance as the "doorway of the heart," the rest of a man's face, his neck, torso, and limbs, his voice and his gait, may also function as signs.[74] If these all should point in the same direction, so much more secure may our judgment be. But what if they do not? We come up against a major obstacle to physiognomy's aspirations to consistency as an explanatory system: what is to guarantee, once all the evidence is in, that the data in aggregate will form a coherent picture? While Polemo's predecessor Loxus, influenced perhaps by his training as a physician, responds to this problem with a rationalistic attempt to adjudicate discordant signs,[75] Polemo invokes "overall appearance"—a concept whose flexibility permits it to function as a useful "fudge-factor" in his calculations.

"There are important signs to be found in the voice, the breath, and in the movement of every part of the body. But it is essential that you seek an *overall impression* so that you may apply it to the body the way a signet ring is applied to the material on which it is to print. . . ."[76] Just exactly how this "overall impression" is to function as a signet ring is not immediately clear. Perhaps the Arabic translator, intuiting how deeply counter-empirical Polemo's procedure is here, has spelled out more clearly than the original text how the "overall impression" is not something formed or stamped by the features of the physiognomical subject, but rather something that the physiognomist stamps upon *them*. Adamantius' paraphrase explains the term as follows:

> The most powerful determining factor is the *overall impression* of the whole man that makes itself visible on all parts of the body. One must look upon this in all

[73] Liddell and Scott gloss ἐπιπρέπεια as "congruity, suitableness" and so obscure its meaning as a technical term for "general appearance" or "overall impression" in physiognomy. See A. MacC. Armstrong, "The Methods of the Greek Physiognomists," *Greece and Rome* 5 (1958), 53n.4. Compare the glosses of Adamantius (2.2,1.349F) quoted below and *Anon. Lat.*, *omnis aspectus qui ex omni circumstantia et qualitate corporis occurrit, quem Graeci* ἐπιπρέπεια *dicunt* (45,2.63F).

[74] *Phys.* 1, Förster vol. 1, 166–68.

[75] Loxus, cited in *Anon. Lat.* 11,2.17–18F.

[76] *Phys.* 1,1.168F. That ἐπιπρέπεια lies behind the Arabic may be seen from Adamantius' paraphrase of this passage (2.1,1.348F).

cases as if it were the seal of the whole. It has no rational principle, in and of itself, but the details, the eye signs and all the rest, synthesize the complete appearance of the man.[77]

Here the image of *epiprepeia* as seal or signet suggests that it is to perform an authenticating function, confirming one's intuitive assessments. A seal is the perfect metaphor for physiognomic oversimplification, since it serves to represent an object's essential identity in a single, easily recognized pattern.

Polemo explains that *epiprepeia* is to function as an indicator of various moral qualities: "depravity, wrath, anxieties or the absence thereof, repressed savagery, hidden intentions, memory, ⟨or⟩ forgetfulness."[78] One is supposed to be able to "remove" individual good signs from a person's overall impression (such as piety or chastity), or even bad signs (arrogance, gambling, envy, cupidity, and perjury).[79] "Once these have been removed, you will find as a result signs that confirm it, and an agreement between them and the signs of the eyes." What purports to be an inductive science, built up from myriad specific observations, becomes a deductive science based on generalized impressions and preexisting prejudices that are confirmed by observed details—some of which can be freely discarded if they do not conform to overall impression.

The use of this term in physiognomy goes back to the second Aristotelian treatise, which recommends *epiprepeia* as the swiftest and surest means of making fine distinctions between superficially similar signs, such as the pallor produced by fear and that attributable to exhaustion.[80] This treatise frequently invokes *epiprepeia* when justifying an alleged connection between physical traits and moral qualities. Some physiognomic observations appear well-grounded in nature: if a man has a distinctly bovine face, we are entitled to conclude that he is sluggish and take the cow as our proof.[81] Similarly one may cite the hawk to prove the rapacity of men who have eyes like birds of prey (813a). But what of temperamental qualities that are not easily found in the animal world, social constructs like servility and effeminacy? For these we "refer to overall impression." The quality of "freeborn dignity" (*eleutheriotēs*) is specially suited to this treatment. Loose-knit shoulders are the mark of the freeborn man (who has presumably never stooped his back to agricultural toil). So those whose shoulders lack freedom of movement are *aneleutheroi*, according to "overall impres-

[77] Adam. 2.1,1.348–49F.

[78] *Phys.* 1,1.168F. Note the text problems in line 10 of the Arabic, and compare *Anon. Lat.* 45,2.63F.

[79] *Phys.* 1,1.170F.

[80] [Arist.], [*Phys.*] 809a.

[81] ἀναφέρεται ἐπὶ τοὺς βοῦς (ibid. 811b).

sion" (811a).[82] Sometimes the physical quality analyzed is itself a social construct: those whose faces are "vulgar" (*mikroprepes*) lack freeborn dignity "with reference to overall impression."[83] Those whose hair droops down onto the forehead also lack freeborn dignity "according to overall impression, since the look is slavish" (812b–813a). Like a servile appearance, effeminacy is in the eye of the beholder. Those who lack a certain characteristically male fullness about the abdomen are effeminate "softies" (*malakoi*, 810b); those whose heads tilt to the right as they walk are pathics (*cinaedi*, 813a). The arbitrariness of this "sign" may be seen from the fact that other treatises claim that pathics tilt to the left.[84] Likewise, those whose voices are high in pitch, smooth in timbre, and generally enervated are pathics "with reference to overall impression and to women" (813a).

These appeals to *epiprepeia* serve the physiognomist like the epicycles of Ptolemaic cosmology: they help the system accommodate recalcitrant "facts." Concepts of gender perform a similar task. Indeed, appeals to the standard of gender-appropriateness[85] are even more frequent in the Aristotelian physiognomy than appeals to *epiprepeia*. The conclusion of this treatise explicitly associates both: "It is a good idea to refer all signs that have been mentioned to overall impression and to gender, male and female" (814b). Polemo likewise moves from *epiprepeia* to gender when he instructs us to determine our overall impression of a physiognomic subject, then to eliminate signs that conflict with it, and then "take a good look at the man and think over whether he seems masculine or feminine to you."[86] At this point Polemo announces his intention to move on to animal signs but warns his reader that knowledge of these will do him no good unless he can distinguish between masculine and feminine types. Polemo counsels us, in cases where we find a predominance of feminine physical features, to "attribute to their possessor those qualities that are indicated by feminine signs," and likewise for men. "You ought to know, moreover, that the male is in all respects stronger, less deceitful, braver, less defective, and more steadfast in adversity than the female. For this reason, you should scrutinize my descriptions carefully."[87]

---

[82] Compare Quintilian, "To shrug or contract the shoulders is rarely becoming, for it makes the neck appear short and produces a gesture that is low-down, servile—and almost fake, particularly when assuming a pose of adulation, admiration, or fear" (*Inst.* 11.3.83).

[83] ἀναφέρεται ἐπὶ τὴν ἐπιπρέπειαν, 811b.

[84] *Anon. Lat.* 55,2.77F.

[85] "With reference to the male," ἀναφέρεται ἐπὶ τὸ ἄρρεν or "with reference to the female," ἀναφέρεται ἐπὶ τὸ θῆλυ.

[86] *Phys.* 1,1.168–70F.

[87] Ibid. 2,1.198F.

In his rhetorical practice, Polemo deprecated speeches built on double meaning, ambiguous intentions, or covert allusions (*eschēmatismenai hypotheseis*).[88] "For hateful to me as the doorway of death is the man who hides one thing in his heart and speaks another," he would say. But just as Polemo was quick to spot "schematized" deportment in others, so he was also quite adept at "schematizing" his own speeches. He gave fabulous performances pretending to be Demosthenes pretending to denounce himself after Chaeronea. He impersonated Solon pretending to ask for the repeal of his own laws. His "Adulterer Unmasked" was a masterpiece of the genre.[89] If that speech were extant, it would be fascinating to comb it for signs of the physiognomist's sensibility at work. Polemo's twin preoccupation with posture and imposture shows that he operated—at some level—with an awareness of how our social identities are fictions. With this in mind, we prepare to scrutinize the physiognomist. How did he use his treatise to present himself?

Polemo's Examples as Self-Presentation

It is much to be regretted that Polemo's preface did not survive. We do not know if the work contained a dedication; we have no clue as to the identity of the implied reader and would-be student of physiognomy whom Polemo addresses at various points in a somewhat condescending tone. It would be useful to know how Polemo introduced himself: did he, like Artemidorus in his manual of dream-interpretation, begin with a graceful pretence of reluctance and confess himself daunted by the magnitude of his task?[90] Not very likely, one might say, given the masterful dogmatism of his approach as we see it in the main body of the treatise. We are left to wonder how he might have positioned himself vis-à-vis his predecessors and potential rivals, and how he would have made a case for the importance of his art. The paraphrase of Adamantius offers a few paragraphs of introduction that probably derive from Polemo:

> If divine men have made any discovery that can be of truly immense benefit to those who study it, it is physiognomy. For nobody would deposit in trust his financial assets, his heirlooms, his wife, or his children—or enter into any sort of

---

[88] Philostratus, *Lives* 524. For the meaning of this term, see W. C. Wright's glossary on p. 570 of the Loeb edition.

[89] Philostratus, *Lives* 542. Perhaps the true title of this speech was "The Adulterer Disguised" (ὁ μοιχὸς ὁ ἐγκεκαλυμμένος rather than ἐκκεκαλυμμένος).

[90] *Onirocriticon*, pr. 1. On prologue form, see A. J. Festugière, *La Clef des Songes* (Paris, 1975), 15–16 with nn.

social relationship—with a person whose appearance radiates the signs of dishonesty, lechery, or double-dealing. As if by some God-given, inerrant, and prophetic art, the physiognomist understands the character and purposes, so to speak, of all men: how to choose associates only from those who are worthy, and how to guard against the evildoing of unprincipled people without having to experience it first. For this reason, wise men should apply themselves with all their strength to working through the indications of this art.[91]

This passage is notable both for its lofty claims to superhuman insight and for its hardheaded insistence on the practical advantages to be gained thereby. It also glosses over the paradox of how something so intuitive can be taught or studied. This tension between physiognomy as an intuitive art and physiognomy as a subject of systematic study reappears in the main body of the treatise. Previous writers had been content to catalog signs; Polemo adds a new dimension: narratives of his own physiognomic triumphs. These are presented in a way that does not obscure the physiognomist's intuitive genius. It is by no means clear that mastering the more technical parts of his manual would prepare his readers to duplicate these feats, any more than an exhaustive study of Galen's technical works on the pulse might prepare us safely to predict the return of the emperor's fever.[92]

These example narratives, however, hold the key to Polemo's self-presentation as an expert.[93] Everything that we know about his predecessors shows them to be interested in generalizations of universal applicability, in the characteristics not of individuals, but of various types. The Aristotelian treatise uses no individual examples in its catalog of types[94] but sketches briefly the physical signs of "a brave man," "a coward," and so on. The anonymous Latin treatise may preserve traces of a few examples from Loxus, but it is impossible to tell whether their brevity and sketchy presentation reflect Loxus' actual practice, or whether the Latin epitomator shortened them himself.[95] Polemo's presentation of original examples goes hand in hand with his insistence on the careful observation and personal experience with which he collected them. Through the authority of autopsy, he seeks to establish himself as the definitive master of his art. "For you to master this science, it will be enough that you learn

[91] Adam. 1.2, 1.298–99F.

[92] See Galen, *On Prognosis* (*CMG* 5.8.1), 12.

[93] These are numbered and summarized in J. Mesk, "Die Beispiele in Polemons Physiognomonik," *Weiner Studien* 50 (1932), 51–67.

[94] A possible exception: under "signs of the *cinaedus*" (pathic), we find "shifty eyes, like Dionysius the sophist" ([Aristotle], [*Phys.*] 808a). Förster took this to be a later gloss. In the light of Polemo's attack on Favorinus, it is interesting that the victim of this slander is a sophist and that the charge is effeminacy.

[95] *Anon. Lat.* 11, 2.19–20F.

thoroughly what I have described to you and then apply what you have learned. For not even I have attained mastery of these things without much study and lengthy observation."[96] Is he exhorting his readers to emulate his methods or to memorize his results?

Polemo makes it clear that he himself went out of his way to collect curiosities. He heard once about a Lydian called Cancer because of his protruding, crablike eyes. "When I heard about his appearance, I kept looking till I found him, because I wanted to know what sort of inner character might be indicated by that configuration of the eyes."[97] Polemo visited Cancer at home (one wonders how he introduced himself) and discovered him to be unintelligent, sharp-tongued, and grasping. His eyes were indeed unique: "both small and incredibly red, entirely unlike the eyes of other men." In this case, as in many others, the quest for *mirabilia* is fundamentally at odds with the study of physiognomy as a science of types.

As a collector of marvelous examples, Polemo in some ways resembles his contemporary Phlegon of Tralles, a freedman secretary of the Emperor Hadrian, whose anthology of ghost stories, sex-changes, and prodigious births still makes good reading.[98] One can imagine him, like Polemo, eagerly inquiring, "Has anything out of the ordinary happened here?" at each stop on the imperial itinerary. Many of his tales concern persons of indeterminate gender (*androgynoi*). In some cases, the double nature of the *androgynos* is evident at birth. Only in these stories, where the infant cannot be assimilated in the binary classification system of its culture, is the anomaly treated as a prodigy requiring intervention by oracles or "freak-prognosticators" (*teratoskopoi*).[99] What these *androgynoi* stories have in common with the physiognomical examples of Polemo is a mode of thinking which uses the extreme to explore the parameters of the nor-

[96] *Phys.* 2, 1.192F.

[97] Ibid. 1, 1.144F.

[98] *On Marvels* (Περὶ θαυμασίων), A. Westermann, ed., *Paradoxographi Graeci* (1839; reprint Amsterdam, 1963), 117–42. I do not know of any translations of this text into a modern language.

[99] In other cases, the *androgynos* is thought at first to be female and then unexpectedly becomes a man with the requisite genitalia (except in one case, where the poor thing is eaten first). Girls who turn into men at puberty seem to have occasioned no social consternation worth mentioning (*On Marvels*, 5–9). Although a *cinaedus* is recorded to have given birth (26), no incontestable male is recorded to have become a female. If a visible penis is the criterion of masculine identity here, then this is understandable, but we must also reckon with the ways in which an ancient reporter's conceptual apparatus might skew his perceptions of anatomical "bare facts." To change from female to male is, on the Galenic view of the differential homology of male and female sexual organs, to progress from the imperfect and less developed female to the full perfection of male humanity (T. Laqueur, *Making Sex: Body and Gender from the Greeks to Freud* (Cambridge, 1990) 25–28).

mal.[100] At the very least, Phlegon's collection indicates a contemporary fascination with the paradoxes of gender that Polemo shared and Favorinus embodied.

In Polemo's collection of *mirabilia*, all but one are sinister. Perhaps this emphasis is due to self-protective common sense: since the thoughts and deeds of a good man are openly displayed to all, only the intentions of the deceitful require the elucidation of physiognomy.[101] Polemo's training as a sophist points to a literary model for the hostile tenor of his example narratives. Sophistic "chats" (*laliai*) were brief discourses usually delivered sitting down to warm up orator and audience before a major performance, but they sometimes, as in Lucian, developed into an art form of their own.[102] Personal criticism of anonymous targets constituted a standard option for the subject matter of such chats: "Often you will ridicule and censure someone anonymously, sketching his portrait, if you like, and defaming his character."[103] Polemo did have a high reputation as a satirist,[104] and the pen portraits in the *Physiognomy* may preserve the tang of his warm-up "chats."

Given his propensity to make sinister discoveries, it is exceedingly difficult to imagine anyone willingly offering himself to Polemo as a subject for physiognomical study. For his part, Polemo preferred to keep his practice covert. He warns that we must be careful not to let people know that we intend to subject them to physiognomical scrutiny, "lest they prepare themselves by altering their deportment and confound

[100] Compare S. Greenblatt:

Whereas the post-Enlightenment world tends to sharpen its sense of individuation through a grasp of the normative, the Renaissance tended to acquire an understanding of the order of things through a meditation on the prodigious. Thus the modern interest, fueled by sociology, in the impersonal structures that govern individual improvisation finds its paradoxical Renaissance equivalent in an interest in prodigies: like sociological structures, prodigies organize individual variations around a norm. "Fiction and Friction," in *Reconstructing Individualism: Autonomy, Individuality, and the Self in Western Thought*, ed. T. C. Heller, M. Sosna, D. E. Wellbery (Stanford, 1986), 36.

[101] The Latin physiognomy discusses this problem in a section that appears to derive from Polemo. Conceding that most of the eye signs discussed are bad rather than good, it points out that vice is multiform (like the hydras, chimaeras, and giants that appear in stories). But the discussion soon becomes muddled, concluding that it is not so much the vices but their signs that are multiform and diverse (*Anon. Lat.* 44, 2.61–62F, a passage that contains at least one serious corruption).

[102] See D. A. Russell, *Greek Declamation* (Cambridge, 1983), 77–79.

[103] Menander Rhetor 2.391: ἀποσκώψεις δὲ πολλάκις καὶ ψέξεις ἀνωνύμως ὑπογράφων τὸ πρόσωπον, εἰ βούλοιο, καὶ τὸ ἦθος διαβάλλων. As a teacher of rhetoric, Augustine once used this technique to good effect: without naming names, he cured a friend's obsession with gladiatorial games by inserting a satiric description of his folly into a lecture (*Confessions* 6.7).

[104] Philostratus, *Lives* 542.

the signs."[105] He envisions a contest of distorted signs and secret scrutiny in which the subject's deception justifies the physiognomist's subterfuge.

In the example narratives, subject and physiognomist are adversaries. The former has secrets that he would rather keep concealed, but they inevitably leave their impression on his body for the latter to read. The signs of private vice are as public as may be—to Polemo, who commands the code. Polemo tends not to name the contemporaries he singles out from his private gallery of *exempla*. They are quintessentially the "other," and their namelessness, while it may preserve them from slander, also prevents them from laying claim to any life of their own. They exist only to serve Polemo's purposes and authenticate his skill.

Polemo's digressions, in which he passes from the systematic presentation of general signs to the narrative presentation of individual examples, represent points of intersection between the authority of scientific tradition and the authority of personal experience. Like many texts of modern ethnography, Polemo's work alternates between the present tense and tribal labels characteristic of scientific description, and the particularized narrative of personal observation that mentions specific persons and employs the past tense.[106] Polemo's examples serve to incorporate the results of his own fieldwork into the impersonal catalog of physiognomical facts preserved by tradition. As first-person narratives they are hardly self-effacing; the omniscient narrator tends to dwarf those whom he describes. Here is the first example:

> I saw once a man from Cyrene, whom I will not name, whose eyes were flecked around the pupil with dots resembling millet-seeds, some red, others black, that flashed like fire. This man was a master of evil-doing, who granted free rein to his greed, his sexual desires, his dissolute habits, and brazen audacity. No respect for divinity restrained him, no honor in human affairs. He was an amalgamation of every vice. Yet I observed him only once, and without a doubt the bad signs confirmed one another. I immediately made my judgment according to the signs that I had observed. Ordinary people, of course, typically notice only one sign, no matter how distinct they all may be. I, for my part, will explain the other signs to you (since I have mastered the subject and studied it thoroughly), even though there is no man alive who could fit the entire subject into a book. But you, after you have learned the other signs and have tried them all out as outlined in my descriptions, will possess the fundamentals of the physiognomic art, just the way a schoolboy is gradually taught his ABCs.[107]

[105] Adam. 1.4, 1.305F.
[106] See M. L. Pratt, "Fieldwork in Common Places," in *Writing Culture: The Poetics and Politics of Ethnography*, ed. J. Clifford and G. Marcus (Berkeley, 1986), 35.
[107] *Phys.* 1, 1.118–20F.

In this example, Polemo sets himself apart from the man he observes, whose lifetime history of vice he is able to read in one brief period of scrutiny. He sets himself apart from ordinary people, whose unsophisticated reliance on single signs leaves them at the mercy of the duplicitous. And he even sets himself apart from his implied reader by comparing him to a schoolboy. In this metaphor of the physiognomic ABCs, Polemo presents himself as a *rhetor* who condescends to act as *grammaticus*.

Sometimes examples expand far beyond the confines of the rubric under which they are introduced. After describing an especially sinister configuration of the eyes, Polemo adds the following warning:

> When you see an eye such as I have just described, you should know that you will never find another eye more perfectly wicked—not even in a wolf or a wild boar. He who has an eye like that will never stop seeking evil, desist from dreadful deeds, or lose his savage nature. I have not seen many eyes of this type, but I have seen one man, a Lydian touring Ionia, whose eyes were such as I have just described to you. [108]

Polemo expands this illustration to include more particulars of physique and character: the man had a drunkard's complexion and spewed boastful words from his effeminate mouth. He hissed through his teeth like a wild boar at bay; his laughter was shrill; his breath was hot.

> And so it was that I knew him for a villain. He was forever planning or executing something offensive and perfecting his atrocities. He was full of violence . . . a homicide dripping with blood. He used to talk openly about his sexual exploits with youths and women and appeared to make the production of bastards his special study. [109]

Here, as so often in ancient invective, charges of sexual malfeasance are lobbed helter-skelter, without any distinction made between male and female partners. What is "effeminate" about this man is his uncontrolled pursuit of pleasure.

Polemo selects one characteristic for elaboration: the Lydian actually took greater delight in harming his friends than his enemies. When his pious neighbors were celebrating a sacred feast, he sent them a food basket by messenger. This gesture regrettably necessitated the cancellation of all festivities, since underneath a promising plate of oysters the basket contained a human head. The horrified celebrants scattered to their homes, cursing the scoundrel who had spoiled their dinner and calling on the gods for vengeance. Only at this point in the narrative do we learn that Polemo himself was polluted by this ghastly offering: "I too was among those cursing him, and I will not cease to curse him as long as I live." [110]

[108] Ibid. 1, 1.126F.
[109] Ibid. 1, 1.128F.
[110] Ibid. 1, 1.130F.

In retrospect we can see why Polemo prefaced this story with the comment, "The most astonishing of all his evil deeds, *which no one saw through,* was this." We have here a case study of a physiognomical failure—or of physiognomy foiled, since the malevolent Lydian, by sending his basket through an intermediary, deprived Polemo of the opportunity to look him in the eye. Polemo's exultant claim, "And so it was I knew him for a villain," must have come after the fact, though it is presented beforehand in the narrative. But we do not linger to puzzle out these inconsistencies because the story continues: "Someone from Syria who knew him informed me that he had polluted food on many previous occasions." Apparently the Lydian with wicked eyes made a habit of bringing along unclean foods to banquets and drinking parties (Polemo's indignation is a reminder of the sacral importance of communal eating in the ancient world); after drugging the wine he served his guests, he would turn his hand to homicide or cruelly insulting practical jokes: suffocating a sleeping guest or shaving off his beard.[111]

Although we are told that this villain's eyes were damp (a sign of gluttony and too much undiluted wine), Polemo subordinates physical description to a generalized defamation of character and behavior: "Whenever he had succeeded in harming someone, I would notice that he was joyful, seized with mirth, muttering unintelligible words. If a malicious project had turned out well, I would see him overjoyed, barking like a dog." This was, indeed, an exceptional man: "I have never seen anyone, male or female, endowed with his disposition." But how can such a fact be useful to a would-be physiognomist? Polemo appears unaware of the way in which the uniqueness of his examples undermines the universal applicability of his art. Indeed, the examples exist only to assert the uniqueness of Polemo's expertise as its practitioner.

Polemo has the confidence of a local priest and from him has learned the full and shocking story of how the evil Lydian sought ritual purification after bungling a particularly monstrous crime. First he poisoned his father. Then he tried to do away with his mother, Neronian style: he took her out to sea in a boat and threw her overboard. The attempt miscarried, however, when the surf washed her up on the beach. Olympius the priest was approached about a purification but could not make any headway with the job: first he stumbled into a newly dug grave, and then the black ram that he brought along for the seaside ceremony dropped dead without a blow. Overcome by these omens of disaster, the priest fled back to the city, now in need of decontamination himself. By closing with this detail, which

[111] These tricks appear to be sinister relatives of the banqueters' παίγνια found in Athenaeus and the Greek magical papyri. See *PGM* 7.167–86 in H. D. Betz, *The Greek Magical Papyri in Translation* (Chicago, 1985), 119–20. These are amusing table tricks and home remedies for social handicaps like garrulity and garlic breath. More hostile intentions appear to motivate *PGM* 11b.1–5 (p. 151 Betz).

echoes the flight of the contaminated banqueters of the previous anecdote, Polemo has created a neat narrative diptych, which highlights his skill without illuminating his methods.

Any example that is the fruit of personal experience provides the narrator with opportunities to introduce himself into his narrative, and in some cases the resulting story is quite elaborate. To illustrate the sinister implications of sunken eyes, Polemo describes the ocular signs of a man whose seditious propensities eventually revealed themselves in treason. Then, as corroboration, he offers to record his personal experience of the traitor.[112]

The tale begins by name-dropping: "I was traveling at one time with the emperor. . . ." A leisurely description of their itinerary brings us at last to the man with sunken eyes. He and his armed companions surround the emperor, who apparently does not perceive the danger. Only Polemo knows that "he did not do this to honor the emperor, or because he was well-disposed to him, but to see how he might do him harm and execute the wicked plans that were giving him no rest." Nothing actually happens, but by voicing his suspicions to us in this early stage of the narrative Polemo presents himself as alive to unseen treachery. Unlike Mordecai at the gates of Ahasueras, the physiognomist does not overhear any conspiratorial conversations. He does not perceive any secret activity, but rather the secret meaning of public activity. For various reasons, however, this narrative cannot achieve the dramatic dénouement favored by Polemo in later examples: a public prediction based on physiognomical evidence that he keeps to himself, soon followed by independent confirmation of its truth. At court Polemo is in no position to point out to the assembled bystanders, "The man with the sunken eyes is a traitor!" Instead, when the emperor retires to prepare for the hunt, Polemo withdraws to discuss matters with his friends "since we had no opportunity for colloquy with the emperor"—a comment perhaps intended to explain why, if Polemo's diagnosis was so sure, he did not draw Hadrian aside to warn him. No, under the circumstances, the traitor must unmask himself, and this revelation is carefully staged.

> My companions and I sat down in conversation. We spoke of the emperor: about how weary he was and how remote from the amenities of life that he was reputed to enjoy. Eventually the subject of *that man* came up, and we expressed astonishment at his disgraceful conduct, his depravity, and the persistence with which he pursued his evil ends. In the midst of our discussion—behold!—we catch a glimpse of someone among the trees. Raising our terrified eyes, we see: yes, it is he, the very villain of whom we speak! He had crept up like a snake in order to overhear. "All this talk," he says, "must be about me." I answered him,

---

[112] *Phys.* 1, 1.138–42F. On the historical background, see G. W. Bowersock, *Greek Sophists in the Roman Empire* (above, n.5), 120–23.

"We have been discussing you, and we are struck by your situation. Come, tell us in your own words how it is that you have imposed this effort on yourself and endure all these disputes." When he heard this, he confessed, "This must be the work of the evil spirits and the desire for evil that they inspire in my soul!" And he began to weep, exclaiming, "Alas, I am done for!" So that is what I have observed about small sunken eyes.

When the man in the grip of an evil spirit is confronted with Polemo, whose specialized knowledge makes him sensitive to the presence of things unseen, the result is a revelation, almost an exorcism.[113] Augustine was not the only person in antiquity to take words overheard by chance as a personal omen,[114] and for the guilty courtier in this story, Polemo's words appear to have some such force. The criminal's self-revelation is presented as an event caused, but not intended, by Polemo and has thus the effect of an independent confirmation of his insight. Polemo's anonymous companions serve as witnesses, by their silent presence in the narrative authenticating his tale. And the anguished exclamation, "Alas, I am done for!" allows the foiled conspirator to imply that Polemo has foiled the plot and ruined his career, a claim that Polemo could not truthfully make himself.

Hadrian never moves out of the background in this story, though his anonymous presence as "the emperor" is essential to the plot. Soon, however, we meet him face to face. After an extended catalog of eye-types that are sinister, or at best ambiguous, it comes as a relief to learn that eyes that are flashing and full of light are *good* (unless they are spoiled by other signs). "I certainly advise the physiognomist not to be hasty in his judgment until all contradictory indications have been thoroughly examined. Certainly the eyes of the Emperor Hadrian were of this kind: full of lovely radiance, swift, and sharp of glance. No man has ever been seen endowed with eyes more full of light."[115] Indeed, Polemo has attributed to Hadrian, Spaniard though he was, eyes of the perfect Hellenic type.[116] This is the only example in which Polemo describes a man's eyes without describing his character, and the only example in which Polemo does not express himself in the first person. And Hadrian, unlike all his other contemporary

---

[113] Compare Apollonius of Tyana, who was able to spot the plague demon of Ephesus disguised as a blind mendicant (Philostratus, *Life of Apollonius of Tyana* 4.10).

[114] Smyrna was famed for its use of this sort of oracle (Paus. 9.11.7) and the city actually possessed a temple of the Κληδόνες. See further references in C. J. Cadoux, *Ancient Smyrna* (Oxford, 1938), 208. For the role of chance words in Augustine's conversion experience, see *Confessions* 8.12.

[115] *Phys.* 1, 1.148F. The Arabic is compatible with either past or present tense and thus provides no evidence for date of composition.

[116] Cf. Adam. 2.32, 1.386F, ὀφθαλμοὺς ὑγροὺς χαροποὺς γοργοὺς φῶς πολὺ ἔχοντας ἐν ἑαυτοῖς.

examples, is named. These deviations from Polemo's usual practice fit together. Hadrian is not a private discovery but public property. To attribute intelligence, courage, and magnanimity to the imperial gaze is a job for the panegyricist, and Polemo is making a statement about himself by refusing to perform it. That statement may be hard to read now in an appropriately nuanced way, but Polemo seems unwilling to compromise his role as the discoverer of secrets by testifying to an acknowledged fact.

Polemo's physiognomical description of Favorinus, which we have met in another context, is notable for the sleight-of-hand dexterity with which Polemo argues from general categories to a particular case and back again, always to the discredit of his rival. The description begins neutrally enough with the observation that a sharp glance and wide-open eyes that corruscate like marble are an indication of insufficient sexual control.[117] Unchastity in itself is not a particularly remarkable condition. But Polemo's focus grows more specific. "This sort of eye is found in men who are not like other men, like a eunuch who has nonetheless not been castrated but was born without testicles." From the unchaste in general, to "men who are not like other men," to a eunuch who is an unusual example even within his unusual kind—the field is narrowing rapidly. Now we find out that Polemo is really heading toward a category of one: "I don't think that I have ever seen but a single example of that type of man; he came from the land of the Celts." The allusion to Favorinus is unmistakable. Nominally camouflaged by the pretense of objective description within impersonal scientific categories, physiognomical character assassination may proceed. "He was libidinous and dissolute beyond all bounds, for his eyes were those of the very worst sort of men and doubtless were similar to that description." It is typical of Polemo's method to support character assessment with physiognomic details, but in Favorinus' case, what do the latter consist of? Here Polemo fails to describe the specific optical signs that he includes in all his other examples but refers us instead to the ocular profile of "the very worst sort of men," a category so broad as to be meaningless. It is almost as if, at the last moment, he could not bring himself to look his rival directly in the eye.

Polemo sketches in the rest of the eunuch's features: his soft, fleshy body, his effeminate voice and languid walk, his use of body lotions and the elaborate attention he paid to his hair, grooming habits that are passive and feminine because they are designed to inspire *others* with lust. Favorinus' voice, perhaps in real life his most outstanding effeminate characteristic, is a prominent feature of this description. Polemo mentions it twice and then insists that "among all mankind I have never before seen

<hr />

[117] *Phys.* 1.160F.

anyone whose appearance or whose eyes resembled his."[118] Polemo concedes that Favorinus was "thoroughly schooled in the Greek language and idiom and generally used that language; he was even called a sophist." But after this oblique acknowledgment of his rival's rhetorical skill, Polemo devotes much more space to a description of his proficiency in magic, poisons, and love-charms: "All of his intellectual talent was focused on these areas." By glossing over Favorinus' achievements as a sophist, and by implying that dubious magical activities were his strongest suit, Polemo has managed to avoid any reference to his rival's status as a philosopher, unless the wary reader is prepared to interpret accusations of magic as an indirect allusion to a rhetorician's interest in philosophy.[119] Yet in this sketch of an itinerant magician, whatever its distortions, the internationally famous sophist must be recognizable in order for the slander to succeed. The uniqueness of Favorinus' physical status, which enables Polemo to refer to him both generically and individually as a category of one, is what makes effective misrepresentation possible.

Having pinpointed (indeed, skewered) Favorinus' characteristics as an individual, Polemo draws ethical consequences from his example in ever-widening circles of generality:

> Therefore I have known eunuchs to be an evil tribe: they are greedy and replete with tendencies to dissipation. You should be aware, moreover, that castrated eunuchs undergo a change in the general appearance, complexion, and physique that they had before castration. In contrast, those who are born without testicles exhibit altered characteristics that are different from those shown by the castrated. Hence *no one is more perfectly evil than he who is born without testicles.* Therefore, when you see the eyes I described at the outset of this discussion, you will find that their owner resembles the class of eunuchs.[120]

The focus broadens from Favorinus the individual eunuch-magician, to "eunuchs, subset non-castrati," to the class of men who merely resemble eunuchs. The way Polemo has juxtaposed his assertions asyndetically, as if they were terms in a syllogism, only serves to highlight the incoherence of his reasoning. Is Favorinus evil because he is a eunuch, or is the "tribe" of eunuchs evil because it contains Favorinus? Why exactly should it be that uncastrated eunuchs are "worse" than castrated ones? Polemo's explanation in terms of "different altered characteristics" appears to be double-talk: generalizations, couched in universalizing "scientific" plurals, on the basis of a single example that he has already admitted to be unique.

Professional rivalry is distorting logic here: Favorinus must be not

---

[118] 1.162F.
[119] Apuleius is only the most obvious example.
[120] *Phys.* 1.162–64F, italics mine.

merely bad, but the very worst of a very bad lot. He is more than Polemo's competitor: he is Polemo's antithesis and, as such, must be superlative.[121] In contrast to the partisan hyperbole of his portrait of Favorinus, the beard-eating caricature chosen to illustrate the category of "evil idiots," when Polemo's original examples resume toward the end of the treatise, provides an unproblematic instance of superlatives used for entertainment.

> So thoroughly was he at the mercy of his loathsome depravities that he was always taking his beard up with his teeth and eating it, twisting hairs from his chin or elsewhere on his body and putting them into his mouth to devour them. This man surpassed in wickedness all the wild beasts and evil men of his time, while surpassing in stupidity all the idiots of his generation. This one man gave clear and ample indications of both qualities.[122]

In vignettes such as these, the physiognomist does not participate in his own narrative but takes aim from behind a duck-blind at the flights of human folly. Polemo's most extended narratives, however, include himself, and he concludes the treatise with four of them in a row. The first, which we might entitle "The Woman at the Temple," illustrates physiognomy transmuted into prophecy by a practitioner of genius. In this exploit, Polemo takes as his subject a woman whose features are almost entirely concealed and uncovers secrets of her destiny of which she herself is unaware.

We find ourselves before the temple of Artemis at Perge in Pamphylia, where by local custom the women go about completely veiled.[123] Polemo picks out from the crowd of shrouded figures entering the temple one who is marked for disaster:

> Great was the admiration of the assembled bystanders (for they all wondered how I was able to pass judgment on her merely by observing her eyes and the tip of her nose) when I exclaimed, "How huge is the disaster bearing down upon that woman and how soon will it strike!" There had been a sign, because her nostrils and nose had become darkened and agitated, while her eyes had turned green and were opened abnormally wide; her head showed too much movement

---

[121] Professional rivalry also appears to have distorted Polemo's judgment in the only independently reported account we have of his competence as a physiognomist. Philostratus records his total failure to read the face of a fellow sophist. Although Marcus of Byzantium's brows and meditative countenance "proclaimed him a sophist," and although "the steady gaze of his eyes intent on secret thoughts" revealed him as a man who constantly meditated in silence upon rhetorical themes, Polemo was sufficiently misled by the roughness of his hair and grooming to exclaim to his students, "Why are you looking at that rustic? *He* will not give you a theme" (Philostratus, *Lives* 528–29).

[122] *Anon. Lat.* 105, 2.130F. The Arabic version of this chapter (*Phys.* 65, 1.280F) is incomplete.

[123] This was also the custom at Tarsus (Dio Chrysostom 33.48–49). Cf. L. Robert, "Deux textes inutilisés sur Pergè et sur Sidè," *Hellenica V*, 68.

and her feet, as she went into the temple, moved about as if she were in pain. These signs, unless you see them in a lunatic, you may be sure portend imminent disaster.[124]

The words are barely out of his mouth when Polemo's prediction receives a spectacular confirmation. A second woman suddenly appears, screaming, to tell the veiled lady that her most beloved child, her only daughter, has fallen into a well and drowned: "When the woman heard this, she threw off her headdress, veil, jewelry, and all her clothes to stand naked, with beaten breast. In her grief she ran off down the road, crying out as she ran, 'Oh, my daughter!'" When her last shred of clothing falls off, men rush out to cover her up with vestments from the temple.

Polemo describes the removal of the woman's enveloping garments, to which he had drawn our attention as a detail of local custom at the beginning of the story, as if the gesture were a literal recapitulation of the metaphorical stripping he had performed a few minutes before with the X-rays of his physiognomical insight. He characterizes her last undergarment with studied precision, "When even the loincloth underneath her clothes, which was of Egyptian or Greek manufacture, fell off," (who but Polemo would have the sangfroid to speculate about the provenance of linens at such a moment as that?) in a way that emphasizes his self-mastery and emotional detachment as an observer. While the awesome penetration of the physiognomist's all-seeing eye rivets the reader's attention, the naked woman's suffering is eclipsed from the scene.

Polemo recounts how he performed another spectacular feat of prognostication while attending a wedding. As he followed the wedding procession on its noisy way through the streets, Polemo startled his companions with an electrifying pronouncement: "'The bride,' said I, 'will be abducted before she reaches the groom's house, and assuredly tonight another man, not her betrothed, will make her his wife.'"[125] A private hunch is one thing, but a public prediction, even when made sotto voce to one's immediate neighbors, carries with it the risk of considerable embarrassment should it fail to prove true. But Polemo, in his narrative, strikes a pose of imperturbability. "While I was waiting for what I had said to be confirmed," he tells us, the wedding procession was ambushed and the bride was carried off—just outside her bridegroom's door! The basis of his prediction was not originally the bride's appearance or behavior; he only found out later that she was an accomplice to the plot. But Polemo had spotted the prospective abductor among the crowd that accompanied the bride. He attracted the physiognomist's attention by his sinister smile and

[124] *Phys.* 68, 1.284F.
[125] Ibid. 69, 1.286F. For an analysis of this story in relation to the social background of erotic magic, see John J. Winkler, *The Constraints of Desire* (New York, 1989), 71–77.

furtive glances. As Polemo came closer to investigate, he observed the young man's heavy breathing, his garments damp with sweat, his quivering nostrils and complexion that kept changing color, "evidently because he was gripped by trembling and by fear of disgrace." Then Polemo observed something queer about the bride's eyes and drew his own conclusions.

This anecdote calls forth another: "Once when I was in the territory of Smyrna, I came upon a wedding party, which I was invited to join. While we were leading the bride to the bridegroom's house in the middle of a great crowd, I decided to practice physiognomy."[126] Here we have Polemo as he wished others to see him: a man whose distinguished appearance elicits wedding invitations from strangers, a detached and resolutely independent observer of the human scene. He makes the same prediction as before, and for similar reasons. The complicitous bride actually gets as far as the groom's house this time but is abducted when she goes out-of-doors again under pretext of paying a visit to the latrine.

Polemo's original text may well have contained additional anecdotes that were designed to illustrate his skill at foretelling future events,[127] but he chose to end his work with a demonstration of a different sort of clairvoyance: the unveiling of a hypocrite.[128] "You should know that physiognomy attains to no higher form of knowledge, among all that I have mentioned, than the knowledge of things past and things to come, to the point that it can uncover events that are alleged to have happened but never in fact took place, and demolish them as fiction." While traveling abroad, Polemo hears of a local merchant whose ship has gone down at sea, taking with it all his goods and his only son. He finds the bereaved man lamenting before a large crowd of fellow-citizens, tearing at his clothes and pulling out his hair: a self-dramatizing performance on a grand scale. Just as we have achieved a satisfactory picture of the scene, Polemo interjects the startling comment, "The man was a dissimulator and adept at deceit." Everything is not what it seems, but, helpless without access to all the evidence, the reader is reduced to the role of Dr. Watson, whose astonishment is extorted by Sherlock Holmes as an admission of intellectual inferiority. "When I came upon him in that state of mourning, I remarked to those around him . . ." Here we have Polemo's typical "revelation to the astonished crowd," a reminder to his readers of the confidence he felt in his as yet unfulfilled prediction, as well as a reminder to us of the way that other sciences besides medicine in the second century could be

[126] *Phys.* 69, 1.288F.
[127] The *Anon. Lat.* (133, 2.144–5F) mentions multiple predictions out of which it promises to give two or three examples (now lost).
[128] *Phys.* 70, 1.290–92F.

practiced as performing arts.[129] In this scene he gives his "chorus" a stake in the outcome of events by suspending his announcement to inform us that the crowd was itself in mourning for the sons, brothers, and fellow-citizens that had gone down with the ship. "I said to them," he resumes, "'In my opinion, at any rate, that man has *not* suffered the loss for which you grieve.'"

The crowd's reaction, here as elsewhere, can only be imagined. It is not described. But they are not left to wonder long, since a messenger arrives forthwith to announce the vessel is safe: previous reports of a shipwreck were in error.

> Of course I had realized that that was the case, for when I looked at that deceiver, although his fear and anxiety seemed great, his eyes were not shedding any tears and the hair on his head and brows had not changed position in any way. I saw that his skin was smooth; I observed how his lamentation resembled laughter, and other signs which I forbear to mention, since I have no desire to go on at length, being well aware of the beginner's intellectual limitations.

It is not made clear why the deceitful merchant perpetrated this charade. Was it an attempt at insurance fraud, a horrid practical joke, or did he succumb to a pathological urge for self-display? Was he perhaps actually innocent of conscious deceit, the victim of a rumor, whose grief (physiognomical truths being absolute), because it had no basis in fact, could not make his appearance play false to his destiny? Polemo does not tell us. Human motives count for little; what fascinates is the challenge of deceit and the frisson of discovery.

After this anecdote, Polemo brings his treatise to a close with the abrupt nod of a busy professor who can no longer conceal his impatience with his sluggish pupils. Compared to the pithy characterizations of animals and eyebrows that he brought into the central sections of the treatise from his Aristotelian model, Polemo's elaboration of these examples has indeed extended to some length, a fact that he acknowledges with a cursory justification:

> I have not been describing things that could be explained in any other way but by narration. Learning, however, does not seem tedious to those who apply themselves studiously and possess the requisite talent; but those who are stupid enough not to believe in it or acknowledge its truth give up in despair. Farewell.[130]

---

[129] On medicine as a performing art, see Galen's *On Prognosis* (*CMG* 5.8.1), where the standard scenario appears to be multiple doctors in competition around a single bedside.
[130] *Phys.* 70, 1.292F.

52   CHAPTER TWO

Dismissed so abruptly from the presence of our instructor, we may well wonder why he bothered to try teaching us at all. In an academic system where professors had to compete for students while avoiding all traces of servility in their search for a clientele, such high-handedness constituted an assertion of professional superiority. To maintain "face" in this situation, every professor had to act as if he took on only the best and that any pupils who left him did so because *they* were inadequate.[131] By closing his treatise in this way, Polemo serves us clear warning that we are not to be beguiled by the charms of his anecdotal presentation into thinking that the expert has stooped to *entertain*. It is not we who as reading audience have tolerated Polemo's performance with patient attention. It is he who has tolerated us.

In conclusion, let us try to recapture the full weight of Polemo's presence as sophist and physiognomist. He was a public performer in a high-wire discipline who faced the constant competitive scrutiny of other men. He was an accomplished courtier, whose successful negotiations with the emperor required a sure sense of what to say and when to be silent. As a master of the physiognomic art, he had trained himself to take in the shifty, timorous, or aggressive gaze of his contemporaries with a calm, impenetrable stare.

Little can be concealed from the penetrating gaze of Polemo's portrait which survives from the ruins of the Olympieion. His eyes, forgoing direct confrontation, incline obliquely a little to the left, rising slightly upward to plumb the inner recesses of the soul.[132] Frozen in stone, this is the expression Polemo bequeathed to posterity to immortalize a climactic moment of self-presentation. After 560 years, the great Temple of Olympian Zeus at Athens stood at last complete. Hadrian presided over the inauguration of this monument to imperial munificence and cultural continuity "as a triumphant speech-achievement of Time itself."[133] The magnificent paradox of this phrase, which resists translation into English, was to be embodied by Polemo himself, whose oration crowned the dedicatory sacrifice. Standing at the base of the temple, where ornate Corinthian capitals rested atop 104 columns of blinding Pentelic marble that towered upward to ten times human height, Polemo, with the magisterial concentration of a master performer, focused his eyes beyond the brilliance of the visible scene. "Fixing his gaze, as was his custom, on the thoughts that

[131] For one sociologist's view of "face," see Erving Goffman, *Interaction Ritual: Essays on Face-to-Face Behavior* (New York, 1967).
[132] This bust is now in the National Museum at Athens (reproduced in the *frontispiece*). Photographs are reproduced in G. Richter's *Portraits of the Greeks* (London, 1965), vol. 3, 285 with figures 2034–2037. Without an inscription, the identification must remain speculative.
[133] ὡς χρόνου μέγα ἀγώνισμα: Philostratus, *Lives* 533.

PORTRAIT OF POLEMO 53

were already present before his mind, he threw himself into his speech, . . . building his proemium on the observation that it was not without divine inspiration that he was moved to speak."[134] No matter how well prepared he was for this occasion, it was essential that Polemo's performance emanate spontaneity, demonstrating to his expectant audience that his inspiration came from beyond himself.

The ability to perform extempore was highly prized in Polemo's culture precisely because each improvisation was a triumph of individual endeavor that could be achieved only within collectively sanctioned limits: a highly circumscribed array of traditional vocabulary and themes. Every sophist began his training by mining tropes and phrases from classic texts by lamplight, and then, wiping off all sooty traces of his labor, held them up to scintillate by light of day. Correct diction was only the beginning; what counted for more was the fluency and grace with which these elements could be combined extempore, so that every turn of the kaleidoscope produced intricate new patterns from the familiar gems. Improvisation transcended memorization; the audiences of the Second Sophistic knew and appreciated the difference.[135] A successful extempore performer was worshiped as an epiphany of the collective past, Hellenic culture made to live again with every re-creation.[136] "The typical circumstances of delivery allowed a rapport between speaker and audience denied to circulated written texts: speaker could work upon audience, and the audience could, especially in impromptu performances, feel the stimulus of participation in the act of creation."[137] All those who saw themselves and their city as participants in the common culture of the civilized world had reason to rejoice as they watched a great sophist negotiate its verbal territory with surefooted mastery. This turf was a minefield of potential solecisms, to be traversed with dazzling confidence at exhilarating speed. The apparent pettiness of the conventions that governed sophistic performance is misleading: such rules only seem trivial to those who do not acknowledge the importance of the game. It takes superlative vision to negotiate invisible obstacles, spectacular insight and audacity to build a verbal edifice to stand beside the Olympieion. Trained by the endless practice of imaginary declamations, as well as the merciless discipline of physiognomy, the eyes that stare outward from Polemo's stone portrait learned long ago to fix themselves on things unseen.

[134] Ibid. 533.
[135] On the role of improvisation in second-century rhetoric, see B. Reardon, *Courants littéraires Grecs des IIe et IIIe siècles après J.-C.* (Paris, 1971), 111–14.
[136] On the re-instantiation of the heroes of the past, compare L. Robert, "Une Epigramme Satirique d'Automédon et Athènes au début de l'empire," *REG* 94 (1981), 360–61.
[137] Thus E. L. Bowie, "The Importance of Sophists," *YCS* 27 (1982), 45.

Polemo and Favorinus, whom we have endeavored to capture at moments of peak performance, were at the same time highly idiosyncratic individuals and typologically resonant cultural icons. It is now time to investigate some key variables in the social construction of the educated man's persona. The next three chapters discuss manly and effeminate stereotypes in body language, in the use of the voice, and in rhetoric. We begin with body language, for which the physiognomists are an invaluable source.

Chapter Three

DEPORTMENT AS LANGUAGE:
PHYSIOGNOMY AND THE SEMIOTICS
OF GENDER

> When you see deep blue eyes that stand still, you may take it
> that their owner is remote from other men, aloof from his
> neighbors, and extremely eager to amass wealth. You should
> avoid him with the greatest caution, even if he be a member
> of your own family, nor should you ever make a journey in
> his company or accept his advice. For he delights in evil and
> sleeplessly plots the ruin of his friends.

THE COMPETITIVE ENVIRONMENT of mutual distrust pre-supposed by this piece of advice will be familiar to any student of village culture in the Mediterranean world of today.[1] But the words are Polemo's, whose second-century *Physiognomy* constitutes a highly elaborated operations manual for a technology of suspicion that was indigenous to his culture.

To follow the thought-patterns of the physiognomist is to enter the forest of eyes that made up what we lightly call today "the face-to-face society" of the ancient Mediterranean city. This was a world in which the scrutiny of faces was not an idle pastime but an essential survival skill. In this world, the practice of divination, in many forms and at various levels of formality, was a ubiquitous reflex in response to uncertainty. Everyone who had to choose a son-in-law or a traveling companion, deposit valuables before a journey, buy slaves, or make a business loan became perforce an amateur physiognomist: he made risky inferences from human surfaces to human depths.

A version of this chapter appeared in *Before Sexuality: The Construction of Erotic Experience in the Ancient Greek World*, ed. D. Halperin, J. Winkler, and F. Zeitlin (Princeton, 1990).

Epigraph: Polemo, *Phys.* 1, Förster, *Scriptores Physiognomonici Graeci et Latini* (Leipzig, 1893), vol. 1, p. 112, hereafter cited in the form 1.112F. Cf. Adam. 1.6, 1.310F.

[1] See E. Friedl, *Vasilika, a Village in Modern Greece* (New York, 1962), esp. 79–81; M. Herzfeld, *The Poetics of Manhood: Contest and Identity in a Cretan Mountain Village* (Princeton, 1985); J. du Boulay, "Lies, Mockery, and Family Integrity," in *Mediterranean Family Structure*, ed. J. G. Peristiany (Cambridge, 1976), 389–406; P. Walcot, "Odysseus and the Art of Lying," *Ancient Society* 8 (1977), 1–19.

Physiognomy detects weakness or wickedness in one's neighbors. While too much dampness in the eye is a sign of cowardice, an eye that is too dry suggests stupidity.[2] What is decisive is a man's behavior when he is watched up close: "Where you see the eyelids lifted high, and where the owner of such an eye breathes deeply while he speaks to you, know then that he is up to no good and meditating evil schemes."[3] Lest you think that only misanthropes have the potential to harm you, Polemo warns against the snares of excessive geniality: "If you detect delight and mildness in someone's eyes, take care that you approve him not. For he is perfidious and hides what is in his heart. He is given over to deception, malignant in disposition and behavior alike."[4] There is indeed something suspect, in most cases, about mirth.

> If you see someone who looks down at the ground while he laughs, whose eyes remain dry amidst his laughter, assign him to the very worst category based on his eyes. Nor does abundant laughter mean any good in an eye that is bad in other respects, especially if the eye looks like it is planning an ambush from within its lair. Should you observe that his forehead, cheeks, and lips move while he laughs, no good will come of *that*, for it shows that he is pursuing someone with devious designs.[5]

Whom can we trust? Polemo's ideal appears to be "decorum without rigidity." If this balance be in place, it is even possible to smile without appearing sinister.

> Where you have noticed dampness in gently smiling eyes, and you observe that the whole face is open and that eyelids and forehead are smooth and relaxed, the possessor of such eyes tends more toward good than bad. You will find in consequence that his character is attractive and benevolent, and in that person you will find fairness, leniency, piety, and hospitality. You will find further that he is intelligent, prudent, quick to learn, and strongly sexed.[6]

Eyes that lack dampness, however, indicate dangerous men, "for you will find that they are schemers, full of excessive ingenuity."

Along with excessive dryness, another danger signal is a fixed stare: "When you see eyes that remain quiet and completely still, almost fixed in the face, know then that man for an implacably hostile enemy." The depraved emperor Caligula had fixed, unblinking eyes (a peculiarity shared by two of his gladiators, who were for that reason unconquerable).[7]

---

[2] *Phys.* 1, 1.110F.
[3] Ibid. 1, 1.112F.
[4] Ibid. 1, 1.152F.
[5] Ibid. 1, 1.152–54F.
[6] Ibid. 1, 1.154–56F, with Adam. 1.17, 1.336–38F, and *Anon. Lat.* 37, 2.55F.
[7] Pliny the Elder, *Natural History* 11.54.144 (Caligula); *Phys.* 1, 1.110F (eyes).

Yet eyes that move too much are just as bad as those that stay too still: Thracians, for example, have eyes so agitated they appear to spin, "because they are inclined to evil-doing but are restrained by powerful fear and timidity from actually doing wrong, although their natural propensity is always in that direction."[8]

Heads I win, tails you lose; benign behavior may mask malignant inclinations. Physiognomy puts no one above suspicion. To blink or not to blink, the effect is the same: "When you see someone's eyes opening and closing in a certain way, you may be sure that their owner is working out plans to commit some crime. And when you observe that those eyes keep opening but their owner appears to want to keep them shut, you may be sure that he has already perpetrated every kind of loathsome atrocity."[9]

The idea that the eyes reveal the hidden thoughts of the mind provides the theoretical justification for their importance to the physiognomist. "You should know, moreover, that the heart, from which the impulses of the soul originate and have their secret start, is the seat of thought. For the eye is joined to the seat of the heart and experiences the disturbance of ⟨the heart's⟩ thoughts and anxieties so that the discourse of the soul shines through."[10] The importance of the eyes was already well known to orators. As Cicero observed, "Delivery is entirely a matter of the emotions, which are mirrored by the face and expressed by the eyes."[11] As an aristocratic naturalist thoroughly trained in rhetoric, the elder Pliny was accustomed to read the language of the human face. Other animals have foreheads, he tells us, but only in man is the brow an *index* of sorrow, gaiety, mercy, or severity. It is only in man that eyebrows register their owner's awareness of his status relationships with others: "With them we indicate assent and dissent; they are our chief means of displaying contempt; pride has its place of generation elsewhere, but here is its abode: it is born in the heart, but rises to the eyebrows and hangs suspended there. . . ."[12]

Cicero's advice to the orator shows the pressure that the unremitting scrutiny of an exacting peer group exerted on masculine deportment: "Consequently, there is need of constant management of the eyes, because the expression of the countenance ought not to be too much altered, lest we slip into fatuity or into some distortion."[13] The eyes were valued as

---

[8] *Phys.* 1,1.110F.

[9] Ibid. 1,1.154F.

[10] Ibid.1,1.110F, cf. 168F.

[11] *De oratore* 3.59.221: *animi est enim omnis actio, et imago animi vultus, indices oculi.* Cf. Quintilian, *Inst.* 11.3.75–76.

[12] Pliny the Elder, *Natural History* 11.51.138, trans. H. Rackham (Loeb Classical Library [Cambridge, Mass., 1956]).

[13] *Quare oculorum esto magna moderatio, nam oris non est nimium mutanda species ne aut ad ineptias aut ad pravitatem aliquam deferamur* (*De oratore* 3.59.222).

indices because they were thought to give unmediated expression to the thoughts and emotions of the inward self. Yet at the same time a person was held accountable for the way his eyes appeared. These two facts added up to a double bind that could only be escaped by flawless self-control—or successful dissimulation. One man's restraint was another man's hypocrisy. The "hall of mirrors" quality that these beliefs gave to social relations would have been complex enough had physiognomy confined itself to ferreting out the malevolence and venality of neighbors and fellow-citizens. But more was at stake. Perhaps because the competitive interaction of public life was a discourse confined to men, and the eligibility of the contestants was never taken entirely for granted, physiognomists also specialized in spotting males who were not real men at all.

THE DECIPHERMENT OF GENDER

The fact that physiognomy was prepared to offer itself as a tool for decoding the signs of gender deviance makes it a fruitful source of information about the sex/gender system that permeated ancient society but rarely articulates itself explicitly in canonical texts. In this system gender is independent of anatomical sex:

> You may obtain physiognomic indications of masculinity and femininity from your subject's glance, movement, and voice, and then, from among these signs, compare one with another until you determine to your satisfaction which of the two sexes prevails. For in the masculine there is something feminine to be found, and in the feminine something masculine, but the name *masculine* or *feminine* is assigned according to which of the two prevails.[14]

The essential idea here is that there exist masculine and feminine "types" that do not necessarily correspond to the anatomical sex of the person in question. This may seem strange to us now, since we have become accustomed to thinking of the human race as divided into two natural kinds, male and female. But recent writing on the history of sexuality reminds us that this was not always so. Perhaps as early as the third or fourth century B.C.E., and certainly from the time of Galen, it was a medical commonplace that men are—anatomically speaking—women turned inside out.[15]

---

[14] *Phys.* 2,1.192F.

[15] Herophilos the Hellenistic anatomist stressed the homologies between male and female reproductive organs (Galen, *On the Seed* 2.2, K4.596–97). For Galen's elaborate formulation of the inverse topology of male and female, see Galen, *On the Use of the Parts* 14.6, trans. in M. May, *Galen, On the Usefulness of the Parts of the Body* (Ithaca, N.Y., 1968), vol. 2, 628–29 = K4.159–60; *On the Seed* 2.1 and 5 = K4.596, 634–36. For a recent discussion, see T. Laqueur, "Orgasm, Generation, and the Politics of Reproductive Biology," *Representations* 14 (1986), 2–5; and *Making Sex* (Cambridge, 1990), 24–43.

The embryology of Hippocrates and Galen envisaged a mingling of male and female seed, in which various proportions were possible: an infant's gender was not an absolute but a point on a sliding scale, depending on the type of seed that predominated or the temperature of the uterine quadrant in which it lodged.[16] Masculinity in the ancient world was an achieved state, radically underdetermined by anatomical sex.[17]

Hence "masculine" and "feminine" (*arsenikos* and *thēlukos*) function as physiognomical categories for *both* male and female subjects.[18] Those of the masculine "type," though strictly speaking of the female sex, may be known by their tendency to bear male children. Similarly, males and females of the feminine "type" will produce female children. Male types will physically favor the right-hand side:[19] eyes, hands, feet, or testes will be larger on that side, and the features of their face will incline to the right. Women who bear the signs of the male type and men who bear the features of the female type are mendacious imposters—presumably because their bodies "lie."[20] The very possibility of mixed gender-signs demanded a science of decipherment.

A science of decipherment that postulates the co-presence of masculine and feminine qualities in the same individual could conceivably support a complementary rather than a hierarchical view of gender. The Hellenistic physician Loxus claims in his discussion of mixed gender-signs that good character requires both masculine courage and feminine wisdom.[21] But such possibilities definitely did not intrigue Polemo, who follows Aristotelian tradition closely in his summary of gender differences in character and physique.

[16] Hippocrates, *On Generation* 6 (Littré 7, 479), trans. in I. M. Lonie, *The Hippocratic Treatises "On Generation," "On the Nature of the Child," "Diseases IV"* (Berlin, 1981), 3; Galen, *On the Use of the Parts*, in May (above, n. 15), vol. 2, 636–38 = K.4.171–72. On the relationship of these theories to those of Aristotle, see A. Preus, "Galen's Criticism of Aristotle's Conception Theory," *Journal of the History of Biology* 10 (1977), 65–85; M. Boylan, "The Galenic and Hippocratic Challenges to Aristotle's Conception Theory," *Journal of the History of Biology* 17 (1984), 83–112; and G. E. R. Lloyd, *Science, Folklore, and Ideology* (Cambridge, England, 1983), 86–111.

[17] Masculinity is similarly constructed in many tribal societies today. See for example G. Herdt, *Guardians of the Flutes: Idioms of Masculinity* (New York, 1981) and *Rituals of Manhood: Male Initiation in Papua New Guinea* (Berkeley, 1982); also T. Gregor, *Anxious Pleasures: The Sexual Lives of an Amazonian People* (Chicago, 1985). For a discussion of masculinity and femininity as admitting of degrees, see M. Mead, *Male and Female: A Study of the Sexes in a Changing World* (New York, 1949), 128–42.

[18] *Anon. Lat.* 3,2.5–6F; this part of the anonymous Latin physiognomy derives from Loxus: cf. Förster (above, note to epigraph), vol. 1, intro., cxxxii.

[19] Just as male children were thought to be engendered by sperm from the right testicle (Leophanes in Aristotle, *Gen. An.* 4. 1, 765a24) and to have occupied the right side of the womb (Galen in Oribasius, *Incerta* 22.3.18). This idea is found as early as Parmenides, fr. 17.

[20] *Anon. Lat.* 7, 2.11–13F. See below for further discussion of deceptive signs.

[21] *nec aliter ingenium bonum constat, nisi virtutem ex masculina, sapientiam ex feminina specie conceperit, Anon. Lat.* 10,2.16F.

The male is physically stronger and braver, less prone to defects and more likely to be sincere and loyal. He is more keen to win honor and he is worthier of respect. The female has the contrary properties: she has but little courage and abounds in deceptions. Her behavior is exceptionally bitter and she tends to hide what is on her mind. She is impulsive, lacks a sense of justice, and loves to quarrel: a blustering coward.

Now I will relate the signs of male and female physique and their physiognomical significance. *You will note which prevails over the other* (in any single individual) and use the result to guide your judgment. The female has, compared to the male, a small head and a small mouth, softer hair that is dark colored, a narrower face, bright glittering eyes,[22] a narrow neck, a weakly sloping chest, feeble ribs, larger, fleshier hips, narrower thighs and calves, knock-knees, dainty fingertips and toes, the rest of the body moist and flabby, with soft limbs and slackened joints, thin sinews, weak voice, a hesitant gait with frequent short steps, and limp limbs that glide slowly along. *But the male is in every way opposite to this description, and it is possible to find masculine qualities also in women.*[23]

The italicized phrases in this quotation reveal the unstated assumption behind the gender-typing system of the physiognomist: "male" and "female" are categories independent of anatomical sex. They are, in their most "perfect" form, highly polarized: "in every way opposite" to each other. But when used as tools to assess the gender status of an individual, these categories function as the opposite poles of an invisible thermometer with which the physiognomist takes the "gender temperature" of his subject. In those individuals whose signs are mixed, the physiognomist must make his judgment according to which sign "prevails over the other," paying particular, we might even say anxious, attention to those whose masculinity is only lukewarm.

"WALK LIKE A MAN, MY SON"

Norms of masculinity definitely existed, though deviations were more often remarked. Polemo's readiness to detect undesirable "feminine" characteristics in men presupposes a firm standard of correctness in masculine appearance and deportment. "You should know that a certain amplitude in a man's stride signifies trustworthiness, sincerity, liberality, and a high-minded nature free from anger. Such men come off successful in their encounters with emperors."[24] A man who can walk like that evi-

[22] μαρμαρύσσοντας. Adamantius preserves this word. Polemo claimed that the eyes of unchaste persons, particularly Favorinus, display "a corruscation like marble" (*Phys.* 1,1.160F).

[23] *Phys.* 2, 1.192–94F (italics added), clarified at some points by the Greek summary of Adam. 2.2,1.350F. Cf. [Arist.], [*Phys.*] 809b–810a.

[24] *Phys.* 50,1.260F; Adamantius 2.39,1.398F.

dently has mastered the trembling that to Galen was the natural, physiological consequence of meetings with one's political superiors.[25] Polemo's impeccably poised gentleman is a lineal descendant of Aristotle's "great-souled man" (*megalopsuchos*), transformed by the political conditions of the Roman empire into a provincial ambassador with an unruffled command of the courtier's art, a man whose step is slow, whose voice is low, and whose speech is measured and deliberate.[26] In the second century, Dio Chrysostom admonished the Alexandrians by the same standard: "Walking is a universal and uncomplicated activity, but while one man's gait reveals his composure and the attention he gives to his conduct, another's reveals his inner disorder and lack of self-restraint" (*Or.* 32.54). The Greek sophist Philiscus lost his liturgical immunity because the emperor took exception to the way he walked, the way he stood, the way he was dressed, and the way he used his effeminate voice at the hearing.[27] As late as the fourth century, Ambrose, the formidable bishop of Milan, refused to receive a priest whose gait showed signs of arrogance, and refused to ordain another man, apparently devout, "because his gestures were too unseemly." Both men subsequently bore out the promise of their deportment by deserting the orthodox church.[28]

Manly modesty appears to be an ideal best expressed in the negative: the real man, or the boy who is on the road to becoming one, is known by the absence of effeminate signs as much as by any positive distinguishing marks. As Clement says, "A noble man should bear no sign of effeminacy upon his face or any other portion of his body. Nor should the disgrace of unmanliness ever be found in his movements or his posture."[29] The orderly man (*ho kosmios*) reveals his self-restraint through his deportment: he is deep-voiced and slow-stepping, and his eyes, neither fixed nor rapidly blinking, hold a certain indefinably courageous gleam.[30] In the zoological

---

[25] Galen in Oribasius, *Incerta* 35 (*On Tremor*): "And in particular, someone who approaches an intimidating authority figure (δυνάστης φοβερός) trembles all over, and if he be commanded to speak, he will not even be able to hold his voice steady."

[26] καὶ κίνησις δὲ βραδεῖα τοῦ μεγαλοψύχου δοκεῖ εἶναι, καὶ φωνὴ βαρεῖα, καὶ λέξις στάσιμος, *Eth. Nic.* 1125a34. Demosthenes concedes the unattractiveness of a hasty gait in *Or.* 37.52 and 55, and in 45.77. Such deportment reveals inner defects; the person with an unattractive walk is not one of the "well-born." For Cicero's condemnation of a hasty gait and mental excitement as impediments to masculine *dignitas*, see *De officiis* 1.131. Similarly, gait distinguishes the "man of honor" in contemporary Algeria from the indecisive, the frivolous, and the sluggish of his own sex and from women in general (P. Bourdieu, *Outline of a Theory of Practice* [Cambridge, 1977], 94).

[27] Philostratus, *Lives* 623. The emperor was Caracalla.

[28] Ambrose, *On the Duties of the Clergy* 1.18.72.

[29] Ἀνδρὸς δὲ γενναίου σημεῖον οὐδὲν εἶναι δεῖ περιφανὲς ἐν τῷ προσώπῳ μαλακίας, ἀλλ' οὐδὲ ἐν ἑτέρῳ μέρει τοῦ σώματος. Μὴ τοίνυν μηδὲ ἐν κινήσεσιν μηδὲ ἐν σχέσεσιν εὑρεθείη ποθ' ἡ ἀσχημοσύνη τῆς ἀνανδρίας (*Paidagogos* 3. 11.73–74).

[30] ὁ δὲ κόσμιος βαρὺ φθέγγεται, βραδὺ βαίνει, τὰ βλέφαρα κινεῖ μέσως, . . . χαροπός, Adam. 2.49, 1.413–14F; cf. *Phys.* 58, 1.274F; *Anon. Lat.* 107, 2.131F.

shorthand of physiognomy, this ideal appears as the man with the leonine walk: "He whose feet and hands move in harmony with all the rest of his person, who moves forward with shoulders calm and carefully controlled, with his neck but slightly inclined—he is the one whom men call brave and magnanimous, for his is the walk of the lion."[31]

PARADIGMS OF EFFEMINACY

The dignified carriage of the leonine man had to be achieved with unfaltering assurance in public, before an audience whose sensibilities were finely tuned to detect bluffing or any deviations from ideal composure. While a mild and gentle appearance of the eyes, for example, is in general a good thing, even the possessor of such a fortunate feature remains perilously close to forfeiting his claim to masculine dignity. The slightest sign of softness or slackening will undo the whole effect. Should he also exhibit eyelids or eyebrows that are not entirely straight, should they appear to tremble just a bit, should the pupils appear to be in motion, "then you may be sure that this is the profile of someone who is really feminine, *even though you may find him among real men.*"[32] Similarly, a certain fold in the eyelids, if they are raised excessively high, invites the diagnosis of gender deviance.[33] A man who breathes like a coward may be an *androgynos* as well, if you can find any other signs that point in that direction.[34]

In his handbook of insults, Suetonius informs us that *androgynoi* "have something of the shape of a man but are feminine in all other respects."[35] The Hippocratic *On Regimen* explains this phenomenon genetically: *androgynoi* are produced when male seed from the female parent overpowers female seed from the male parent. This combination is the least desirable in a continuum of masculine possibilities, according to which men who are

---

[31] *Anon. Lat.* 76, 2.99–100F; cf. *Phys.* 50, 1.262F. This ideal endured. As a protocol official at the court of Haile Selassie informs us:

A man who has been singled out by His Distinguished Majesty will not jump, run, frolic, or cut a caper. No. His step is solemn: he sets his feet firmly on the ground, bending his body slightly forward to show his determination to push through adversity, ordering precisely the movement of his hands so as to avoid nervous disorganized gesticulation. Furthermore, the facial features become solemn, almost stiffened . . . they are set so as to create no possibility of psychological contact. One cannot relax, rest, or catch one's breath next to such a face. The gaze changes too. (R. Kapuściński, *The Emperor: Downfall of an Autocrat* [New York, 1983]).

[32] *Phys.* 1, 1.158F. Cf. Adam. 1.19, 1.341F, quoted in n.101 below..

[33] *Phys.* 1, 1.166F.

[34] Ibid. 51, 1.264F; Adam. 2.41, 1.403F.

[35] τὰ μὲν ἄλλα γύνις ὤν, ἔχων δέ τι ἀνδρόμορφον, *On Insults* 61 in the edition of J. Taillardat, *Peri blasphemiōn* (Paris, 1967), 52.

both spiritually "brilliant" and physically strong are the product of male seed from both parents, while male seed from the male parent, if combined so as to dominate female seed from a female parent, will produce men who are somewhat less brilliant but still completely manly (*andreioi*).[36] Polemo tells us how to spot the adult *androgynos*:

> You may recognize him by his provocatively melting glance and by the rapid movement of his intensely staring eyes. His brow is furrowed while his eyebrows and cheeks are in constant motion. His head is tilted to the side, his loins do not hold still, and his slack limbs never stay in one position. He minces along with little jumping steps; his knees knock together. He carries his hands with palms turned upward. He has a shifting gaze, and his voice is thin, weepy, shrill, and drawling.[37]

These are precisely the feminine mannerisms that the Roman educator Quintilian told his pupils to avoid. He warned them that the ideal orator should not indulge in any melting glances of the eyes; he should pay attention to the effects achieved by his eyebrows so as to avoid both constant motion and rigidity; he should hold his head straight lest it "signify languor" by tilting to one side; he should avoid any appearance of servility in the carriage of his shoulders, just as he should avoid hasty movements of the feet and any sort of swaying or oscillation in his body movement.[38]

Polemo claims that, as with other vices, *androgynoi* come in two kinds: mild and tame or rough and wild.[39] You can tell which is which from the relative dryness, roughness, and hardness, or moistness, smoothness, and softness, of their signs. We do not hear more of the wilder sort of *androgynos*. Polemo focuses on the softer and damper sort of effeminacy that is revealed by such feminine clues as a small, rounded chin; soft, unstable knees; fleshy hips; and a fluid gait in which no part of the body holds still.[40]

These strictures in Polemo are but an elaboration of stereotypes already present in the Hellenistic physiognomy attributed to Aristotle. There the

---

[36] Ch. 28 (Littré 6.500–502).

[37] φωνὴ λεπτὴ ἐπικλάζουσα λιγυρὰ σχολαία πάνυ: Adam. 2.52, 1.415–16F. My translation is a composite of this passage, *Phys.* 61, 1.276F (which breaks off), and *Anon. Lat.* 98, 2.123–24F.

[38] *Inst.* 11.3.76 (eyes), 78–79 (eyebrows), 69 (head), 83 (shoulders), 126 (feet), 128–29 (swaying), cf. 165. Compare Seneca, "A sexually impure man is revealed by his gait, his gestures, sometimes by his answers, by his finger touching his head, and by the shifting of his eyes" (*Ep.* 52.12).

[39] Adam. 2.58–59, 1.420–24F; *Anon. Lat.* 104,2.126–28F. Perhaps the "rough and wild" type of effeminate should be connected with the hirsute hypocrites attacked by Juvenal in *Satire* 2.

[40] *Phys.* 24,1.224F (chin); 8,1.204F (knees); 10,1.206F (hips); 50,1.262F and *Anon. Lat.* 76,2.100F (gait); cf. Suetonius, *On Insults* 66.

fainthearted man (athumos) reveals himself with eyes that are both dry and weak (keklasmena)—a quality that signifies, we are told, both effeminate softness and dejection or lack of spirit. On top of this, "he is stooping in his carriage and apologetic in his movements."[41] From here it is but a step to the cinaedus, whose eyes are likewise weak, whose knees knock together (gonukrotos), and whose head tilts to the right. He gesticulates with limply upturned hands. He has two gaits: either he sways his loins from side to side or he holds them tight and stiff (kratountos tēn osphun). He also has a shifty gaze.[42]

The word androgynos (which I have been translating as "effeminate") in its most literal sense describes an appearance of gender-indeterminacy, "he who is between man and woman."[43] The word cinaedus, on the other hand, describes sexual deviance, in its most specific sense referring to males who prefer to play a "feminine" (receptive) role in intercourse with other men.[44] But the two terms become virtually indistinguishable when used to describe men of effeminate appearance and behavior. The Latin physiognomy offers a profile of the cinaedus that is substantially identical to Polemo's portrait of the androgynos: a tilted head, a mincing gait, an enervated voice, a lack of stability in the shoulders, and a feminine way of moving the body. A cinaedus may also be known by certain mannerisms: he shifts his eyes around in sheep-like fashion when he speaks; he touches his fingers to his nose;[45] he compulsively obliterates all traces of spittle he may find—his own or anyone else's—by rubbing it into the dust with his heel; he frequently stops to admire what he considers his own best feature; he smiles furtively while talking; he holds his arms turned outward; he laughs out loud; and he has an annoying habit of clasping other people by the hand.[46] Clement of Alexandria seethes, in his invective against women's luxury, "[These women] delight in intercourse (sunousiais) with androgy-

---

[41] ἐν τῷ σχήματι ταπεινὸς καὶ ταῖς κινήσεσιν ἀπηγορευκώς, [Arist.], [Phys.] 808a.

[42] Ibid. 808a. A knock-kneed walk is characteristic of women according to Aristotle, Hist. Anim. 538b10. Compare the younger Seneca's description of an affected, mincing gait as a sign of effeminacy: tenero et molli ingressu suspendimus gradum: non ambulamus sed incedimus ("We tiptoe along with delicate soft steps: we don't walk, we sashay") (Natural Questions 7.31.2).

[43] qui inter virum est et feminam (Anon. Lat. 98, 2.123F).

[44] I have transliterated the Greek term κίναιδος as cinaedus to make it match its Latin equivalent. The word may derive from κινεῖσθαι τὰ αἰδοῖα, "wiggle one's privy parts." For the image of the cinaedus in Classical Athens as the stereotype of the man who violates the dominant social definition of masculinity, see J. Winkler, The Constraints of Desire (New York/London, 1990), 45ff. (= Winkler and F. Zeitlin, et al., eds., Before Sexuality [Princeton, 1990], 171–204). Amy Richlin argues that the cinaedus was more than a stereotype and that there was in real life a passive homosexual subculture in Roman society ("Not Before Homosexuality: The Materiality of the Cinaedus and the Roman Law against Love between Men," Journal of the History of Sexuality 3 (1993), 5232–73.

[45] On the impropriety of this gesture, compare Quintilian, Inst. 11.3.80 and 121.

[46] Anon. Lat. 115, 2.134–35F. This passage probably derives from Loxus (Förster [above, note to epigraph], vol. 1, intro., cxxxii).

noi, and crowds of *cinaedi* flow in, with mouths that will not shut. Contaminated in body and speech, they are men enough for obscene service, ministers of adultery. . . by lewdness of word and gesture endeavoring to please."[47] Here what is deviant in the behavior of these *androgynoi* and *cinaedi* is not the gender of their sexual object choice (a preoccupation of contemporary North Americans and Northern Europeans),[48] but the style of their erotic pursuit. A man who actively penetrates and dominates others, whether male or female, is still a man. A man who aims to please—any one, male or female—in his erotic encounters is ipso facto effeminate.[49]

The second-century lexicographer Pollux considered the words *androgynos* and *cinaedus* synonyms (6.126–27). His entire list of possible synonyms for *cinaedus* is instructive for the range of meaning represented. Apparently one could hurl the epithet *cinaedus* as an all-purpose term of abuse to express generalized, not specifically sexual, moral reproach. In such cases *cinaedus* functions as the equivalent of terms like *loathsome*, *licentious*, or *reprehensible*.[50] Another group of synonyms in Pollux's list emphasizes softness and effeminacy: *soft, feminized, she-man*.[51] Accusations of passive homosexual activity and prostitution account for the remainder of the synonyms: *catamite, vendor of his youthful beauty, prostitutes' colleague*, and the like.[52]

A person could even become a *cinaedus* against his will. All his enemies had to do was to inscribe on a piece of obsidian the figure of a castrated man, gazing downward to the genitals lying at his feet, and enclose this figure in a golden box with the "stone" of a *kinaidion*-fish. Then any man who touches the stone will become impotent, and any man who can be made to carry the stone unwittingly will become soft (*malakisthēsetai*). But he who is tricked into *eating* it will become a complete *cinaedus* (*kinaidos teleios*), who will never change back to his natural state.[53] This magical

[47] *Paidagogos* 3.29.2–3.

[48] In Turkey and Morocco, by contrast, as long as males play the active, insertor role in a sexual relationship, there is no question of their being considered homosexual (J. Carrier, "Homosexual Behavior in Cross-Cultural Perspective" in J. Marmor, ed., *Homosexual Behavior* [New York, 1980], 111).

[49] In Greek culture, as David Halperin points out, "erotic reciprocity was relegated to the province of women" (*One Hundred Years of Homosexuality* [New York/London, 1990], 133). Thus the man who seeks to please women becomes tainted with their passivity.

[50] βδελυρός, ἀσελγής, ἐπίψογος.

[51] μαλθακός, ἐκτεθηλυσμένος, γύννις.

[52] καταπύγων, τὴν ἡλικίαν πεπρακώς, ταῖς πόρναις ὁμότεχνος.

[53] μὴ ἀποκαθιστάμενος εἰς τὸ κατὰ φύσιν. [Harpokration], *Kyranides* 1.10.49–67 in D. Kaimakis, *Die Kyraniden, Beiträge zur klassischen Philologie* 76, 1976 (Meisenheim am Glan). See C. Faraone, "Sex and Power: Male-Targeting Aphrodisiacs in the Greek Magical Tradition," *Helios* 19 (1992), 95–96. In Pliny (*Natural History* 32.146), *Cinaidi*-fish are yellow (after the pallor of a debauchee's complexion?).

recipe from the first or second century C.E. clearly shows a conceptual structure in which emasculation happens by degrees.

Further evidence for the spectrum of possibilities behind the term *cinaedus* lies submerged in the horoscopes of Firmicus Maternus. As a source for information about the way sex/gender stereotypes were structured into a system in antiquity, astrological treatises, the neglected practical handbooks of another popular science, constitute a useful supplement to the works of the physiognomists.[54] Firmicus' astrological textbook lists dozens of permutations of the stars under which one might be born a *cinaedus*. The most significant thing about these horoscopes is the way they divide the field into those for whom being a *cinaedus* is a publicly recognized part of their identity and those for whom it is not.

Of those *cinaedi* whose identity is publicly recognized, most numerous are the horoscopes of male prostitutes (*publici cinaedi*), whose careers bring them public disgrace.[55] Some *cinaedi* are destined to be pantomimes, who were often considered prostitutes *ex officio*.[56] Prostituted *cinaedi* often appear as the astrological twins of female prostitutes (*meretrices*). They are born under the same signs, and their passive sexual role-playing is sometimes singled out for special mention.[57] Indeed, horoscopes are a good place to look for what counted as functional equivalency in the gender roles destined for males and females born under the same sign. Sometimes a straightforward equation appears to operate between *cinaedi* and female prostitutes. At other times we glimpse more complex relationships. When Mars and Venus, for example, rising in the morning, have a conjunction in a masculine sign, females are born mannish and sterile (*viragines sterilesque*). But these same planets, rising in the evening in a feminine sign, cause males to be born *cinaedi*—if Saturn comes into the picture at all.[58] Here the message seems to be that feminine males, in their gender deviance, are to some extent—but not completely—analogous to masculine women. They are born under a structurally homologous planetary conjunction, which is modified by the inversion of the conditions under

---

[54] In this chapter I discuss only passages in the astrologers that specifically use the term *cinaedus*. But other passages are certainly relevant. Manilius and Firmicus Maternus agree, for example, that when Taurus rises rear-end first in a bevy of Pleiades, men will be born who will show that they regret their sex by their effeminate gait and their fondness for depilation and women's clothing (Firmicus Maternus 8.7 and Manilius 4.518, 5.140–56). F. Cumont, *L'Égypte des Astrologues* (Brussels, 1937), 181–83, lists various passages in the astrological corpus that touch upon sexual behavior.

[55] They are "condemned" or "struck" by public disgrace (*damnati/pulsati publica infamia*). See Firmicus, *Mathesis* 7.25 passim; 8.19.7; 8.25.4; 8.27.8; a graffito from Pompeii shows that the "public" *cinaedus* was a category known to popular as well as technical discourse: *Crescens publicus cinaedus* (*CIL* 4.5001).

[56] *Mathesis* 8.20.8; 8.23.3.

[57] Ibid. 6.31.5; 8.23.3; 8.25.4; 8.30.2.

[58] Ibid. 7.25.4.

which it appears (morning/evening, masculine sign/feminine sign). But symmetry has its limits: *cinaedi* sometimes require the additional influence of the unpredictable planet Saturn to queer their horoscopes.[59]

Not all those *cinaedi* born to take a public role were destined for the disgrace of prostitution. Some were born to become temple officials, who might become rich enough to qualify as one of the "fortunate *cinaedi*" (*cinaedi felices*).[60] Others were destined to become court officials of high prestige[61] or, under a similar set of stars, men of great wealth (*cinaedi divites*) (7.25.23). And there were also, most intriguingly, men born to be *cinaedi*—sophisticates, "who are famous for their charm and urbanity."[62]

Yet there was also an entirely different class of *cinaedi* whose deviant sex role was not part of their acknowleged public identity, and who for that reason were objects of hermeneutical suspicion to their uneasy peers. These were the hidden *cinaedi* (*cinaedi latentes*). They are mentioned in the horoscopes numerous times, but we never learn any details about their social status—only that they practice their alleged vice in secret.[63] Born under astrological conjunctions that are similar but slightly superior to those that produce public *cinaedi*,[64] the hidden *cinaedus* might be anywhere. It is precisely this sense of the omnipresence of potential deviants that kindled the vigilance of physiognomists, expert and amateur.

STOIC COSMETOLOGY

Although physiognomists and astrologers may have used them more systematically than did laymen, the "signs" of effeminacy were a commonplace constellation in the nontechnical discourse of antiquity. In comedy,

[59] But more typical is *Mathesis* 7.25.5, where sterile viraginous females are born under exactly the same astrological configuration as male *cinaedi*.

[60] Ibid. 7.25.4,10,14. Perhaps it was the deterministic element of astrological thinking that made possible a limited form of social acceptance for those whose gender identity did not accord with their biological sex, along the lines of some Native American societies, in which a belief system that attributed the development of individual "careers" to an extra-societal destiny left room for the gender-crossing of the *berdache*. On the phenomenon of the *berdache*, see H. Whitehead in S. Ortner and H. Whitehead, eds., *Sexual Meanings* (Cambridge, 1981), 80–115.

[61] *in maxima honorum gloria constituti: Mathesis* 7.25.22 (which may reflect the expansion of the imperial bureaucracy after Diocletian). Astrologers also knew the perils of high position: 8.21.11 describes the horoscope of those *cinaedi* "who die because of the anger of the emperor" (*qui regis indignatione moriantur*).

[62] *cinaedi gratia semper urbanitatis perspicui, Mathesis* 8.25.1. Their horoscope is, astrologically speaking, the feminine equivalent of the horoscope of those who become "well-born hymnodists, to whom the secret lore of the gods is entrusted" (*hymnodici nobiles, quibus deorum secreta credantur*).

[63] *Mathesis* 7.25.7,9,12,19,21,23; 8.29.7.

[64] Ibid. 7.25.21,23.

for example, a character might indignantly disclaim them: "*I* have absolutely no idea how to use a twittering voice or walk about in effeminate style (*katakeklasmenōs*), with my head tilted sidewise like all those pathics that I see here in the city smeared with depilatories."[65] In his attack on effeminate mannerisms at Tarsus, Dio Chrysostom speaks darkly of "those who violate nature's laws" in secret, but whose true character is revealed by the *symbola* of their debauchery: by their voice, glance, posture, hairstyle, gait, shifting eyes, receding neck, and by certain upturned gestures of the hand.[66] "For you must not think that the notes of songs or pipes and lyre reveal sometimes masculinity (*to andreion*), sometimes femininity (*to thēlu*), but that movements and actions do not vary according to sex and afford no clue to it" (33.52). Dio called effeminate mannerisms *symbola* because masculine deportment and grooming habits constituted a system of social communication. According to Clement of Alexandria, one man is entitled to "read" another's grooming habits in the manner of a physiognomist. The details he observes function as oracular signs to reveal unseen behavior: "Just like a physiognomist, he can divine from their appearance that they are adulterers and effeminates, who go hunting for both kinds of sex. . . ."[67]

In Clement's view, to depilate one's beard and body while coifing one's head was to announce a preference for unnatural acts. Clement feels entitled to take this reading of the effeminates' body language because the beard is agreed to be the distinctive mark of a man (*to andros to sunthēma*). It serves as a symbol of Adam's superior nature (*sumbolon tēs kreittonos phuseōs*, 19.1). Hairiness in general is the mark of a manly nature (19.3). In similar fashion, Epictetus also saw the secondary sex characteristics as *signs* (*sumbola*) which function linguistically. They "announce from afar, 'I am a man.'"[68] According to Dio, there is no portent so terrible as when "someone who is a man, and retains a man's distinguishing marks (*charaktēras*) and characteristic voice, being unable to remove the signs of Nature (*ta*

---

[65] Kock, *CAF* 3.470, quoted by Clement in *Paidagogos* 3.11.69.

[66] τὰ δὲ τοιαῦτα ξύμβολα τῆς ἀκρασίας μηνύει τὸ ἦθος καὶ τὴν διάθεσιν, φωνή . . . ("Signs like these reveal their character and condition: their voice . . . ") (*Or.* 33.52). For the oration at Tarsus as evidence for the degree of openness with which gender deviance might be discussed in the Eastern empire, see R. MacMullen, "What Difference Did Christianity Make?" *Historia* 35 (1986), 329.

[67] Ἀτεχνῶς καθάπερ μετωποσκόπος ἐκ τοῦ σχήματος αὐτοὺς καταμαντεύεται μοιχούς τε καὶ ἀνδρογύνους, ἀμφοτέραν ἀφροδίτην θηρωμένους (*Paidagogos*, 3.15.2). Clement's second-century manual of etiquette for wealthy Christians in Alexandria reflects largely pre-Christian aristocratic values. Clement's familiarity with pagan literary and philosophical tradition raises the question of the extent to which he can be relied on as a witness to the social realities of his own time. H. I. Marrou concluded that in Clement "*une description peut être livresque sans cesser d'être historique.*" H. I. Marrou, *Clément d' Alexandrie: Le Pédagogue* (Paris, 1960), 89.

sēmeia tēs phuseōs)," tries instead to cover them up and adopts the vocal mannerisms of an effeminate (33.60).

Modern readers, accustomed to consider excessive preoccupation with physical appearance as, at worst, a sign of psychological narcissism, are sometimes puzzled or dismayed by the vitriolic intensity with which ancient moralists attack elaborate male grooming as if it were physically dangerous. Clement had special doctrinal reasons for asserting the coinherence of body and soul, but he shares with pagan moralists the assumption that "feminine" grooming habits will alter more than the surface appearance of the man who indulges in them. Like an illness, these habits will infect his essential masculinity: "If such people do not decontaminate themselves by getting rid of these embellishments, they cease to enjoy sound health and decline in the direction of greater softness until they play the woman's part."[69] A man's natural hair was the product of the same abundance of inner heat that concocted his sperm.[70] Depilation therefore could be considered a particularly dangerous practice. It was a way of going soft, of giving in to the pleasure of passivity.

Stoics liked to moralize about hair because it was a term in the symbolic language of masculinity that could be construed as not merely a conventional sign, but as a symbol established by Nature itself. It was in this spirit that Musonius praised the beard as "a covering provided us by Nature" and as "a symbol of the male, like the cock's crest and the lion's mane" (fr. 21). Epictetus counseled an elaborately coifed and depilated young student of rhetoric, "Leave the care of your hair to Him who made it" (*Discourses* 3.1.26). Nature made women smooth and men hirsute. If a man born hairless is an ominous sign (*teras*), what are we to make of a man who depilates himself? Under what label should we exhibit *him*? (3.1.27–29). Such a creature of hybrid sex should "eradicate—what shall I call it—the cause of his hair" so that he makes himself entirely female and no longer forces other people to make mistakes when they attempt to categorize him (3.1.31).

Clement offers a Christianized view of Stoic doctrine on this subject. God decreed hairiness for Adam and created Eve from the only hairless

---

[68] Οὐκ εὐθὺς μακρόθεν κέκραγεν ἡμῶν ἑκάστου ἡ φύσις "ἀνήρ εἰμι· οὕτω μοι προσέρχου, οὕτω μοι λάλει, ἄλλο μηδὲν ζήτει· ἰδοὺ τὰ σύμβολα." (Does not the nature of each one of us announce from afar: "I am a man. Approach me as such. Address me as such. Behold the signs.") *Discourses* 1.16.11. Chief of these signs is the beard, but the voice also serves to differentiate the sexes (1.16.12).

[69] Μὴ γὰρ καθαρεύοντες καλλωπισμοῦ οὐχ ὑγιαίνουσιν, πρὸς δὲ τὸ μαλθακώτερον ἀποκλίναντες γυναικίζονται, *Paidagogos* 3.15.1.

[70] Aristotle, *Gen. An.* 765b; 783b. Compare 727a: because their lower body temperature does not permit complete concoction, women lack any extra residue with which to make facial and body hair. Very hirsute men are especially lustful because they are especially hot: Aristotle, *Problems* 10.24.

part of Adam's body.[71] Clement finds that another divinely ordered mark of the male is activity, as opposed to passivity, in social and sexual behavior: "To do (*to dran*) is the mark of the man; to suffer (*to paschein*) is the mark of the woman." He immediately offers a physiological explanation for these social differences between the sexes: "For what is covered with hair is by nature drier and warmer than what is hairless. This is why the male is hairier and warmer than the female, why males with testicles are hairier and warmer than those castrated, and why the mature male is hairier and warmer than the immature" (3.19.2). Since the secondary sex characteristics (particularly the hair and the voice) are "read" socially as signs of the inner heat that constitutes a man's claim to physiological and cultural superiority over women, eunuchs, and children, those who tampered with the most visible variables of masculinity in their self-presentation provoked vehement moral criticism because they were rightly suspected of undermining the symbolic language in which male privilege was written.

Those who saw the end result of depilation as impious also considered the process ridiculous. When Clement describes men who allow themselves to be plucked in public, he emphasizes the indignity of the postures they must assume (they twist about, uncovering their genitals, dance burlesquely, and bend over backward while failing to change color in positions that should put anyone to the blush). He also stresses the incongruity of adopting such postures in a public space consecrated to the display and training of masculinity: among the assembled youth of the city and in the middle of the gymnasium "where manly excellence is tried" (3.3.20). In this parody constructed by a Christian moralist, we see all Quintilian's strictures on maintaining masculine decorum through economy of body movement turned, as it were, inside out.

THE MOLDING OF MEN

Masculinity, in the conceptual world inhabited by physiognomists, astrologers, popular moralists, and their audiences, constituted a system of signs. It was a language that anatomical males were taught to speak with their bodies. The process began at birth. In upper-class households that followed the advice of Greek physicians, it was the nurse's duty to assist, if not enforce, the infant's physical development along appropriately "natural" lines. This was done, according to a second-century gynecologist, by massaging and modeling each part of the body "so that imperceptibly that

[71] When "all that was soft and smooth" was thus removed from him, Adam was left all male, a natural symbol of his own masculinity: "But he—since he had given up his hairless element—remained a man and shows ostensively what a man is" (ὁ δέ—προήκατο γὰρ τὸ λεῖον—ἔμεινέν τε ἀνὴρ καὶ τὸν ἄνδρα δεινκύει), *Paidagogos* 3.19.2.

which is as yet not fully formed may be molded into conformity with its natural characteristics."[72] Squeezing and stretching, even hanging the body upside down, she was instructed to mold the infant body into shape: pressing hollows into the buttocks "for the sake of comely appearance" (*euprepeia*), and paying particular attention to the shape of the head. It was her responsibility, by assiduous effort, to elongate a snub nose and push back one that showed signs of becoming too aquiline. Should the foreskin appear inadequate in length—a possible cause of embarrassment in adult life—the nurse was to pull it into position and tie it, if necessary, with string (3.34.[103]). Even the scrotum did not escape these lessons in conformity. Swaddling was designed to achieve much the same results. Gender typing began at birth, for girls were swaddled more tightly than boys at the breasts and more loosely at the loins to encourage their bodies to take on "the shape that in women is more becoming" (2.15.[84]). After two months of corrective immobility, the bands of swaddling were gradually released, but for older children the daily modeling continued. Galen recommended that children be forced to submit to this procedure before they be allowed to eat breakfast. This early discipline (*askēsis*) was an aggressive process, in which the nurse was supposed to "make an attack" on the child, "schooling the body to good health and condition and at the same time schooling the mind to obedience and self-control."[73]

The self-control achieved through such discipline in childhood manifested itself in adolescent decorum. A well-schooled young man would know how to avoid body language that might signal sexual availability: "Let his face be open, with a clear brow, and with eyes that are neither too wide open nor enervated-looking. His neck should not be bent. His limbs should not be slack but held up with a certain sinewy tension. . . . His bearing and body movement should arouse no expectations in the lustful. May modesty and manliness bloom upon his face!"[74] We owe this descrip-

[72] ὥστε λεληθότως τὸ ἀκμὴν ἀδιαμόρφωτον εἰς τοὺς κατὰ φύσιν διατυπωθῆναι χαρακτῆρας, Soranus *Gyn.* 2.32 (101); cf. Galen in Oribasius *Incerta* 17, Rufus in Oribasius *Incerta* 20.6. Plutarch refers to this practice as a well-known necessity (*Mor.* 3E). A. Rousselle, *Porneia* (Oxford, 1988), 47–62, is an attempt to reconstruct, on the basis of such medical texts, the sensory education of the upper-class Roman child. Plato speaks of nursemaids molding souls with folktales the way they mold children's bodies with their hands (*Rep.* 2.377c).

[73] τότε γὰρ ἐπιθέσθαι μάλιστα αὐτοῖς χρή, τὸ μὲν σῶμα πρὸς ὑγίειαν ἅμα καὶ εὐεξίαν ἀσκοῦντα, τὴν ψυχὴν δὲ εἰς εὐπείθειάν τε καὶ σωφροσύνην, Galen in Oribasius, *Incerta* 17.5.

[74] ἔστω καθαρὸν τὸ πρόσωπον, ὀφρὺς μὴ καθειμένη, μηδὲ ὄμμα ἀναπεπτάμενον μηδὲ διακεκλασμένον, μὴ ὕπτιος ὁ τράχηλος, μηδὲ ἀνιέμενα τὰ τοῦ σώματος μέλη, ἀλλὰ μετέωρα ἐντόνοις ὅμοια . . . καὶ σχηματισμοὶ καὶ κινήσεις μηδὲν ἐνδιδοῦσαι τοῖς ἀκολάστοις ἐλπίδος. Αἰδὼς μὲν ἐπανθείτω καὶ ἀρρενωπία. . . . Zeno in Clement, *Paidagogos* 3.11.74. Compare Aristophanes from the fifth century B.C.E.: "*He* would not make his voice weak (μαλακή), molding it to please an adult admirer, or walk about while acting as a procurer with his eyes." *Clouds* (979–80).

tion to Clement of Alexandria quoting Zeno over a lapse of more than four hundred years—a fact which testifies to the durability of this ideal. As an ideal it is by no means unambiguous, since talk of "bloom" suggests that youthful modesty in one's deportment is in some paradoxical way sexually desirable.[75] One cannot help arousing the sexual interest of the lustful, but one's deportment can prevent them from lusting with any expectation of success. Hence Quintilian carefully advised his pupils, "The eyes should never be rigid and distended, languid or torpid, wanton or rolling; nor should they ever seem to swim or look watery with pleasure, or glance sideways, or appear amorous, or as if they were asking or promising something."[76]

It is no coincidence that we find these strictures on sexual decorum in a rhetorical handbook. The process of forging masculine deportment that could begin as early as infancy continued during literary education, when the linguistic mastery that was the exclusive prerogative of upper-class males was attained under pain of physical punishment at the hands of the *grammaticus* and under pain of social humiliation in the school of the rhetor. At this stage of their education, young men learned, while declaiming, to maintain decorum under conditions of competitive stress.

Their instructors performed publicly also, before a wider audience, in ritualized contests that mesmerized the leisured elite. Polemo once told a gladiator dripping with the sweat of the terror of death that in his agony he looked like a person who was going to declaim.[77] The agonistic element in these literary duels was never far beneath the surface. After Dionysius of Miletus, for example, heard Polemo plead at a court hearing, he was heard to remark, as a senior practitioner of a rising star, "The athlete has strength, but it doesn't come from the *palaistra*." When Polemo heard about this, he wasted no time in summoning Dionysios to hear a declamation and, after a successful performance, he took the imagery of athletic competition one step further: going straight up to his critic, he braced him shoulder to shoulder in the pose of those who are about to begin a wrestling match and mocked him wittily with the proverbial tag for the degenerate, "Once, once upon a time they were strong, the men of Miletus."[78]

From confrontations like these emerged the infamous professional quarrels of the sophists, such as the feud between Favorinus and Polemo,

[75] This contradiction is best seen in Aristophanes' *Clouds* (966, 973ff., 1014), where Just Logic palpably drools over his own description of the chaste young paragons of the "old education." See K. Dover, ed., *Aristophanes, Clouds* (Oxford, 1968), lxiv–lxvi.

[76] *Rigidi vero et extenti, aut languidi et torpentes, aut stupentes, aut lascivi et mobiles, et natantes et quadam voluptate suffusi, aut limi et, ut sic dicam, venerii aut poscentes aliquid pollicentesve numquam esse debebunt* (*Inst.* 11.3.76, trans. modified from that of Rev. John Watson [London, 1876]).

[77] Philostratus, *Lives* 541.

[78] Philostratus, *Lives* 525–26. Compare Cicero, *De legibus* 1.2.6, where the vigor of an orator's style is criticized for lacking the refinement of the *palaistra*.

in which their pupils naturally took sides. Participation in these quarrels, far from being a mere epiphenomenon, should be seen as an integral part of male socialization. After all, one reason that these rivalries became so intense was that they came to represent competing paradigms of masculinity, as well as competing claims to power and status. Philosophers, as well as sophists, were interested parties in the struggle, and some of them used the beards that were a traditional component of the philosophical costume to claim high ground.

Fueling the controversy was an element of genuine ambiguity and confusion among the students that derived from the internal inconsistencies of the culture in which they had been raised: anyone who has been compelled to submit since birth to highly intrusive processes of nurture exacted in the name of nature might be expected to experience some uncertainty on the question of exactly where one ends and the other begins. Serious-minded young men who consulted the philosopher Epictetus with an eye to learning "how one may preserve the integrity of one's persona on all occasions"[79] would find their Stoic guide sliding dizzyingly between a constructionist and an essentialist view of masculinity. In this treatise masculine integrity appears as both a natural phenomenon and a cultural construct. To be a noble man is to aspire to stand out from the social fabric, to be the *red stripe in the toga*. To preserve one's integrity as a man is to be like the athlete who refuses to consent to a medical amputation of his *genitals*, or like a philosopher who would rather die than submit to a tyrranical order to shave his *beard*. When the sage compares the courage of a *mature bull* to the virtue a man perfects by year-round *training* (*askēsis*), ("A bull does not come into being overnight, nor does a noble man, but it is necessary to *train* out of season"), the confusion between the natural and the cultural appears complete.

Rhetoric focused these issues more concretely than did philosophy. When a quarrel broke out between Timokrates, a physician turned Stoic philosopher, and the sophist Scopelian, the disagreement focused on Scopelian's practice of submitting his body to the treatments of pitchplasterers and hair-pluckers—an issue of personal grooming that symbolized intensely felt differences of opinion over the role of refinement in masculine style. In this contest between hirsute philosophy and depilated rhetoric, all the leisured youth of Smyrna took sides. Polemo chose his paradigm according to physiognomical principles. Though hitherto a pupil of both men, he threw his weight to Timokrates, "whose hair, during debate, stood up straight on his head and his cheeks, like the mane of a *lion* springing to attack."[80] From this perspective Polemo's quarrel with the smooth-skinned Favorinus appears inevitable.

[79] Πῶς ἄν τις σῴζοι τὸ κατὰ πρόσωπον ἐν παντί, *Discourses* 1.2.

[80] Philostratus, *Lives* 536. Some orators appear to have brushed their hair back from the forehead to achieve this terrifying effect (Quintilian *Inst.* 11.3. 160). The lion is the chief

PARADIGMS ROUGH AND SMOOTH

Moralists claimed that deviations such as Scopelian's from the leonine norms of masculine public deportment were a sure sign of sexual passivity in private: "He who disowns his manhood by the light of day is sure to be proved a woman at night."[81] But some people were skeptical of their pretensions, since the pose of "hairier than thou" was in itself a form of posturing.[82] As Athenaeus observed, men who groom themselves cheaply and roughly to advertise their own philosophical austerity "call other men *cinaedi* if they wear perfume or dress a bit daintily."[83] It is important to remember that the strictures of hirsute moralists did not command universal assent. Might not a perfectly respectable gentleman, as Athenaeus implies, dab on a bit of perfume? *Were* all dandies pathics? If depilation, dainty grooming, and singsong speech were universally ridiculed as explicit signposts of sexual passivity, we must wonder why any man would court censure by adopting such practices unless he wished explicitly to advertise himself a pathic. The answer seems to be that these habits, while they might in some circumstances constitute a shorthand key to their practitioner's sexual preferences, might also bear a more generalized penumbra of meaning and indicate nothing more than his aspirations to elegance. After all, these mannerisms—from depilation to ingratiating inflections of the voice—were refinements aimed at translating the ideal of beardless ephebic beauty into adult life,[84] and as such might appeal to women and boys, with whom one could not by definition play the pathic role, as well as to some adult men, with whom one could.[85]

---

exemplar of those species in which masculine signs predominate, *Phys.* 2, 1.194–8F. Compare the lengthy list of virile traits that Vettius Valens assigns to the constellation Leo: ἐλεύθερον, πυρῶδες, εὔκρατον, νοερόν, βασιλικόν . . . ἡγεμονικόν, πολιτικόν . . . ὀργίλον ("of freeborn temperament, fiery, restrained, intelligent, kingly, a natural leader, statesmanlike, proud") (1.2, 9 Kroll).

[81] ὁ γὰρ ὑπὸ τὰς αὐγὰς τὸν ἄνδρα ἀρνούμενος πρόδηλός ἐστι νύκτωρ ἐλεγχόμενος γυνή, Clement, *Paidagogos* 3.3.20.

[82] The hypocrisy of such *poseurs* is a standard target of satirists: see, almost at random, Martial 1.24, 9.47; Juvenal 2.1–15; Lucilius, *Greek Anthology* 11.155.

[83] *Deipnosophists* 13.565c. An advice manual for the medical profession warned doctors against using too much perfume but conceded that a little bit of grooming refinement is acceptable in the attempt to please patients (Hippocratic *Precepts* 10, probably first century C.E.). On men's use of perfume, see J. Griffin, *Latin Poets and Roman Life* (London, 1975), 10–11.

[84] Dio Chrysostom's brief "history of depilation" describes how those who first tried shaving their beards found that their faces became "pretty and boyish beyond their years" when rid of that down" (*Or.* 33. 63). For the ephebe as the youth who, once he becomes hairy, will cease to attract, see Plutarch, *Erōtikos* 770bc and Ps.-Lucian, *Erōtes* 10, 26.

[85] See Polemo, *Phys.* 49, 1.258F, quoted below. Ps.-Lucian *Erōtes* 9 describes a young man who uses cosmetics in order to attract women. Lucian's *Teacher of Rhetoric* recommends to

It is as if the bristling lion competed with a counter-paradigm, an image of masculine smoothness and refinement whose exponents, basking (one assumes) in idleness and *luxuria*, did not bother to promote or defend their style in writing.[86] Some of them may have been those *cinaedi-sophisticates*, mentioned by the astrologers as "famous for their charm and urbanity."[87] But others were surely wealthy and cultivated gentlemen of unremarkable sexual habits who, like the orator Hortensius, permitted themselves the luxury of displaying their cultivated taste in their dress and mannerisms. Hortensius' oratorical delivery was famous for its grace of physical movement,[88] which seems to have occasioned some hostile comment. We should note, however, his spirited retort to insinuations of effeminacy, "I would rather be called a dancing girl, yes, a dancing girl, than like you, Torquatus, a stranger to the Muses, to Aphrodite, and to Dionysos."[89] When polemical moralists oversimplify the sexual significance of such a stance, they are deliberately eclipsing the middle ground. Not every Greco-Roman gentleman could be expected to transact civic business—much less attend a dinner party—in the shaggy garb of a cynic philosopher. A certain amount of refinement was in order; it was just a question of degree, a matter of taste: depilate the armpits, of course, but not the legs. This was where Seneca felt that one should draw the line.[90] The best place to draw the line might shift according to one's audience, as the Cilician sophist Alexander found out the hard way while on an embassy on behalf of his native city: the refined grooming habits that had enhanced his appeal in the East went over very poorly with the dour and caustic Antoninus Pius.[91]

This very Alexander, whose exquisite getup and grooming alone sufficed to excite the admiration of the Athenians, and whose extravagant

---

would-be imitators a dissolute program of private life (featuring depilation and oral sex) that is intended to appeal to *both* women and other adult men (*Teacher of Rhetoric* 23).

[86] On young Roman aristocrats' choosing such a style, see J. Griffin, *Latin Poets and Roman Life* (London, 1975), 5–6. On the possibility of the existence of a class of men in Classical Athens who "freely and deliberately chose not to live by the fictions of self-mastery," see J. Winkler, *The Constraints of Desire* (New York/London, 1990), 63–64. The price of this freedom would have been "voluntary apostasy from the arena of political warfare."

[87] Firmicus Maternus, *Mathesis* 8.25.1.

[88] Valerius Maximus 8.10.2.

[89] ἄμουσος, ἀναφρόδιτος, ἀπροσδιόνυσος, Gellius, *Attic Nights* 1.5.

[90] *Ep.* 114.14. Note that in context this dictum is intended as literary criticism: depilation is but the vehicle for a metaphor about oratorical style, a fact that fortifies the contention of this study that in antiquity judgments about speech were sexualized because speech was an essential variable in the social construction of masculinity.

[91] Philostratus, *Lives* 570–71. Philostratus states that he was thought to be trying to make himself look younger. The emperor objected specifically to the arrangement of his hair, the polished state of his teeth and nails, and his lavish use of perfume. Marcus Aurelius, on the other hand, appointed him Imperial Secretary (ibid. 571).

rhythmic variations inspired the emulation of Herodes Atticus, was a pupil of none other than Favorinus himself, which suggests that the "smooth" style could be taught or in some way inherited.[92] As Ramsay MacMullen argues, there was considerable variety in Roman attitudes to both effeminacy and depilation, and some segments of upper-class society were more accepting of these practices than were others.[93] But the lack of first-person testimony on the part of those espousing the "smooth style" hampers our appreciation of this variety of attitudes and may be due to constraints on the sort of masculine persona that people felt entitled to adopt in writing.[94] Depilation appears to have been a topic that an author could not handle in writing without distancing devices, among which the brine of invective appears to have been preferred for its sterilizing effect. Yet there can be no doubt that norms of masculine behavior were enforced largely through threat of censure and ridicule, and physiognomical scrutiny belonged to a large-scale coercive social process.[95] While some men aspired to the sort of *chic* that could "carry off" elegant grooming habits that normally invited accusations of effeminacy, others feared mockery so greatly that they submitted their flabby breasts to correction by the surgeon's knife. It is proper to operate in such cases, the doctors write, "because this deformity carries the reproach of effeminacy."[96]

PHYSIOGNOMICAL DECEPTION

The desire to improve one's physiognomical profile may not often have resulted in solutions as radical as surgery, but the impulse was a natural response to the competitive pressures of a face-to-face society. An anonymous physiognomist observes, "The investigation of humans is rendered difficult by the fact that each man strives to conceal his proper faults." He continues, "The true character of a human being may be obscured by assiduous effort and ⟨deceptive⟩ behavior, so that it frequently happens that a single individual may exhibit a complex disposition ⟨compounded

---

[92] Ibid. 576.

[93] "Roman Attitudes to Greek Love," *Historia* 31 (1982), 484–502 (a discussion that is couched, somewhat anachronistically, in terms of "homosexuality.")

[94] For example, Persius' account of a sunbathing dandy being accosted by a shaggy rustic who attacks his depilatory practices with crude agricultural metaphors is not presented in the first person but begins hypothetically in the second ("But if you should be sitting in the sun, nicely oiled, and someone you don't know accosts you . . . ") *Satires* 4.33–42.

[95] On Roman sexual satire as a form of aggression, see A. Richlin, *The Gardens of Priapus* (2nd ed. Oxford, 1992).

[96] τῆς γοῦν ἀπρεπείας ἐχούσης ὄνειδος τὸ κατὰ τὴν θηλύτητα χειρουργεῖν ἄξιον, Paul of Aegina 6.46 (*CMG* 9.2.86). This operation definitely existed in the second century: Rhases attests that it was recommended by Antyllos.

of various animal signs⟩, whereas animals are simple, naked, take no precautions, and show their ⟨true⟩ nature out in the open."[97] These precautions are but the *askēsis* or regimen of the nurse applied by the adult to his
own self-fashioning. In order to detect them, the physiognomist should
examine carefully any man who is "taking precautions to safeguard himself (*praecaventem aut praemunientem*)—though he too will be uncovered by
the skilled practitioner."[98] If we watch closely, we may observe a fellow
citizen betray himself in conversation at the baths: "His voice laid bare his
slavery to sexual desires." We might see another "confess by a sudden
sneeze that he was no man at all." This is the famous story of Cleanthes and
the catamite.[99] There was a physiognomist of wide repute (the Stoics
identified him with Cleanthes) who made it his special business to detect
brave men and cowards, pretentious imposters, pathics, and adulterers—
just the way most people can identify at first glance a dog or an ox. His
reputation for inerrancy inspired certain wags to test his skill: they brought
before him a tough-looking hirsute man with horny hands and shaggy
mantle and demanded a diagnosis. The physiognomist looked this specimen up and down and finally declared himself stumped. But just as the
shaggy fellow turned to leave, he sneezed—at which the physiognomist
cried out triumphantly, "He's a *cinaedus!*"

This rare vignette of a physiognomist in action permits us to observe the
latent agonistic element in physiognomy made explicit in performance.
The physiognomist must prove himself in front of an audience that would
be only too delighted to witness his discomfiture. The physiognomical
subject, it is taken for granted, has something to conceal. He "wins" if the
physiognomist fails to pry it out of him. In this case, the "subject" (or
"suspect") almost succeeds in concealing the secret of his unmanly passivity beneath an assumed exterior of hyper-masculine signs: a hard body
(*sklēros*); shaggy eyebrows that meet above the nose (*sunophrus*); a conspicuous absence of any signs of grooming (*auchmōn*); roughened hands; legs
hairy right down to the ankles; hair cut badly with no attention to aesthetic
effect.[100] Physiognomists therefore must always be alert to deception. Signs that
one's subject is overcompensating are a dead giveaway. "People who are
unable to keep their eyelids straight or their eyebrows level but tremble
slightly there while their gaze keeps shifting—these people are *androgynoi*

---

[97] *Anon. Lat.* 132, 2.144F, a passage that probably derives from Loxus.
[98] *Anon. Lat.* 11, 2.19–20F.
[99] Ibid. 11, 2.20F; Diogenes Laertius 7.173; Dio Chrysostom 33.53–54.
[100] Compare the farcical scenario with which Lucian taunts the ignorant book-collector:
"Suppose one of your cinaedic cronies were to start walking around with a club in his hand
and a lion-skin on his back. Would any one mistake *him* for Heracles? No: his gait, his glance,
his voice, and his limp neck would instantly give him away" (*Ignorant Book-Collector* 23).

who are forcing themselves to be men."¹⁰¹ As the anonymous Latin treatise says, "They are eager to conceal this fault and by that very fact are
more easily exposed by the experienced observer."¹⁰² The same goes for
the neck. Some people are stiff-necked because they are stubborn and
stupid. "But other people who have stiff necks are sort of steering themselves and straining artificially with tremendous effort, although they
are actually completely enervated. These *androgynoi* who then straighten
themselves out *think* that they are concealing their feminine lust"—but in
vain: their own efforts expose them: "For it is by the twitching of their
lips and the rotation of their eyes, by the haphazard and inconsistent
shifting of their feet, by the movement of their hips and the fickle motion
of their hands, and by the tremor of their voice as it begins with difficulty
to speak, that effeminates are most easily revealed."¹⁰³ The expert physiognomist claims to see, behind the disguise of the deliberately stiffened
neck, the minutest intermittent trembling. "Their necks are unable to
remain sufficiently firm but tremble slightly when the tension becomes
too great" (Adam.). Hence "all forms of pretense are of no avail" (*Anon.
Lat.*).

Polemo distinguished bodily movements that are natural and unaffected
(*autophues kai apronoēton*) from those that involve some form of pretense.
"You must also practice physiognomy on those who schematize themselves in certain postures and move themselves in ways that have been
carefully thought out"¹⁰⁴ (an interesting warning from a sophist who
specialized in "schematized" themes). Deception operates on various
levels. Polemo sees the first type of feigned deportment in the postures we
adopt to further our social and political ambitions. "Some contrive to
convey an appearance of dignity as they solicit political office and influence
in their city or seek prestigious marriage alliances; sometimes people
transform themselves to give an appearance of poverty or thrift or make
themselves over to give an appearance of ⟨false⟩ joy or gloom, by which
means they dispose themselves so as to appear most acceptable to those
who are in a position of power."¹⁰⁵ Some people stand tall and "put on the
appearance of wealth and good character." At other times, one needs to
hang one's head and present oneself as "poorly dressed, uncouth, pitiful,

¹⁰¹ οὗτοι ἀνδρόγυνοι ὄντες ἄνδρες εἶναι βιάζονται, Adam. 1.19,1.341F.
¹⁰² *Anon. Lat.* 39, 2.56–57F.
¹⁰³ Adam. 2.21,1.368–70F, with *Anon. Lat.* 54,2.75–76F.
¹⁰⁴ ὅσοι δὲ σχηματίζουσιν ἑαυτοὺς καὶ κινοῦνται ἐπιτετηδευμένως, Adam. 2.38,1.397–
98F. Cf. *Phys.* 49, 1.256–58F and *Anon. Lat.* 74,2.94–97F. My translation is a synthesis of
these three passages, which all derive from the same original.
¹⁰⁵ Adam. 2.38,1.397F, with *Anon. Lat.* 74,2.95F: *prout acceptissimum esse potioribus arbi-
tratur.*

and hardworking"—depending, we may assume, on whether one is asking for forgiveness of interest or demanding the repayment of a loan.[106] The second sort of pretense in deportment outlined by Polemo is the sort that people adopt to ingratiate themselves with others by using the charm of their personal appearance. Here it is not a question of assuming a false identity, but of enhancing one's looks for possibly immoral ends. "These signs are contrived in the area of personal adornment and clothing with which men deck themselves out to please other men and women. Some men pursue boys with these techniques. Others, such as pathics (cinaedi), who have a woman's sexual desire, use these techniques to catch men the way prostitutes do."[107] In the words of another physiognomist, these are men who "have set themselves up in the woman's role and elaborate an affected style of deportment in order to attract other men."[108]

Finally Polemo describes the kind of pretense in deportment that is adopted by men who really are androgynoi and are endeavoring to conceal that fact. The sort of affectation in question here does not involve external appearance and personal adornment, but something more elusive. It is analogous to the deception practiced by men who adopt an arrogant mode of speech in order that they themselves may be thought proud, or by men who adopt the speech-patterns of the brave in order to appear courageous.[109] This is the sort of deception practiced by "those who are by nature effeminate but mold themselves on the masculine pattern."[110] Such people "actually try to remove suspicion from themselves by straining to assume a more virile appearance. They imitate a youthful stride, hold themselves with a peculiar firmness, intensify their gaze and voice, and with their whole body they adopt a rigid bearing."[111] But underneath this hypermasculine rigidity lurk signs of their real nature. "They generally slacken both voice and neck, relaxing their hands and feet, and are easily betrayed by other transient signs. For both sudden fear and unexpected joy shake them from their carefully prepared pretense and recall them to their true nature."[112] These overcompensating gender-indeterminates are easily

[106] Anon. Lat. 74, 2.95F.

[107] Phys. 49, 1.256–58F.

[108] aut mulierum loco se ipsos constituunt, quo viros in se provocare possint, affectatum atque elaboratum corporis motum habent (Anon. Lat. 74,2.96F). Compare Caelius Aurelianus, On Chronic Diseases 4.9 (131).

[109] Phys. 49,1.258F.

[110] τῶν ἀνδρογύνων μὲν ὄντων φύσει, πλαττόντων δὲ ἑαυτοὺς εἰς τὸ ἀνδρεῖον, Adam. 2.38,1.398F.

[111] Verum suspicionem a se removere conantes virilem sumere speciem sibimet laborant. Nam et incessum pedum iuvenilem imitantur et semet ipsos rigore quodam confirmant et oculos et vocem intendunt atque omne corpus erigunt (Anon. Lat. 74,2.96F).

[112] Anon. Lat. 74,2.96–97F.

"caught in the act" (phōrōntai), and despite their zealous imitation of a man's gait, voice, and gaze, an unexpected emotional shock, like the sneeze of Cleanthes' catamite, can collapse the entire house of cards.[113] This concern with false deportment was not merely a physiognomist's fantasy. Medical science also took note of the phenomenon. The methodist physician Caelius Aurelianus, while conceding that "no man will easily believe that pathics really exist," asserts that they actually do.[114] Driven by lust to act in ways contrary to human nature, they adopt the dress, walk, and other attributes of women. This is not a bodily affliction but a defect of a diseased mind, and for this reason it is subject to some startling reversals. "Often out of fear, and in rare cases out of respect for certain persons to whom they are beholden, these pathics suddenly change their character and for a brief while try to demonstrate the signs of virility (virilitatis quaerunt indicia demonstrare). But since they have no sense of limits, they often subject themselves to excess in the other direction and do more than what is appropriate to manly strength (plus . . . quam virtuti convenit faciunt) and so involve themselves in worse vices."[115] Caelius Aurelianus does not make clear exactly what dangerous feats of overcompensating behavior he has in mind here, but he shares with the physiognomists a conviction that effeminate men may try to reverse their signs and deliberately alter the profile that they present to the world—whether more out of fear or reverence, we cannot say.

Perhaps the taut suspension required of the ideal man's physical carriage is emblematic of the constant strain involved in maintaining a truly masculine profile in the face of such exacting standards, where an appropriate level of masculine tension in gaze, walk, and gesture must be cultivated by continuous exertion but must never be allowed to appear put on. The failures, which made the effort behind the act appear too obvious, were stigmatized as the clumsy efforts of overcompensating imposters— perhaps because they threatened to reveal the deportment of masculinity for the construct of conventions that it really was.

The physiognomists, astrologers, and popular moralists of antiquity thought in terms of degrees of gender-conformity and gender-deviance. They shared a notion of gender identity built upon polarized distinctions (smooth/hirsute, pantherine/leonine) that purported to characterize the gulf between men and women but actually divided the male sex into legitimate and illegitimate members, some of whom were unmistakable androgynes, while others were subtly deceitful imposters. Masculinity

[113] Adam. 2.38,1.398F.
[114] On Chronic Diseases 4.9(131). On this text see P. H. Schrijvers, Eine Medizinische Erklärung der Männlichen Homosexualität aus der Antike (Amsterdam, 1985).
[115] On Chronic Diseases 4.9(132), reading timentes, rather than tumentes.

DEPORTMENT AS LANGUAGE   81

was still thought to be grounded in "nature," yet it remained fluid and
incomplete until firmly anchored by the discipline of an acculturative
process. It was in this area of slippage between anatomical sex and constructed gender that the crypto-*cinaedus* found room to design his disguise
and the physiognomist found the signs to decode it.[116]

[116] For the notion of "slippage" applied to theories of gender in a slightly different con-
text, see S. Greenblatt, "Fiction and Friction," in *Reconstructing Individualism: Autonomy,
Individuality, and the Self in Western Thought*, ed. T. C. Heller, M. Sosna, and D. E. Wellbery
(Stanford, 1986), 30–52, here 44.

Chapter Four

AERATING THE FLESH: VOICE TRAINING AND THE CALISTHENICS OF GENDER

The Physiognomy of the Voice

D IO CHRYSOSTOM reveals the role he expected speech to play in the maintenance of gender boundaries in a censorious lecture addressed to the inhabitants of Tarsus. His target is an unpleasant personal habit of the citizenry: nasal snorting.[1] To bring home the shocking impropriety of this mannerism he proposes a thought experiment: "Suppose an entire community were struck by the following peculiar affliction: all the males suddenly acquired women's voices and no one, whether boy or adult, was able to say anything in manly fashion. Would that not seem unbearable—worse, indeed, than any plague?"[2] Yet even this, he argues, would be easier to bear than the present situation. The Tarsian snort is worse than men speaking with women's voices because it is the sort of sound that belongs to gender indeterminates (*androgynoi*). Indeed, it befits the castrated! In the *a fortiori* structure of his argument, we see how gender ambiguity is more alarming than outright exchange of vocal roles. Similarly, the voice that blurs the boundaries of gender is more hideous than the voice that crosses the boundaries of species. Hecuba, howling like a dog, is less ill-omened than "someone who is a man and has both the distinguishing marks of a man and the voice appropriate to a man" but, being unable to remove the signs of his nature (*ta sēmeia tēs phuseōs*), is transformed by the Furies: "perverted, completely enervated!" Such a person learns how to emit "a voice that belongs neither to man nor to woman nor to any other creature. He does not even imitate the cries of a whore at work but vocalizes as if he were engaged in the most disgusting and profligate activity [pathic sex], *and* he does it in public in the broad light of day!"[3]

---

[1] The precise definition of the practice he calls ῥέγκειν has eluded commentators; perhaps it is extinct. Polemo's *Physiognomy* alludes to something similar: a snorting, nasal style of speech that is associated with devious, antisocial behavior: *si eum ronchantem vides, tamquam si eius vox infra nares exeat, ei mendacii studium multam invidiam et aviditatem sodalibus nocendi tribuas* (52,1.266–68F). For other discussion see C. P. Jones, *The Roman World of Dio Chrysostom* (Cambridge, 1978), 73–74. C. B. Welles, "Hellenistic Tarsus," in *Mélanges de l'Université Saint-Joseph* (Beirut) 28 (1962), 43–75, argues unconvincingly that the whole business of nasal noise is simply a metaphor for the Tarsians' neglect of philosophy.

[2] *Or.* 33.38.

[3] Ibid. 33.60.

Dio's tirade continues, "But not even indeterminates and eunuchs make that sound at all times or to all persons: rather it is something private among them that functions as a password."[4] Here we see the voice operating on several levels as a signifier of gender identity. On the primary level, it serves to distinguish the sexes. "Male" and "female" voices are, in principle, distinct enough that it is possible for Dio to imagine a complete reversal of the "normal" and "natural." At another level, the voice can be the red flag that warns of an ominous blurring of gender identity, as in the case of the *androgynoi* and eunuchs. And finally, the voice that signifies ambiguity to *us* becomes a very specific signifier in a private language owned by *them*.

Physiognomical treatises refer frequently to the voice. In the handbook attributed to Aristotle, we are taught to read a low voice as a sign of courage, a high voice as a sign of cowardice.[5] This discussion becomes very muddled when it tries to align the qualities of vocal slackness and tension along the bravery-cowardice grid. The basic problem seems to be that the characteristic tautness and intensity of the masculine body-habitus must not be associated with a high-pitched voice. A similar logical snafu results when Aristotle tries to ascribe the lower pitch of the male voice to the tension placed on the vocal passages by the testicles functioning like loom-weights.[6] The Latin physiognomy instructs us to read bravery in a voice that is "somewhat harsh and energetic, conspicuously noble, and emits breath calmly."[7] You can tell a timid man easily: like his hair, his voice is soft (*mollis*).[8] It is also resonant (*sonora*). We will return later to the question of whether deviations from the idealized norm of masculine vocal quality were conceded to bestow certain expressive and aesthetic advantages.

A man's lack of sexual self-control reveals itself in his speech: the incontinent man has a high-pitched voice.[9] Presumably his lack of control assimilates him to the feminine. *Cinaedi*, of course, are easily known by their voices: high-pitched, smoothed-soft, and enervated "as one can tell by referring to women and the overall impression."[10]

For those whose activities included public speaking, flaws in vocal control could combine with other signs to make a very unfortunate impression. Even a highly successful teacher of rhetoric might wonder as an old man whether his vulgar way of walking (brought on by gout), and per-

---

[4] ἀλλὰ ἴδιον αὐτῶν ὥσπερ ξύμβολον, *Or.* 33.39.

[5] [Arist.], [*Phys.*] 806b.

[6] *Gen. An.* 787b–788a.

[7] *Anon. Lat.* 90, 2.120F: *vox durior et vehementior, magnanimitate praecellens, anhelitus quoque tranquillus.* Cf. the κόσμος of Adam. 2.49, 1.413F: βαρὺ φθέγγεται, βραδὺ βαίνει.

[8] *Anon. Lat.* 91, 2.120F.

[9] Adam. 2.48, 1.413F; *Anon. Lat.* 94, 2.121–22F; *Phys.* 57, 1.274F.

[10] οἷοι δὲ ταῖς φωναῖς ὀξείαις μαλακαῖς κεκλασμέναις διαλέγονται, κίναιδοι. ἀναφέρεται ἐπὶ τὰς γυναῖκας καὶ ἐπὶ τὴν ἐπιπρέπειαν. [Arist.], [*Phys.*] 813a.

haps something unpleasant about his voice and facial expression, was impairing his popularity.[11] Failure to strike the right note of manly dignity could sink a speaker's case. The sophist Philiscus, for example, appearing before the emperor in an attempt to resist the liturgical requirements of his native region, gave offense by the way he walked and by the way he stood. His clothing seemed inappropriate and his voice quasi-feminine (*mixothēlus*); his speech lazy, careless, and off the point. The emperor harassed him with interruptions and finally exclaimed with displeasure, "The hairstyle shows what sort of man he is, and the voice what sort of orator."[12] Thus it is not surprising that many people considered the development of these variables too important to be left to chance. The voice in particular was subjected to regular discipline, and both physicians and educated laymen believed that the training of the voice affected not only a man's speech, but also the well-being of his entire body. Since concern for the well-being of the body was in many ways the hallmark of the age, a brief exploration of this phenomenon will provide a context for beliefs about vocal exercise.

THE ASKĒSIS CULTURE

The second century afforded many opportunities for self-improvement to those whom we might term "the worried well."[13] But their hypochondria can be read as an index of optimism as well as an index of worry: an assertion of confidence in the perfectibility of human habits and the psycho-physical constitution that they produce. *Askēsis*—the Greek word for *exercise* from which *asceticism* is derived—was the watchword of the day. Exhorted by moralists and philosophers to transform his existence into a kind of perpetual training program, a right-thinking gentleman of this period was by no means inclined to treat his body with benign neglect. On the contrary, he would have carefully assessed each quotidian habit for its effect on his well-being. He aspired to a body that was light and dry, to flesh minimally tainted with unwholesome humors, to pores unclogged by the lingering effluvia of his digestive processes. It is important to remember that, though people in the twentieth century tend to conceive of

---

[11] Libanius, *Or.* 2.18. Cf. R. A. Pack, "ΦΥΣΙΟΓΝΩΜΟΝΙΚΑ in Libanius' *Antiochikos*," *AJP* 56 (1935), 347–50.

[12] Philostratus, *Lives* 623.

[13] A pessimistic assessment of this phenomenon is to be found in G. W. Bowersock, *Greek Sophists in the Roman Empire* (Oxford, 1969), 71, 75, and in E. R. Dodds, *Pagan and Christian in an Age of Anxiety* (Cambridge, 1965). M. Foucault, *The Care of the Self* (New York, 1986), sees a preoccupation with self-mastery where the former authors see hypochondria and despair.

disease as the intrusion of alien substances into the body from outside (be they toxic chemicals or microorganisms), the ancients were much more likely to perceive their bodies as being at risk from the accumulation of naturally occurring substances produced on the inside.

With a surprising degree of unanimity, the doctors and educated laymen seem to have agreed that the ideal body is light, warm, rarefied rather than dense in texture, and dry rather than damp. Though medical sects differed in the ways they conceptualized the factors that maintained or disrupted this well-balanced bodily constitution, they took for granted the importance of *pneuma* and the existence of humors.[14] *Pneuma*, drawn in by the breath and also by the pores, supports the body's vital heat. As an animating principle, it is far more than just "air." It is the vital principle associated with the soul, with semen, and with the higher forms of intelligence.[15] Indeed the conceptual connection of breath with soul is a basic feature of the Indo-European inheritance.[16] Flesh well aerated by *pneuma* will be dry rather than damp, warm rather than cool, and rarefied rather than dense.[17] Pores are important because they incorporate *pneuma*. Pores are also important because they extrude undesirable substances through transpiration.[18] (This is one of the assumptions that lies behind Galen's exposition of the benefits of massage.) In general educated people felt a preference for flesh that was rarefied and light, as opposed to dense and heavy, because of its association with health and intelligence.[19]

There was considerable popular interest in such matters. Like philosophers and sophists, physicians might be found giving learned displays in public places—on subjects like "pores and *pneumas* and excretions."[20] Crowds of aristocratic Romans gathered to watch Galen demonstrate by dissection the physical mechanisms of voice production.[21] A generation before Quintilian we find a physician recommending that adolescents, in addition to their philosophical and rhetorical studies, attend medical lectures, "so that they may become accomplished counselors of their own health." For, he continues,

> There is practically no moment, either of night or day, in which we have no need of the medical art, but in walking and sitting, in massage and bathing, in eating

---

[14] Methodist theory minimized the differences between the humors but took it for granted that an excessive accumulation or depletion of fluids within the body would have harmful effects on health.

[15] For the association of *pneuma* with sperm, see for example Galen, *On the Use of the Parts* (K4.183). Excessive loss of sperm depletes the body's vital *pneuma* (*On the Seed* K4.588).

[16] R. B. Onians, *The Origins of European Thought* (Cambridge, 1951).

[17] Antyllus, *On Hygienic Declamation* (Oribasius 6.10) 15–24 in *CMG* vol. 6.

[18] *On Hyg. Decl.* 7–9, 18.

[19] Ibid. 13, 15–16.

[20] Dio Chrysostom, *Or.* 33.6.

[21] Galen, *On Prognosis,* (*CMG* 5.8.1) 5. 7–21.

and drinking, in sleeping and waking, and in every activity throughout our lives, we have need of good counsel to avoid impairment and make the best use of our existence: to be constantly referring everything to physicians is tedious and impractical.[22]

Indeed, the youth who aspired to embody the ideals of his culture had to develop an exquisite sense for the nuances of his physical state in order to select the best course of corrective action from among a wide range of subtly calibrated possibilities. Did he bathe? Then he must consider when and how and in what sequence to take the waters. These decisions in turn required him to assess the nuances of his physical condition. Was he suffering from inflammatory or ulcerous fatigue?[23] Decisions about baths brought others in their train. Massage first—or afterward? Dry or oiled, with muslin cloths or bare hands, gentle or brisk, brief or prolonged? Outdoors, indoors, in the shade? In a breezy or a windless place?[24] One's choice among all these alternatives should be guided by the status of one's body: did one need to put on weight, for example, or reduce? But in general, massage increased one's intrinsic warmth, facilitated the elimination of excreta through the pores, and stimulated respiration.[25] The proliferation of alternative methods testifies to the care taken to make the best of a good thing.

Few foods were neutral. The edible universe was pervasively charged with opposing qualities, a system more complex, and therefore less reducible to order, than the *yin* and *yang* of Chinese dualism. Wheat warmed, but barley cooled, the flesh.[26] Lentil porridge was drying, but peeled barley made you damp.[27] All one's choices in food and drink could be classified according to the humors they were likely to produce or the part of the body that they would help or harm. Beyond the choice of raw ingredients, there was the choice of methods of preparation. Those for whom *askēsis* was a serious concern could seek advice from medical sources on how to remove unwholesome humors from the flesh they ate or on how to bake bread as *dry* as possible without burning it to a crisp.[28]

Concern for one's daily regimen also extended to the bedroom. How many hours should one sleep, and in what position?[29] Should one have

[22] Athenaeus, *On Healthy Regimen* 7 (Oribasius, *Incerta* 21).

[23] Galen, *Hygiene* 3.5–9 (K 6.189–218). Trans. R. M. Green, *Galen's Hygiene* (Springfield, 1951).

[24] A full exposition of the techniques and varieties of massage may be found in Galen, *Hygiene* 2.3 (K6.92–105).

[25] Ibid. 2.2.

[26] Oribasius 3.31–32; Celsus 2.27.

[27] Oribasius 3.33–34. Barley was in many regions the staple food of the poor.

[28] Galen, *On the Properties of Foods* 3.41 (K6.745–47); Dieuches in Oribasius 4.5.

[29] Antyllus in Oribasius 6.1–2, 5; Galen in Oribasius 6.4; Galen, *Hygiene* 6.5 (unhealthy sleeping habits and too much sex can ruin a good constitution).

sex? And afterward, would baths or breathing exercises make a more effective restorative?[30]

Exercise was a widely accepted method of improving one's bodily constitution. There was some rivalry between professionals who offered instruction in these matters, as we can tell from Galen's treatise "On Whether Hygiene Is a Matter of Medicine or Gymnastics,"[31] but the doctors, being more articulate than the gymnasts, have had the last word. In addition to running and the sports of the *palaistra*, activities that by no stretch of the imagination could be called athletic also came to be considered forms of exercise: being carried about in a sedan chair, for example.[32] Two factors may explain this development: the desire of doctors to assert their authority in matters of physical culture, and the desire of busy men to maintain their health without recourse to the dust of the gymnasium, the dangers of warfare, or the tedious logistics of hunting expeditions.[33] Galen devotes a chapter of his *Hygiene* to "A Regimen for Those with Lives Restricted by Work," directed at "people who used to take exercise in the gymnasium before their bath, until they got involved in a busy life."[34] Men who serve in the highest ranks of government are no better off than "slaves or businessmen" if they have to dance attendance on the emperor or governor all day. Health requires autonomy.[35]

Galen warns scholars too not to be induced by their intellectual exertions to neglect the exercise of their bodies.[36] He in fact disapproved of people who worked out too frequently in the gym. That sort of exercise renders the flesh crass and contributes nothing to the soul's progress in virtue. Such persons are not fit for military service, imperial government, or local politics: "One would do better to turn one's business over to pigs."[37] So how was one to avoid the extremes of unwholesome inactivity and excessive muscle-buildup? Galen recommended handball, but many doctors considered that, for a busy gentleman, *vocal exercise* was the obvious choice.

[30] Galen, *Hygiene* 3.11. For the linkage of dietary and sexual hygiene, see 6.7: "For those with faultless constitutions, it is not necessary to refrain completely from sex relations, as has been previously said for dry constitutions [6.3–4]. But it must be considered whether it is advantageous for those in such a [busy] life to eat once or twice [a day]." Rufus (early second century) outlines a healthy diet for those who wish to engage in sex (Oribasius 6.38.10–17). Laymen shared these concerns: Plutarch, "Health Precepts," *Mor.* 129E, 136B.
[31] K5.806–98; cf. *Hygiene* 2.9. For their part, gymnastic trainers claimed that intellectual conversation at dinner spoiled the food and made the head heavy (Plutarch, *Mor.* 133B–E).
[32] Antyllus in Oribasius 6.23 gives a full exposition of passive exercise (αἰώρα). It stimulates the body's innate heat and dissipates excess ὕλη.
[33] Galen, *Small Ball Workout* (K5.900–901).
[34] *Hygiene* 6.7.
[35] Ibid. 6.5.
[36] Galen in Oribasius 6.11.7.
[37] *Small Ball Workout* (K5.905).

VOCAL EXERCISE

Several treatises on vocal exercise survive in the digest of medical texts that Oribasius put together for the emperor Julian.[38] The sixth book of this compendium is devoted to exercise, beginning at the minimum level of physical activity, as it were, with a discussion of sleep and wakefulness. Next come excerpts from a second-century medical treatise on vocal exercise.[39] This author dismisses casual conversation as being of no use to the sick. Declamation, however, is something else altogether. It provides a valuable exercise of the chest, the vocal organs, and especially the body's vital heat. It augments, purifies, tones, and refines this natural heat and renders the solid parts of the body vigorous, pure, and resistant. Declamation soothes stomach ailments and conditions of excessive phlegm; it helps pregnant women who crave unusual foods. It is good for people with poor appetite, for those who fail to gain weight, for people with palsy, dropsy, and asthma and is particularly appropriate for convalescents. The voice can be injured by immoderate amounts of casual conversation, by loud shouting, and by uttering sounds too great in intensity and too high in pitch. It also can suffer from disuse. Vocal exercise ameliorates all these conditions, relieving the congestion that conversation produces in the head, and correcting the damage done by high-pitched sounds because it pulls the voice down to low tones. It is a useful form of restorative therapy for the entire body when one is enervated by fatigue.

The reader whose interest has now been aroused will want to know how best to integrate this salubrious discipline into the daily routine. One should begin by emptying one's bowels and taking a light massage of the lower body. Then one should sponge one's face and warm up with some preliminary chat—or, better yet, go for a little walk before beginning to declaim. Educated persons should declaim a passage from memory; epic hexameters are best. The passage should exhibit the "polish" thought to characterize the middle style, with frequent alternations between rough and smooth consonants. Perhaps Sisyphus rolling his rugged rock would fit the bill.[40] Those unfamiliar with epic may use dramatic, elegiac, or lyric

---

[38] Ἀναφώνησις was the technical term. I have translated it sometimes by the phrase "vocal exercise" and sometimes by "declamation." The Latin equivalent was *declamatio* and first appears in this sense in the *Rhet. ad Her.* 3.20 (*exercitatio declamationis*). Vocal exercise in general is discussed by A. Rousselle, "Parole et inspiration: Le Travail de la voix dans le monde Romain," *Pubblicazioni della Stazione Zoologica di Napoli*, Section 2,5 (1983), 129–57.

[39] Oribasius 6.7–9, from Book Four of Antyllus' handbook of therapeutics, which classifies vocal exercise among "those health practices that lie within the power of the individual." Oribasius may be consulted in *CMG* vol. 6 or in the edition of Charles Daremberg, with French translation, *Oeuvres d'Oribase* (Paris, 1851), vol. 1.

[40] Ἀναφωνείτω δὲ ὁ μὲν οὐκ ἄπειρος παιδείας ἃ μέμνηται, καὶ ἃ δοκεῖ γλαφυρὰ εἶναι, καὶ ὅσα πολλὰς μεταβολὰς ἔχει λειότητός τε καὶ τραχύτητος. Εἰ δὲ ἀνεπιστήμων ἐπῶν

passages, in descending order of preference. At any rate, recitation from memory is more effective than reading aloud. It is best to start declaiming one's passage on the lowest notes, drawing the voice down as low as possible. From there one should ascend to the top of the scale (though one must not stay there long), and then bring the voice downward by degrees until the lowest notes are reached again.[41]

The anonymous author of the next treatise, "On Hygienic Declamation" (Oribasius 6.10), makes more extravagant claims for the art: "Having learned from experience that the exercise of the voice, when properly performed, is the most effective of all forms of instruction for the protection and preservation of health, I have taken pains to write down to the best of my ability both the nature of this therapy and the methods it employs" (1).[42] The author promises to present "the true method of vocal training (askēsis) that promotes longevity and secure good health." We are no longer in the realm of empirical therapy for particular conditions. With its elaborate grounding in physiological theory, this treatise presents vocal exercise as a way of life.

Pneuma is all-important. Vocal exercises promote the diffusion of *pneuma* through the body. But the *pitch* at which the voice is used governs the effectiveness of this process. Low tones dilate the neck and throat; a large volume of *pneuma* is blown through the vocal organs; the rest of the body is relaxed and loose because of the rarefaction. To produce high tones, neck and throat are constricted and compressed, and the remainder of the body contracts proportionally (6). Therefore, the author decrees, one must abandon the training of the higher notes, those exercises that advance upward by degrees from the lowest notes, and "the ingenious elaboration of progressive exercises." "For how," the anonymous author asks, "do melodious sound and a good voice protect the health of the body?"[43] This prohibition implies that progressive exercises were a common practice; indeed they seem to be exactly the sort of ascending and descending chants recommended by Antyllus, though he also cautions about dwelling too long on the high notes.

Pneuma is drawn into the body not only through the bronchial tubes, but

---

εἴη, ἰαμβεῖα λεγέτω· τρίτην δὲ χώραν ἐλεγεῖα ἐχέτω· τετάρτην δὲ μέλη (Oribasius 6.9.2–3). On the three genera dicendi, of which the "middle style" is γλαφυρός, see D. A. Russell (ed.), 'Longinus' On the Sublime (Oxford 1964), xxxiv–xxxvi. On Sisyphus: the sound and rhythm of Od. 11.593–98 were discussed by Dionysius of Halicarnassus (On Literary Composition 20).

[41] "What is the Proper Way to Perform Ἀναφώνησις?" (Oribasius 6.9), also from Antyllus Book Four.

[42] Oribasius 6.10.1. Paragraph numbers in the text refer to sections of this treatise, which differs from the material attributed to Antyllus in its use of the first person singular, and in its categorical condemnation of high notes; it is probably the work of another author (H. Schöne, ΠΕΡΙ ΥΓΙΕΙΝΗΣ ΑΝΑΦΩΝΗΣΕΩΣ, Hermes 65 [1930], 94).

[43] τί γὰρ ἂν εἰς ἀσφάλειαν σώματος εὐμέλεια καὶ χρηστοφωνία συμβάλλοιτο, Oribasius 6.10.7.

also through the invisibly dilated pores on the surface of the body. Hence those whose flesh is dense and whose pores are narrow have small voices and produce weak sounds. This is why, the author claims, children, women, and eunuchs have weaker voices than men do: their pores are narrower (sick people for similar reasons have weaker voices than do healthy ones) (10).

So training the voice rarefies the body by dilating the pores. By contrast, other forms of exercise thicken and compact the flesh. While vocal exercise makes the body light, athletic exercise makes it heavy, massive, and ponderous (15). Because of the rarefaction it produces, vocal exercise develops flesh that is "pliable and adapts easily to all activities," while flesh formed by other sorts of exercise is "resistant, tough, and insensitive." It is for this reason, the author observes, that athletes generally are more thickheaded than other people (16).

Besides improving the texture of one's flesh, vocal exercise will adjust its humidity, promoting excretion of excessive moisture through dilated pores during reading aloud and speaking (17–18). We are told that those who extend their range to the lowest notes possible and force the sound will find their interior humidity dramatically reduced (23). Anyone who looks can observe this from the abundant vapor that comes out of the mouths of those who are reading aloud and from the excretion of stale humors through their appointed conduits—not only through what we call expiration, but also through coughed-up saliva and phlegm—all means by which the body rids itself of morbific influences (24). (Here we are forcibly reminded of the extent to which reading and speaking were experienced by the ancients as *physical* activities).

Perhaps it is the temperature of one's flesh that requires adjustment. For those whose cool temperature requires warming up, what remedy could be more appropriate than the activity of disciplined breathing? The motion of *pneuma* produces friction that awakens and kindles our internal heat (19).

For all these reasons, the author concludes, one should read aloud and recite at every opportunity, relaxing the whole body; and when the flesh is fluid enough for rarefaction, one should make an effort to dilate the bronchial tubes and the other air passages, speaking at the lowest frequencies of the voice but renouncing those ingeniously elaborated progressive exercises that ascend to the highest notes. High pitch, he insists, spoils the power and intensity of the voice, although, he concedes, it does foster "melodiousness, tonal variety, and the graceful modulations of musical phrasing" (23).[44] But none of these aesthetic advantages promote the health of the body.

[44] ἰσχύος μὲν γὰρ καὶ δυνάμεως καὶ ἐπιτάσεως πόρων ἀλλοτριώτατον φωνῆς ὀξύτης, εὐμελείᾳ δὲ καὶ ποικιλίᾳ φθόγγων μεταβολαῖς εὐκράτοις μελῶν πρόσφορον, ὧν οὐδὲν ἂν εἰς σώματος ὑγιεινὴν ἀσφάλειαν εὑρεθείη χρήσιμον.

In conclusion, we are warned, vocal exercises should not be practiced casually or in an unprepared fashion; this applies particularly to those who are not accustomed to using them. One should never attempt them when full of unwholesome and corrupted humors, nor should one practice vocal exercise in cases of flagrant indigestion, lest the putrid vapors become more widely distributed in the body as a result (25).

This treatise thus presents the voice as an instrument of physiological reform, which, when properly used, can actually ameliorate the practitioner's psycho-physical constitution by warming, aerating, and drying the flesh. But this does not mean that attainment of their culture's ideal body-type came within everyone's grasp. The full benefits of vocal exercise are not equally available to all who may practice it. The treatise makes it clear that women, children, and eunuchs *always* have an undesirable configuration of the pores. Theirs are just too small (10). As a result, they are inevitably deficient in *pneuma*. The suboptimal physical condition of women, children, and eunuchs is presented as a given, something over which they have no control. Yet the fundamental premise of vocal exercise is that *men* who practice it can dilate their pores through their own efforts, that the disciplines of *askēsis* actually can produce an improvement in their physical condition. Why, then, cannot women, children, and eunuchs do the same? The answer has to be that they can never aerate themselves with *pneuma* as well as men can because they cannot produce low notes.

Given the acknowledged aesthetic advantages of practice on the high notes,[45] why would medical writers feel compelled to develop a theory that privileges low notes? Experts generally tell people what they already want to believe. Physiological theories, though the creation and in some sense the exclusive property of experts, tend to articulate a conception of the human body that is consonant with lay beliefs about purity and pollution, about the right relation of matter and spirit, and the appropriate polarization of masculine and feminine. Second-century physicians were not free to choose their culture's physical ideal, only to elaborate it. And in their prescriptions for voice-training, against all possible aesthetic considerations, there weighed, heavily, considerations of decorum. After all, for half a millenium, a low voice had been known to be a sign of a nobler nature.[46]

A LAYMAN'S ENDORSEMENT: PLUTARCH

Plutarch speaks scornfully of persons in positions of political authority who try to give an impression of immense dignity (*semnotēs*) by using an

---

[45] Oribasius 6.10.7, 23.

[46] καὶ δοκεῖ γενναιοτέρας εἶναι φύσεως ἡ βαρυφωνία, Aristotle, *Gen. An.* 787A; *Eth. Nic.* 1125a34.

artificially low voice.[47] His comment shows us two things: both that a low voice *was* popularly considered dignified, and that the voice was considered a controllable variable in self-presentation. Plutarch is also able to show us that theories about vocal exercise had actually penetrated beyond the technical world of medical handbooks to inform the daily habits of a cultured gentleman's life. In his treatise "Health Precepts," under the rubric of "Exercises Suitable For Scholars," Plutarch discusses the benefits of vocal exercise, which he claims are to be obtained not only from the practice of declamation in the narrow sense, but also from speaking aloud in general.

> The daily use of the voice in speaking aloud is a marvelous form of exercise, conducive not only to health but also to strength: not the strength of the wrestler, which lays on flesh and makes the exterior solid like the walls of a building, but a strength that engenders an all-pervasive vigor and a real energy in the most vital and dominant parts.[48]

Instead of making the practitioner's body fleshy and dense, vocal exercise increases warmth, tones the blood, clears every conduit, and by evacuating the moist digestive residues, prevents them from clogging up the body. Therefore we should make ourselves accustomed to this exercise by speaking continuously! Should this prove too much of a strain, we can read aloud or practice vocal exercises. (Reading aloud, since we use the words of others, bears the same relationship to intellectual discussion that passive exercise does to active). After vocalizing, but before going for our walk, we should use gentle massage to diffuse to the extremities the *pneuma* ingested during vocal exercises. The man who has thus resolved the tension of his inner *pneuma* will remain untroubled by digestive residues and, should circumstances prevent his going for a constitutional, will come to no harm.

> Wherefore neither a sea voyage nor a stay in a hotel should serve as an excuse for silence—not even if everyone laughs at you. For certainly it is no disgrace to exercise in a place where it is no disgrace to eat. But what really is shameful is to feel intimidated and self-conscious in front of sailors, muleteers, and innkeepers, who do not laugh at travelers who take their exercise by playing ball and shadow-boxing but only laugh at the man who uses his voice, even though in *his* exercises he teaches, questions, learns, and uses his memory.[49]

[47] "To an Uneducated Ruler," *Mor.* 780A. Faith in this method of enhancing one's dignity was widespread: Cicero wrote of using a deep voice to appear *gravis* (*Orator* 56).

[48] *Mor.* 130AB, trans. modified from F. C. Babbitt, *Plutarch's Moralia*, vol. 2 (Loeb Classical Library, London and Cambridge, Mass., 1928).

[49] Ibid. 130EF. Compare the persistence of the sophist Hippodromos, who practiced declamation "even while on vacation in the country, and while traveling, whether by land or by sea" (Philostratus, *Lives* 618).

Plutarch cautions us against straining the voice when our fitness is impaired by indigestion, intercourse, or fatigue and concludes with a cautionary anecdote about the famous sophist who died from lecturing with a fishbone stuck in his throat.

Another glimpse of how vocal exercise might have worked in practice comes from a Methodist work on chronic diseases, which discusses the treatment of persons afflicted with mania. In the early stages of their cure, they are to be gently moved about in "passive exercise." As they grow stronger, they should be made to walk and perform vocal exercise, presumably of the simpler sort: scales and repetitive chants. Then the patient should be made to read aloud (sometimes from texts marred by false statements, the better to exercise his mind!).

> As the treatment progresses, rhetorical exercises and discourses should be introduced (*meditationes adhibendae vel disputationes*). And in this case the speeches should all be arranged in the same way, so that the introduction is delivered in a gentle voice, the narrative portions and proof more loudly and intensely, and the conclusion in a subdued and kindly manner, according to the precepts of those who have written on vocal exercise, which the Greeks call *anaphōnēsis*. Let an audience be present, made up of persons familiar to the patient, who by their kind attention and praise as they listen to his words will relax the speaker's mind. In fact, any pleasant physical exercise promotes good health. After his rhetorical exercises and discourses, the patient should be immediately given a gentle massage and taken for an easy walk. If the patient is unacquainted with literature, give him problems appropriate to his particular skill: agricultural problems for a farmer, navigational problems for a sea captain. And if he is without any skill whatsoever, give him questions on commonplace matters, or let him play checkers.[50]

The idea of vocal exercise being therapeutic for both body and soul, as it were, may appear less startling if we recall the importance of the voice in magical and religious practice. The intoning of the seven Greek vowel sounds was ubiquitous in magical ritual; under a paranoid emperor, a person caught chanting the vowels in the public baths to soothe a stomach complaint might find himself accused of treason.[51] Orphic and Pythagorean convictions about the power of music in the soul and in the cosmos encouraged some men to believe that attempts to reproduce the music of the spheres with the lyre and with the voice could assist the soul in its

---

[50] Caelius Aurelianus, *On Chronic Diseases* 1.162–65, which is a Latin translation of a lost second-century treatise of Soranus. My translation is a modification of that of I. E. Drabkin, *Caelius Aurelianus: On Acute Diseases and On Chronic Diseases* (Chicago, 1950), 549. Compare Seneca's letter to a sick friend, where he assumes that the doctor will prescribe reading aloud to exercise the sufferer's *spiritus* (*Letters.* 78.5).

[51] Ammianus Marcellinus 19.2.28.

passage home.[52] Philosophers disturbed by the emotional intensity of their dreams might "harmonize their soul to the lyre" at dawn, presumably by chanting vocal exercises on a fixed series of pitches.[53]

From the description quoted above of vocal exercise being used to treat mental illness, it appears that *anaphōnēsis* could be more than a regimen of chanting scales: the delivery of extempore discourses was also considered therapeutic. Since extempore discourses presuppose a rhetorical education, a modern reader is bound to wonder to what extent the benefits of vocal exercise were confined to the upper classes. Though Antyllus mentions hypothetical patients who may lack the literary training to declaim hexameters from memory, and Caelius Aurelianus proposes alternative subjects of discussion for farmers and sea-captains deficient in *paideia*, it is possible that these proposals are just "theory talk" unrelated to social reality. When, for example, Galen recommends small ball exercise because the inexpensive equipment makes it "accessible, so to speak, even to the very poor,"[54] one cannot assume that his indigent contemporaries were actually subjecting themselves to the rigors of hygienic exercise routines. The extant written evidence about ancient society derives almost exclusively from educated males of elite social background whose conceptual apparatus allowed them to slide unawares from writing of themselves as exemplars of perfected humanity (*optima pars humani generis*) to taking themselves and their experience as normative for everyone (*pars pro toto*). This tendancy presents a major methodological obstacle to subsequent investigators who want to know what less privileged members of society actually did.

Even if we confine ourselves to investigating what the privileged few *expected* of others, plenty of questions remain. Medical experts writing for the elite evidently were able to imagine undereducated males improvising health-giving discourses on occupationally appropriate subjects, whatever they actually prescribed for such persons. But what did they expect of females? In certain circumstances they apparently were quite willing to recommend vocal exercise for women.

VOCAL EXERCISE FOR WOMEN

Everybody in the second century knew that women's bodies were colder and damper than men's.[55] This stands to reason because, as Galen ex-

---

[52] Cicero, *Dream of Scipio* (*De republica* 6.18); Orphic poems, fr. 308. See M. L. West, *The Orphic Poems* (Oxford, 1983), 31–32.

[53] Dio Chrysostom, *Or.* 32.57.

[54] καὶ τοῖς πενεστάτοις, ὥς εἴρηται, εὔπορος, K5.901. Compare Soranus on menial jobs as appropriate exercise for impecunious wet-nurses (*Gyn.* 2.14.29).

[55] Τὰ σώματα τῶν γυναικῶν ὑγρότερα καὶ ψυχρότερα εἶναι, πᾶς ἂν ὁμολογήσειεν, Oribasius, *Incerta* 4.1, perhaps from Rufus of Ephesus (early second century). On women as

plains, the testicles are a source of heat.[56] Some people concluded that women should follow a drying and warming regime to counteract their constitutional humidity.[57] Both society doctors and magicians retailed drying recipes to prevent unappetizing lubrication during intercourse.[58] An anonymous medical author maintains that women need exercise just as much as men do. He recommends running for girls, promenades and carriage-drives for matrons. Excessive effort is bad for either sex, but women run the particular risk of impairing their menstrual regularity.[59] Athenaeus of Attaleia believed than women should take exercise appropriate to their sex. He recommended housework.[60] Some medical writers recommended vocal exercise for women as therapy for specific conditions. Because of its beneficial effects on the pores, vocal exercise appealed to doctors of the Methodist sect like the second-century Soranus of Ephesus. He usually recommended vocal exercise in conjunction with various forms of gently jiggling exercise like massage, baths, walks, reading aloud, and riding in litters. These activities are beneficial for the appetite disorders of pregnancy, uterine flux, false pregnancy, and for "hysterical suffocation" accompanied by the loss of speech.[61] Wet nurses with lactation problems can also profit from doing vocal exercises.[62] Infants are to take their vocal exercise in the only way they can: by crying.[63]

Whenever medical authors specify the nature of the vocal exercise that they recommend for women (and they do not always do this), we see it distinguished by certain feminizing traits. Soranus, for example, recommends a highly inflected or singsong recitation, precisely the sort of affected execution that Quintilian deplored in men reading aloud.[64] A medical regimen for pregnant women recommends singing and the recitation of lyric poetry as the safest form of exercise.[65] Singing and poetry, as well as vocal exercises, could serve all women as a constitutional correc-

---

"wet," see A. Carson, "Putting Her in Her Place" and A. Hanson, "The Medical Writers' Woman" in *Before Sexuality*, ed. Halperin et al. (Princeton, 1990), 137–143, 317–19.

[56] *On the Seed*, K4.572–74.

[57] Oribasius, *Incerta* 4.2.

[58] Galen K14.485, PDM 970–84 (= H. D. Betz, *The Greek Magical Papyri in Translation* [Chicago, 1986], 243).

[59] Oribasius, *Incerta* 4.4, 6–7.

[60] Oribasius, *Incerta* 5. Athenaeus flourished in the mid-first century. Clement of Alexandria also recommends housework as exercise (*Paidagogos* 3.49,67).

[61] Soranus, *Gyn.* 1.15.49; 1.16.54; 3.11.44; 3.9.38; 3.4.28. An English translation is available by O. Temkin, *Soranus' Gynecology* (Baltimore, 1956, rpt. 1991).

[62] Soranus specifies that midwives should be literate (*Gyn.* 1.1.3), but all that he requires of wet-nurses in this regard is that they should speak Greek (2.12.19, end).

[63] Soranus, *Gyn.* 2.17.39; Rufus in Oribasius, *Incerta* 20.26.

[64] χρῆσθαι . . . ἀναφωνήσεσίν τε καὶ ἀναγνώσεσιν μετὰ πλάσματος, Soranus *Gyn.* 1.15.49; [lectio] non . . . in canticum dissoluta nec plasmata . . . effeminata, Quintilian, *Inst.* 1.8.2.

[65] κάλλιστος δὲ ὁ πόνος καὶ ἀσφαλέστατος ᾠδὴ καὶ μέλος πονεῖν, Oribasius, *Incerta* 6.35, attributed by Oribasius to Galen, but more likely from Rufus.

tive, "for it is my opinion that a woman enjoys the greatest health when she also exercises her voice."⁶⁶ We do not often find song and poetry recommended in the medical writers as therapeutic techniques for men. Antyllus mentions lyric only for the would-be declaimer who cannot manage to recite epic, iambic, or elegiac verses from memory.⁶⁷ Conversely, we never hear of women giving speeches as a form of vocal exercise. Thus it remains likely, though we cannot be certain, that vocal exercise for women consisted of practicing scales and singing or reciting poetry, while vocal exercise for men consisted of practicing scales and delivering speeches.

Girls approaching puberty are in particular danger of the dread *plēsmonē*, a sort of morbid bloat: their growth slows down, but the effects of overeating and inactivity are not yet counteracted by the purging power of the menses.⁶⁸ Exercise can help at this delicate time: running, long walks, gymnastics, and choral song, which is providentially therapeutic. "Choral song appears to have been invented not only for the honor of the god, but also for health. The exertion is double: both in dancing and in song."⁶⁹ While these activities do serve to warm up the flesh, too much activity brings dangers of its own, and girls who exercise must be cautious lest they become too masculine: "It is a good thing to stir up the inner heat and warm the constitution with exertions, but only so far as to remain female, and not to change to a manly-looking appearance."⁷⁰ Here, as in the social construction of the *cinaedus*-role, gender appears to be a continuum on which an individual is not precisely located by anatomical sex alone.

Soranus observes in several places that too much vocal exercise results in loss of menses. To begin with, women who lead an active life menstruate less than indolent women do, and Soranus cites professional vocalists as an example of this tendency.⁷¹ Women who engage in singing contests⁷² sometimes do not menstruate at all, because the excess material in their bodies is forced to move around by their exertions and is thus used up.⁷³

⁶⁶ Oribasius, *Incerta* 4.15 [Rufus?].

⁶⁷ Oribasius, *Incerta* 6.9.3.

⁶⁸ Rufus, *Regimen for Girls* (Oribasius, *Incerta* 2.1). The standard Hippocratic remedy for this condition is early marriage and defloration. For the movement of post-Hippocratic gynecologies toward a concept of women's health independent of reproduction, see A. Hanson, "The Medical Writers' Woman," cited above, n.55, 330–33.

⁶⁹ Ibid 2.12–13.

⁷⁰ ἀνακινεῖν γὰρ τοῖς πόνοις τὸ θερμὸν καὶ τὴν ἕξιν θερμαίνειν συμφέρει, ἀλλὰ ὥστε μένειν θήλειαν, καὶ μὴ ἐξίστασθαι πρὸς τὸ ἀρρενωπόν (ibid 2.15).

⁷¹ αἱ φωνασκοί, Soranus, *Gyn.* 1.4.22.

⁷² Or singing performances at the games? (φωνασκίαι ἀγωνιστικαί).

⁷³ Soranus, *Gyn.* 1.4.23. Aetius derives similar views from Rufus and Aspasia, a woman writer on gynecology about whom nothing is known: "Singers and dancers naturally do not menstruate, because in them there is nothing left [for menstruation], since excessively violent exercise consumes it." This phenomenon is due to heat: "When therefore a woman is hotter than normal, either on account of a natural temperament or on account of excessive exercises, she will be without the menstrual purgations" (Aetius, *Gyn.* 51).

Such failure to menstruate is physiological, rather than pathological, the doctor says, and characteristic of "masculine-looking women and infertile singers and athletes."[74] If a woman desires to conceive and she is infertile because of an athletic life-style or habitually vigorous vocal exercise (*gymnastikē agōgē ē anaphōnēseis eutonoi*), "she should behave more delicately as a corrective for her active mode of life, in order that her body may become more feminine."[75]

While it is possible that ancient female gymnasts sometimes exhibited the amenorrhea that has been reported in twentieth-century athletes and ballet dancers, suppression of the menses has not been reported in opera singers. So either the female vocalists of antiquity were also anorexic athletes, or their reported infertility is a fiction based on *a priori* reasoning. Ancient doctors evidently could imagine the menses as performing in women a function analogous to the function of exercise and physical activity in men. "Nature recognizes that men rid themselves of surplus material through exercise and athletics, whereas women accumulate it in considerable quantity because of the domestic and sedentary life they lead . . . [therefore] she has provided to draw off the surplus through menstruation."[76] In another passage Soranus says that just as physical activity stimulates perspiration and just as vocal utterance stimulates the excretion of saliva, so intercourse facilitates menstruation.[77] Galen explains the anatomical role of the *nymphē* (clitoris), which protects the womb by comparing it to the uvula which protects the pharynx: women's reproductive organs are analogous to the organs of (men's) speech.[78] Analogies made up a large part of explanation in ancient medical theory, and they often tell us less about the physical phenomena that they were designed to elucidate than they reveal about the assumptions doctors felt entitled to use in the elucidation. The analogies we have just been looking at show that menstruation and intercourse were sometimes conceived as the feminine counterparts to masculine speech and physical activity. In small amounts, speech and other forms of exercise can correct disequilibria

[74] ἀνδρώδεις καὶ στεῖραι φωνασκοί τε καὶ γυμναστικαί, Soranus, *Gyn.* 3.1.7.

[75] τρυφερώτερον αὐτὰς ἀκτέον κατ᾽ ἐπίστασιν τοῦ ἐμπράκτου τῆς διαίτης, ἵν᾽ ἀκμὴν θηλύτερα τὰ σώματα γένηται, ibid. 3.1.9.

[76] Ibid. 1.6.27. Soranus is quoting the views of others (compare the Hippocratic *Diseases of Women* 1.1). He himself did not think menstruation was helpful to health, but only necessary for childbearing (1.6.29). Galen, in a discussion of menstruation and venesection, says that women need menstrual purging of surplus matter because they live indoors, do not engage in vigorous activity, and do not expose themselves to the sun. Women, if they are regularly purged by menstruation, never suffer loss of voice (thought to be caused by hysterical suffocation) (K11.165).

[77] Soranus, *Gyn.* 1.7.31.

[78] Galen, *On the Use of the Parts* 15.3. On the homologies between the oral cavity and the womb in Greek medical language, see G. Sissa, "Maidenhood Without Maidenhead," in *Before Sexuality*, 360; and A. Hanson and D. Armstrong, "The Virgin's Voice and Neck," *BICS* 33 (1986), 97–100.

of the female body, but practiced to excess, the doctors warn, they destroy
femininity.

THE ROLE OF THE VOICE IN THE MAINTENANCE
OF GENDER BOUNDARIES

Ambivalent medical views about the role of the voice in women's health
must be situated in the larger ambivalence of long-standing cultural beliefs
about women and speech. A single anecdote should suffice to remind us of
how deeply rooted was the reluctance of a society that prized eloquence
above all other human skills to tolerate any form of public speaking in
women: Pythagoras' wife once accidentally uncovered her arm while out
of doors. When someone exclaimed, "Good-looking arm," she replied,
"Not public property!" The masterful combination of feminine modesty
and feminine brevity in this retort appealed to second-century moralists:
"The arm of a virtuous woman should not be public property, nor her
speech, *and she should as modestly guard against exposing her voice to outsiders as
she would guard against stripping off her clothes.* For in her voice as she's
gabbing can be read her emotions, her character, and her physical condition."[79] Physiognomical exposure through the voice, the theme with
which this chapter began, is especially threatening for women, who must
not be heard lest they be seen.

   The very word that Plutarch selects to characterize a woman speaking is
not the basic Greek word for talking (*legein*), but what linguists would call
a marked form that connotes babble or idle chatter (*lalein*). Plutarch's use
of the marked form in this context points to the possibility that women's
speech and men's speech, in some vital but largely irrecoverable sense,
were felt to be qualitatively *different*. If speech itself is gendered, then the
possibility of confusion of gender boundaries is inherent in any spoken
enterprise. Here follow three examples that highlight the various dangers
of blurring gender boundaries in speech: the masculinization of women,
the feminization of men, and the paradoxical implosion that threatens
when gender roles are reversed.

   Musonius Rufus, the first-century Stoic philosopher, gave discourses
on whether women should receive the same education given to men. He
was well aware of the response that would meet his suggestion that women
should study philosophy; "Some will say it's inevitable that women who
frequent philosophers will become self-willed and brazen, when they give

---

[79] καὶ τὴν φωνὴν ὡς ἀπογύμνωσιν αἰδεῖσθαι καὶ φυλάττεσθαι πρὸς τοὺς ἐκτός· ἐνο-
ρᾶται γὰρ αὐτῇ καὶ πάθος καὶ ἦθος καὶ διάθεσις λαλούσης, Plutarch, *Mor.* 142D; the same
story appears in Clement, *Stromata* 4.522C.

up staying at home and go about in public with men, when they practice declaiming and talk like sophists (*kai meletōsi logous kai sophizōntai*), solving syllogisms while they ought to be sitting at home working their wool."[80] The popular assumption is that practicing a manly style of discourse will inevitably result in a masculine freedom of behavior. Musonius tries to evade this objection by specifying the *content* of the discourses to be delivered by aspiring women philosophers ("to the extent that they practice speaking, they ought to practice speaking about their work"), but his solution rings hollow, since what is "gendered" is not merely the content of verbal performances but the very concept of eloquence itself. This becomes clear in another essay when he considers the question of whether daughters should receive the same education as sons do. He is resolutely egalitarian, insisting on the identity of the moral qualities that should be cultivated in men and women, until it comes to eloquence. There he draws the line: "And I don't mean to imply that verbal acuity and dreadful cleverness are appropriate for women, if they are going to practice philosophy as women—I don't even completely approve such qualities in men."[81]

Women's speech was apparently considered to be different from men's in quality: first, and most obviously, in its higher pitch, but also in the indefinable gestures and mannerisms that accompanied it.[82] For all we know, women's speech may have also differed from men's in noticeable points of vocabulary and idiom. What does Fronto mean when he says that the poet Atta "excelled in women's language"?[83] A woman's voice was even believed to change during menstruation—at least enough to give a spiritually sensitive man an instant headache.[84] That these subtle differences might be considered contagious, we can see from John Chrysostom's response to the asexual cohabitation of men and women devoted to the religious life. In so living, Christians were challenging some of the dearest prejudices of Greco-Roman society, and in repudiating their vision of Christianity, Chrysostom resorted to these very prejudices, articulating with particular vividness beliefs that had been formed by centuries of pagan culture. He finds it highly inappropriate that "a virgin should learn

---

[80] Fr. 3, *That Even Women Should Study Philosophy*. Text and translation by C. Lutz available in *YCS* 10 (1947).

[81] Ibid., fr. 4 (end).

[82] Contemporary spoken English, for example, exhibits sex differences on the level of phonology: women use a wider range of pitches and exhibit more variation in intonation (S. McConnell-Ginet, "Intonation in a Man's World," *Signs* 3 [1978], 541–59). Such intonation in men is stereotyped as effeminate.

[83] *Ad M. Caesar* 4.3.2.

[84] Heraiskos, who could detect the presence of the god in an animated statue by the physiological changes it produced in his body, specialized in detecting female impurity (*Suidas* s.v. Διαγνώμων).

to discuss things frankly with a man." It is not just the virgin who is at risk: the man who spends his time in her society, who sits besides her as she works her wool, may find that "feminine habits and feminine speech wipe themselves off on his soul."[85] Appealing to the immemorial stereotypes of physiognomy, Chrysostom warns that such intercourse makes a man effeminate, like a once-terrifying lion shorn of his proud mane. Intimacy with a woman on equal terms affects both the manner and the matter of his speech: "And if he talks, all he will be able to talk about is weaving and wool, since his tongue has been *discolored* by the quality of women's speech."[86]

Further evidence for a belief that the touch of feminine mannerisms and feminine behavior damages the male power of speech appears in one of Seneca's declamations, "The Man Who was Raped in Women's Clothes," subtitled, "A sexually tainted man should be barred from public speaking."[87] It describes the catastrophic consequences of gender role-reversal. A good-looking young man made a bet that he would go out in public in women's clothes. Out he went, and ten youths raped him. He took them to court and won his case, but then the magistrate prohibited him from speaking in public. The law invoked by the magistrate in this fantasy originated in ancient Greece, but the paradoxes it could produce intrigued Roman schoolboys and their masters; by late antiquity men who had "used their bodies in women's fashion" were indeed prohibited by law from appearing as advocates in any Roman court.[88] By winning the case against his rapists, the youth convicts himself of effeminate behavior. Masculine eloquence avenged the insult he suffered as a woman, but public admission that he played the role of a woman threatened to vitiate his eloquence and destroy his standing as a man. This declamation must have generated multiple ironies in performance, as professional teachers coached their crack-voiced charges to impersonate the transvestite youth, yet for all the risqué charm with which this popular tale permitted the exploration of zones of anxiety, it would also function much like a "myth-

---

[85] ἤθη καὶ ῥήματα γυναικεῖα εἰς τὴν ἑαυτῶν ἐναποματτόμενοι ψυχήν, "Against Those Who Keep Virgins from Outside the Family," PG 47.509.

[86] τῆς γλώττης αὐτοῦ τῇ ποιότητι τῶν γυναικείων ἀναχρωσθείσης ῥημάτων, PG 47.510. The idea that someone's character is damaged when his speech is contaminated by association with unworthy persons also appears in the treatise on child-rearing attributed to Plutarch: the young masters ought to be attended by slaves "of well-turned Hellenic speech, so that they may not be discolored by association (συναναχρωννύμενοι) with foreigners and persons of low character and take on some of their contemptible qualities," Mor. 4A.

[87] Contr. 5.6.

[88] Digest 3.1.6. For the right to practice public speaking in a political context as limited to Athenian citizens who correctly performed their gender role, see J. Winkler, The Constraints of Desire (New York, 1990), 45–70 (= Before Sexuality [Princeton, 1990], 171–209).

as-social-charter" to validate deeply held fears about the reversal of gender roles in speech.

THE LIMITATIONS OF THE "IDEAL" MALE VOICE

Philostratus expressed surprise that Prodicus of Chios had been a success-ful ambassador "even though he was hard to hear and had a very deep voice."[89] Apparently it was possible to have too much of a good thing. The ideal "orderly man" had a low voice according to the physiognomists, but they conceded that it was hollow and lacked carrying power.[90] A voice that was low and hollow might lack flexibility, as in the case of the physi-ognomical paragon who displays "manly greatness of soul."[91] Flexibility, however useful in actual rhetorical performance, was physiognomically suspect. A high-pitched voice that is smooth and flexible reveals the an-drogynos.[92] But even the physiognomists concede that this sort of voice could be pleasant to listen to.[93] Indeed, as medical writers on vocal exercise agreed, there were definite aesthetic advantages to be gained from using a wider range of pitch and a more flexible style of vocalizing than was traditionally permitted to the ideally dignified male voice. Thus it came about that the role of the voice as a boundary of gender was sometimes severely strained by men themselves, who, whether seduced by the fas-cination of role-playing the "other," or purely for dramatic effect, could not resist adopting the falsetto of women, cinaedi, and eunuchs, subgroups they officially despised. This paradox highlights the ambiguity of a cul-tural system that used a secondary sex characteristic like the voice as a mark of gender while at the same time subjecting it to the rigorous cal-listhenics of the askēsis mentality. Since the voice was believed to be subject to alteration, either intentionally by exercise or unintentionally as the

---

[89] καίτοι δυσήκοον καὶ βαρὺ φθεγγόμενος, Lives 496. Plato commented on Prodicus' indistinct low voice (Protagoras 316a).

[90] loquitur gravius, vocem infirmi potius spiritus quam expressam et claram habet quam Graeci τὴν κοιλοστομίαν vocant. (Anon. Lat. 107,2.131F). Quintilian defines the fault of κοιλοστομία thus: cum vox quasi in recessu oris auditur (Inst. 1.5.32). Cf. Philostratus, Life of Apollonius of Tyana 3.38, where βαρὺ φθέγγεται καὶ κοῖλον describes the preternaturally adult voice of a boy possessed by a demon. The emperor Nero's voice is described in the same terms; Nero's fault lies in the way he softens the effect with ingratiating mannerisms and crowd-pleasing modulations (Pseudo-Lucian, Nero 6).

[91] Adam. 2.42,1.405F, ὅσοι δέ κοῖλον καὶ βαρὺ καὶ ἀκαμπὲς ἠχοῦσι, γενναῖα τούτοις τὰ ἤθη.

[92] Ibid. Pitch was not everything: certain kinds of low-pitched voices were simply boor-ish.

[93] cuius vox prope garrula nec ingrata interdum est (Anon. Lat. 98, 2.124F).

result of unwholesome sexual habits, it might be diagnostic of gender difference in various degrees but could never function as a definitive boundary.

The next chapter studies these issues as they are treated in the rhetorical writers and moralists of the age, in an attempt to see how voice training practices that were well-known, if not always widely approved, by elite rhetoricians were refracted in their conceptual schemes. What are the possibilities and dangers that voice training brought to the pursuit of rhetorical excellence as they conceived it? What judgments do we find in Seneca, Quintilian, and Aelius Aristides on the appropriation by males of the high-pitched tones so characteristic of the "singing style" of contemporary rhetoric? This leads us to the anti-Asianist polemic of rhetorical writers (usually couched as an attack on effeminacy of voice and gesture) and the contrast between the crowd-pleasing ululations practiced by the "singing" orators and the more sober style of their serious-minded critics—in short, the contrast between hirsute and depilated rhetoric parodied by Lucian in the *Teacher of Rhetoric*.

Chapter Five

VOICE AND VIRILITY IN RHETORICAL WRITERS

Voice Training and the Roman Orator

"WHICH OF YOUR contemporaries," wrote Seneca to his sons, "—quite apart from his shortcomings in talent and diligence—is sufficiently a man?"[1] Seneca's remark raises a crucial question in oratorical pedagogy: what should be the proper relation between natural endowment, training, and perfected manhood? The correct use of the voice touches on all three of these factors: the voice is the physical instrument through which the orator's natural endowment finds expression, it can be enhanced or corrupted by training, and it also functions as a sign in the symbolic language of masculine identity.

Sometimes Roman rhetorical writers mention vocal exercise explicitly; sometimes they comment in passing on vocal mannerisms that they dislike. I will examine the views of five major figures on voice training and vocal deportment: the author of the *Ad Herennium*, Cicero, the two Senecas, and Quintilian. Any endeavor to make sense of their views must be undertaken in the face of several difficulties. First of all, the authors themselves are ambivalent. Is training the voice a sign of refinement or decadence? Where is the line between manly rigor and effeminate charm? What techniques may the orator appropriate from the stage? It is also difficult to pin down precisely what practices and sound effects an author endorses or condemns. For instance, the Romans lacked a well-developed language for expressing the notion of pitch. Moreover, the terminology of voice training was not standardized: *anaphōnēsis*, *declamatio*, and *exercitatio vocis* are terms that often overlap, without being strictly synonymous. Even a single word, like *declamatio*, does not always have the same meaning in every context. And for most of these terms, with the exception of the descriptions of *anaphōnēsis* in the medical texts surveyed in the previous chapter, we lack a systematic explication of the procedures involved. Vocal exercise was too well known to require explanation when mentioned in passing. Technical manuals have not survived.[2]

---

[1] *Quis aequalium vestrorum quid dicam satis ingeniosus, satis studiosus, immo quis satis vir est?* (*Contr.* 1. preface 9).

[2] Like the φωναοκικὸν βιβλίον of Theodoros: Diogenes Laertius 2.189, cf. *IG* 4.591.

Rhetorical writers, in general, wanted to present themselves as a class apart from voice trainers and consequently veered away from opportunities to present concrete details.[3] Their general statements about the stylistic preferences of their contemporaries are not to be taken at face value either. Because a speaker's vocal deportment was considered diagnostic of his character, the general Roman tendency toward moralizing nostalgia may have inclined Latin writers to represent the current state of rhetoric as more decadent than in fact it was. In a value system that prized rhetorical skill as the quintessential human excellence, and in a society so structured that this perfection could be achieved only by adult males, arbiters of rhetoric were also arbiters of masculine deportment.

The Ad Herennium

As early as 92 B.C.E., a new school of rhetoric that offered instruction exclusively in Latin, with heavy emphasis on voice training and gesture, had occasioned sufficient alarm among traditionalists that it was closed by the censors.[4] The attraction of new techniques was not so easily rooted out, however, and ambitious young Romans continued to resort to voice training. The first discussion of declamatio extant in Latin appears in a treatise of the 80s B.C.E., the Rhetorica ad Herennium. The author of this handbook accepts voice training as a reasonable, even essential, part of the orator's preparations and appears to envision the ideal orator as one who can achieve vocal flexibility without sounding like either a woman or an actor. In his discussion of delivery, he presents a schematic analysis of how training and natural endowment contribute to the size, strength, and flexibility of the orator's voice:

> Vocal size is chiefly the product of nature; careful treatment augments it somewhat but chiefly serves to maintain it. Vocal stability is chiefly the product of careful attention; declamatory exercise augments it somewhat but chiefly serves to maintain it. Vocal flexibility (that is, the ability to moderate our speaking voice at our convenience) must be formed chiefly by declamatory exercise.[5]

---

[3] Aristotle, Poetics 19, 1456b10; Rhetoric 1403b20ff. ("Delivery seems to be a vulgar business."); Dionysius of Halicarnassus, Demosthenes 53.

[4] On the controversial school of Plotius Gallus, see Suetonius, Lives of the Rhetors 2; Seneca, Contr. 2. preface 5; Cicero, De oratore 3.24.93–94. Gallus published a treatise on gesture (Quintilian, Inst. 11.3.143) and was still teaching in the 50s. See S. F. Bonner, Education in Ancient Rome (Berkeley, 1977), 71–73.

[5] Magnitudinem vocis maxime conparat natura; nonnihil auget, sed maxime *conservat adcuratio. Firmitudinem vocis maxime conparat cura; nonnihil adauget, et maxime conservat exercitatio declamationis. Mollitudinem vocis, hoc est ut eam torquere in dicendo nostro commodo possimus, maxime faciet exercitatio declamationis. Rhet. ad Her. 3.11.20. (The asterisk indicates an area of variant readings in the manuscript tradition).

This author does not consider it his province to give instruction in how to care for the voice. We are told to seek such information from "those who are not ignorant of this art." This appears to be a condescending reference to voice trainers,[6] and perhaps also to physicians, who would prescribe vocal chants and regimes of diet and exercise to protect and strengthen the voice. It is important to note that, unlike some later writers, the author of the *ad Herrenium* does not condemn those who resort to voice training. His mission, however, is to discuss the benefits of declamatory exercise, which he considers to be practice in the delivery of complete speeches in which one varies the intensity of one's voice according to the dictates of content and structure. As such, *declamatio* is not an art to be turned over to experts of lower order and remains properly within his own province as a rhetorical educator.

This author's assumptions about the voice as an index of gender show through in his condemnation of high-pitched outbursts: "Shouting at high pitch wounds the voice; it also offends the listener, for it has in it something unbefitting a free man, a quality that is more suited to female screaming than to speech of manly dignity."[7] He does not imply that high-pitched tones damage more than the voice itself. They do not physically feminize the speaker, but, by the merest hint of the presence of some feminine quality, they impair the virility of his self-presentation in the eyes of others. On the other hand, he appreciates the expressive possibilities of a low voice and recommends the deepest possible chest tones to enhance the staccato utterances of "broken debate" and, at lower volume, passages of pathetic amplification. But we must beware, the author cautions, of crossing the invisible line that divides oratory from acting: "To achieve dignity in the conversational style of speech, it is appropriate to produce from a full throat the calmest tone possible at the lowest possible pitch, as long as we do not pass from the behavioral norms of oratory to those of tragedy."[8] In deportment and gesture, we should show the same reserve, avoiding extremes both of elegance and vulgarity, "lest we give the impression that we are either actors or manual laborers."[9]

Cicero

Cicero too requires that students of oratory should not imitate the methods of actors by applying themselves to the study of gesture: "But all

---

[6] The concept of *phonaskia*, like the verb, is known from the fourth century B.C.E., but *phonaskos* as a professional title is not attested before the first century C.E. (J. Schmidt, *RE* 20A (1941), 522–26; E. Fantham, "Quintilian on Performance," *Phoenix* 36 (1982), 257n.43.)

[7] *Acuta exclamatio vocem vulnerat; eadem laedit auditorem, habet enim quiddam inliberale et ad muliebrem potius vociferationem quam ad virilem dignitatem in dicendo adcommodatum.* (*Rhet. ad Her.* 3.12.22).

[8] Ibid. 3.14.24.

[9] Ibid. 3.15.26.

the same, let no one recommend to young students of rhetoric that they learn gesture by practicing like actors."[10] The same goes for voice training. Although in one passage he presents vocal exercise the way the author of the *Ad Herennium* does, as something acceptable, even recommended (though not somehow a seemly subject for discussion in a rhetorical handbook),[11] at other times he is more explicitly contemptuous of an art that he perceives to be a by-product of the stage:

> What is more essential for an orator than his voice? Nonetheless, no one who aspires to eloquence will, on my advice, become a slave to his voice, the way Greek actors do, who for years at a time practice declamation sitting down, and who daily, before they speak in public, gradually warm up the voice while lying in bed, and then, after performing, sit down and take their voices from the highest notes back down to the lowest and so in some fashion or other recuperate. If *we* did that, our clients would lose their cases before we had recited our paean or chant the prescribed number of times (*De oratore* 1.59.251).

Fortunately, Cicero's penchant for satirical description has led him into giving away details of the practices he rejects. Some exercises were performed lying down (one thinks of Nero, who placed a sheet of lead on his chest to enhance the effectiveness of this maneuver).[12] Others involved intoning scales in a sitting position. And, in spite of a textual corruption,[13] it seems clear that some forms of vocal exercise involved the chanting of a metrical text. This form of *declamatio* corresponds to the practice of *anaphōnēsis* as described by Antyllus. Of course, Cicero attributes these practices to Greek tragic actors, but the context implies clearly that rhetoricians have been resorting to them as well.

One could base one's objections to orators' use of actors' techniques on a high-minded Platonic distinction: orators, who engage in "the real thing," have no business learning their technique from actors, who are only engaged in mimesis.[14] Or one could resort to *ad hominem* arguments about the morals of the stage. But where later authors stress the effeminacy of the actor, Cicero merely emphasizes the comparative manliness of the orator.

[10] *Tamen nemo suaserit studiosis dicendi adulescentibus, in gestu discendo histrionum more elaborare.* (*De oratore* 1.59.251). I am assuming that all the speakers are mouthpieces for Cicero.

[11] *De oratore* 3.60.224: *vox . . . quae primum est optanda nobis, deinde quaecumque erit ea tuenda. De quo illud iam nihil ad hoc praecipiendi genus quemadmodum voci serviatur, equidem tamen magnopere censeo serviendum.*

[12] Suetonius, *Nero* 20: *et ipse meditari exercerique coepit neque eorum quicquam omittere, quae generis eius artifices vel conservandae vocis causa vel augendae factitarent; sed et plumbeam chartam supinus pectore sustinere.*

[13] It is not clear exactly what word was originally paired with *paean*. Some conjecture *hymnum*. I have translated the corrupt word as "chant."

[14] *De oratore* 3.56.214.

In his discussion of gesture, he recommends a virile posture that is emphatically not a product of the theater.[15] As he later wrote in the *Orator* (18.59):

> The first-class orator will use gesture, but never to excess, his posture will be erect and elevated. . . . There will be no unmanly softness in the neck, and the fingers should not make delicate gestures or move in time to the rhythm. He will instead regulate himself with his entire torso, by the vigorous and manly modulation of his upper body (*trunco magis toto se ipse moderans et virili laterum flexione*).

Cicero does seem to regard the orator as a paradigm of masculine deportment, but he does not present his ideal as being under severe stress from any widespread counter-paradigm of effeminate behavior. We know that Cicero himself was criticized by Calvus for being "limp and enervated" (*solutus et enervis*) and by Brutus as "emasculated and loose in the loins" (*fractus atque elumbis*).[16] So Cicero's own standards may not have been very exacting in these matters, and as someone who wanted to escape the accusation of "Asianism" by enlarging the "Atticist" position to include himself, he may not have been in a position to make an issue of effeminate styles in oratory.

When Cicero discusses deportment in the *De officiis*, he exhorts us to avoid both "effeminacy" and "boorishness" in "standing, walking, sitting, reclining, and in the motions of our face, eyes, and hands,"[17] but he does not caution us against effeminate use of the voice. The pitch at which orators spoke does not seem to have been a particularly vexed subject for Cicero. His own youthful difficulties with vocal production he ascribes to lack of variety and excessive tension (*contentio vocis*).[18] Plutarch interprets this to mean that he spoke at too high a pitch;[19] indeed it appears that Cicero thought of pitch and intensity as rising and falling together. He recommends that speakers vary the pitch and the intensity of their discourse[20] but does not evince any hostility to high notes per se. Such

[15] *laterum inflexione hac forti ac virili non ab scena et histrionibus sed ab armis aut etiam a palaestra* . . . (*De oratore* 3.59.220). In his discussion of deportment in *De officiis* (1.130), he cautions against both *palaestrici motus* and *histrionum gestus*.

[16] Tacitus, *Dialogus* 18.5. We are assured by the speaker that these were Brutus' very words. This use of *elumbis* is not paralleled elsewhere, but the point of the insult probably is that a person with a dislocated hip walks with a swaying, stereotypically effeminate gait (cf. [Aristotle] [*Phys.*] 808a *s.v.* Κιναίδου σημεῖα: περινεύοντος . . . τὴν ὀσφύν). Cicero was criticized by his contemporaries for being, among other things, *Asianus, in conpositione fractus*, and *paene viro mollior* (Quintilian, *Inst.* 12.10.12).

[17] *status incessus, sessio accubitio, vultus oculi manuum motus teneat illud decorum. Quibus in rebus duo maxime sunt fugienda, ne quid effeminatum aut molle et ne quid durum aut rusticum sit* (*De officiis* 1.128–29).

[18] *Brutus* 313–14.

[19] *Life of Cicero* 3.

[20] *De oratore* 3.61.227.

variation, he claims, is pleasant to listen to and preserves the strength of the voice. Indeed, when he tries to imagine how the contemporaries of Demosthenes would have received the singsong perorations of an "Asianist" orator, he does not ridicule such performances for being high-pitched but characterizes their drooping ululations as *inclinata*, the very word that he uses elsewhere to describe the dignity conveyed by a low-pitched voice.[21] Quite probably what Cicero disliked was excessive variation in vocal pitch, rather than high notes in themselves. When writing on this subject, he sometimes uses the terms *inclinata vox* or *inclinatio vocis* to mean "lowered voice" and sometimes to mean a voice that noticeably rises and falls in pitch.[22] For instance, he commends with these words the dignified oratorical demeanor of Crassus: "Not much flinging the body about, no vocal swerves, no pacing up and down."[23] What mattered was the absence of flamboyant variation.

In two passages where Cicero discusses singing in the theater without comparing it to oratory, he makes it clear that he disapproves of vocal gyrations as unmanly and degenerate. "How much more effeminate and luxurious are trills and runs and falsetto notes in singing than plain notes firmly held!"[24] Indeed, when this kind of elaboration is practiced to excess, not only persons of good taste but even the masses begin to protest. In the *De legibus* he observes that the original musical numbers from the plays of Livius and Naevius are no longer performed with old-fashioned "pleasing austerity" (*severitas iucunda*): "Now they *ululate* them, twisting their necks and rolling their eyes in time to the music."[25] While he clearly harbors qualms about certain vocal techniques, what is absent in Cicero is any impassioned concern that the excesses of the stage are infecting rhetorical practice.

The Elder Seneca

In the first century C.E., when the elder Seneca commented to his sons on the lassitude of their contemporaries, he embedded his speculations on the

[21] *Orator* 17.57: *inclinata [voce] videri gravis*; ibid 8. 27: *inclinata ululantique voce more Asiatico canere*.

[22] The *Oxford Latin Dictionary* (ed. P. G. W. Glare, Oxford/New York: Oxford University Press, 1982) does not make this distinction, taking *inclinata vox/inclinatio vocis* in all these passages to mean "lowered voice."

[23] *Non multa iactatio corporis, non inclinatio vocis, nulla inambulatio* (*Brutus* 43.158).

[24] *Quanto molliores sunt et delicatiores in cantu flexiones et falsae voculae quam certae et severae!* (*De oratore* 3.25.98). If *falsae voculae* are falsetto notes, then Cicero is complaining about high pitch as well as *coloratura* gymnastics: A. S. Wilkins, *M. Tullius Cicero De Oratore* (Oxford, 1892), 461.

[25] *nunc fit ut eadem exululent, cum cervices oculosque pariter cum modorum flexionibus torqueant* (*De legibus* 2.15.39).

decline of rhetoric in the context of a generalized lament for the decadence of the age.[26] In this invective we can see a hardening of attitudes toward effeminate mannerisms in voice, dress, hair-style, and bodily movement. Small wonder, Seneca claims, that rhetoric has retrogressed. The young men of today are too indolent to study anything properly. Instead they devote their attention to dancing and singing, activities that impair, rather than develop, their masculine dignity. They enhance their degradation by curling their hair and deliberately weaken their voices to imitate the ingratiating accents of female speech. They compete with women in bodily softness and sexual passivity, decking themselves out with refinements that are positively unclean. Such is the specimen youth of our age.[27] Those who are born soft and limp (*emolliti enervesque*) and then do nothing but depilate themselves will never fit Cato's picture of an orator: "Now go and try to find orators among those plucked and polished types, men only in their lust."[28] At once both smooth-skinned and libidinous, the young rhetoricians of Seneca's imagination represent a monstrous hybrid of feminine and masculine qualities. He does not, in this passage, attribute their decadence to a depraved manner of speech. Rather, it is the other way round: depraved speech is both a sign and a consequence of corrupted morals.

In a milder mood, he admits that as a youth his own taste ran to effeminate rhythms. He and his friends used to memorize reams of decadent bombast by the declaimer Fuscus. Then they would sing his flourishes aloud with idiosyncratic modulations.[29] Before quoting some of these passages to his sons, he says, "Their overrefinement and effeminate rhythm (*fracta conpositio*) may offend you when you reach my age. Meanwhile I am sure that you will be delighted by those very vices that will offend you later on."[30] Fuscus' style apparently exemplified "Asianist" excesses, though Seneca does not explicitly use that term.[31] It is noteworthy that he chose a sexual rather than an ethnic or geographical stereotype to characterize the traits he disliked.

[26] Cf. *Contr.* 2. preface 2 and *Suasoriae* 6.9 (*insectatio temporum*). The *convicium saeculi* was itself a set piece: J. Fairweather, *Seneca the Elder* (Cambridge, 1981), 20; G. Kennedy, *The Art of Rhetoric in the Roman World* (Princeton, 1972), 446–64.

[27] *cantandi saltandique obscena studia effeminatos tenent, et capillum frangere et ad muliebres blanditias extenuare vocem, mollitia corporis certare cum feminis et inmundissimis se excolere munditiis nostrorum adulescentium specimen est* (*Contr.* 1. preface 8–9).

[28] *Ite nunc et in istis vulsis atque expolitis et nusquam nisi in libidine viris quaerite oratores* (*Contr.* 1. preface 10).

[29] *Recolo nihil fuisse me iuvene tam notum quam has explicationes Fusci, quas nemo nostrum non alius alia inclinatione vocis velut sua quisque modulatione cantabat* (*Suasoriae* 2.10).

[30] Ibid. 2.23.

[31] J. Fairweather, *Seneca the Elder* (Cambridge, 1981), 246–51, cf. 200–201. This book takes a minimalist view of the Asianist-Atticist controversy, whose importance tends to be overstated in classic works such as E. Norden's *Die Antike Kunstprosa* (Stuttgart, 1958).

Although Seneca denigrates effeminate performance practices, he does not associate them specifically with vocal exercise. Voice-training techniques are known to him, but he makes no derogatory remarks about them; he has evidently rationalized vocal exercise as medically necessary. This move may help to explain the "culture of hypochondria" that scholars sometimes deplore in the high empire: medical attentions paid to one's body became in this period a socially acceptable way for a man to "give in to softness" without exposing himself to the charge of effeminacy. Yet we can see that Seneca is not entirely comfortable with this rationalization—he goes out of his way to show how his paradigmatic orator, Latro, made no use of *anaphōnēsis* at all. Latro's voice was strong but unattractive; its huskiness was the result of no natural defect but of hard work and a refusal to pamper it.[32] Latro took no pains with vocal exercises: his rough-hewn provincial manliness would not put up with learning them. He refused to take his voice through gradually ascending and descending exercises; he would never pause to disperse the sweat of his labors with a therapeutic massage or recruit the strength of his lungs with healthful walks.[33] Indeed, he paid so little heed to the cautious precepts of medical wisdom that he would sometimes work through the night and eat before declaiming![34] As we learned in the previous chapter, this is a very dangerous thing to do. Celsus, for example, counseled scholars against working immediately after the evening meal.[35] Seneca, aware of these facts, can hardly suppress his consternation at the risks his hero habitually took. No one could dissuade him from working after his evening meal, and the by-products of his disturbed digestion were driven by his nocturnal efforts to his head, there to impair his eyesight and discolor his complexion.

Thus in Latro's time the prescriptions and prohibitions of vocal exercise were well enough known that one could make an impression by disregarding them. Seneca seems to be favorably impressed by his hero's toughminded refusal to sing scales, though he admits that, as a result, his voice was not all it might have been. But while it seemed to Seneca in some way admirable to refuse to embellish the voice, he was clearly shocked by Latro's refusal to take elementary precautions to protect it. He interprets the claims of precautionary measures in the light of physiological theory,

---

[32] *vox . . . lucubrationibus et neglegentia, non natura infuscata.* (*Contr.* 1. preface 16).

[33] *Nulla umquam illi cura vocis exercendae fuit; illum fortem et agrestem et Hispanae consuetudinis morem non poterat dediscere; . . . nihil vocis causa facere, non illam per gradus paulatim ab imo ad summum perducere, non rursus a summa contentione paribus intervallis descendere, non sudorem unctione discutere, non latus ambulatione reparare* (*Contr.* 1. preface 16).

[34] *Contr.* 1. preface 17. Aristotle knew that it spoils the voice to exercise it after meals: "all those who practice voice production, such as actors and chorus members and so forth, practice their exercises in the morning on an empty stomach" (*Problems* 11.22).

[35] *De Medicina* 1.2.5. Cf. Cicero, *De oratore* 1.115; Quintilian, *Inst.* 11.3.26.

much as the second-century Greek doctors do, but he does not seem to endorse any further claims that vocal exercise can actually improve one's constitution.

The Younger Seneca

A generation later, we find that Seneca the Younger has been well trained by his father. He disapproves of exercise performed to embellish the voice, but he takes it for granted that vocal exercises belong in the standard medical regimen for convalescents and is willing to grant that *intentio vocis* has its place in a scholar's physical fitness program. Yet he worries that valetudinarianism can be carried to ungentlemanly extremes. Physical exercise of the time-consuming and body-building sort is inappropriate for educated persons. Exercising the biceps, building up the neck, and strengthening the torso is a foolish occupation, hardly befitting an educated man.[36] Devotion to this sort of physical culture entails a degrading submission to instruction from slaves and provokes a hearty appetite for food, whose abundant consumption dulls the acuity (*subtilitas*) of the spirit. As flesh expands, it stifles the soul, and the effort one must expend to build such muscle exhausts the spirit and leaves it unfit for intellectually demanding work. Less elaborate exercises (running, jumping, and swinging hand weights) appeal to Seneca because they take little time and presumably require no servile supervision. In a series of zigzags, he counsels us to return as quickly as possible from the body to the mind, but not to bury ourselves forever in our books; the mind needs a break, but it should be relaxed rather than made lax. He concludes by recommending passive exercise: riding about in a litter jiggles the body without interfering with our ability to read, converse, or give dictation![37]

It is in this context that Seneca brings up vocal exercise: "Nor need you scorn to exercise your voice, though I forbid you to raise it by measured degrees and then lower it again. What if you should next propose to take lessons in walking!"[38] This advice is at best ambiguous. What is it that Seneca objects to about practicing scales? Voice is clearly associated in his mind with gait. They are both aspects of a man's behavior that affect other people's assessment of him: variables in his self-presentation, as it were, but variables that a man should be ashamed to be found cultivating. Social snobbery plays a part here: Seneca objects to a new breed of professionals, "spurred by insolvency to invent novel techniques." Let a *phonascus* in your life and soon you will have another such person to regulate your steps and

[36] *Letters* 15.2.
[37] Ibid. 15.6. *Gestatio* is the equivalent of αἰώρα.
[38] *Nec tu intentionem vocis contempseris, quam veto te per gradus et certos modos extollere, deinde deprimere. Quid si velis deinde quemadmodum ambules discere?* (*Letters* 15.7).

guide each spoonful to your mouth, a person whose audacity will know only the limits that your patience and credulity supply. Hence, according to Seneca's prejudices, any kind of vocal exercise complicated enough to require a trainer is socially degrading and therefore unacceptable.

Since he forbids practicing scales, it is difficult to determine just what sort of vocal exercise Seneca deems acceptable. He imagines his readers objecting that if we are not allowed to warm up with scales, we will be obliged to plunge into impassioned speech without any preparation. Seneca suggests that we avoid this problem by varying the intensity of our discourse while keeping the transitions gradual. He does not specify whether this technique is to be practiced separately as a warm-up exercise or whether it is to govern the declamatory performance itself. He sums up sound practice with an epigram: we should not act to exercise the voice but instead try to get the voice to exercise us.[39]

Seneca has no ambivalence about exercise performed as part of a medical regimen, as we see from a letter he composed for a sick friend:

> The doctor will advise you how much to walk and how much to exercise so that the inactivity imposed by ill health does not degenerate into idle indulgence. He will tell you to read in a louder voice and exercise your breath through the activity of its passages and cavities. He will tell you to take boat rides to stimulate your flesh with gentle vibration. He will prescribe what foods you are to eat, and when you should drink wine to recruit your strength and when you should abstain to spare your cough.[40]

Here we find vocal exercise in what Seneca would consider its rightful place, amid the physical activities, dietary restrictions, and mental diversions that doctors of the period recommended as restorative therapy.

On the question of performance practice, Seneca did not hesitate to "read" the misuse and excessive embellishment of the voice as a sign of moral degeneration. "And so wherever you find that decadent rhetoric is popular, there, without a doubt, mores have also degenerated from what they should be."[41] He deplores the introduction into rhetorical performance of vocal mannerisms derived from singing and the stage. The style of today is "broken" (*infracta*) and "modulated like a song" (*in morem cantici ducta*). Here, as elsewhere in Latin rhetorical criticism, the words *fracta* and *infracta* connote effeminacy through a kind of semantic double-determination. Words or voices that are "broken" are weak, and therefore feminine; rhythms that are "broken" (in Greek, *keklasmenoi*) soil the dignity of prose with the unmanly ethos of certain lyric meters.[42]

[39] *Non enim id agimus, ut exerceatur vox, sed ut exerceat* (*Letters* 15.8).
[40] Ibid. 78.5.
[41] Ibid. 114.11.
[42] See, for example, Demetrius, *De elocutione* 198.

Like a physiognomist, Seneca eagerly scans his subject's grooming and deportment for signs of rot. He associates gait with speech as indicators of corrupt mores. A man's stride reveals the condition of his soul: "Don't you see how a man whose spirit lacks vigor will drag his limbs and move his feet sluggishly? How an effeminate man will reveal his softness in his very step? How an energetic and aggressive man will speed up his pace?" (*Letters* 114.3) Maecenas was a case in point: his life-style was notorious, his very walk proclaimed him a *delicatus*. Speech and clothing mirrored the same fault: "Was not his speech as loose as he?"[43] Effeminacy, like irascibility and excitability, reveals itself through the voice.[44] Seneca associates hair with speech as an index of character and virility: after describing the voice of the effeminate man, he goes right on to say, "You can see this example being followed by people who remove or thin their beards, who trim the mustache closely or shave it off." It seems natural to him to use hair as a metaphor for speech. When characterizing the contrast between those who strive for ornate diction and those who affect archaic simplicity, he writes, "The former depilate even the leg, the latter not even the armpit."[45]

The same train of association can be seen at work in a philosophical essay when he passes straight from an elaborate satire on the self-conscious hairstyles of his contemporaries to an indictment of their passion for singing with unmanly inflections: "How incensed they become if the barber gets careless, as if he were trimming a real man! . . . And what about those who spend all their time composing songs, listening to them, and learning them, while they twist the voice, whose proper course was designed by Nature to be perfectly simple, into the most slothful modulations."[46] The association between hair, voice, and virility at work in these passages is not merely a product of Seneca's unconscious mind; the physiognomical texts have shown us that these variables in a man's deportment were widely scrutinized as clues to the extent of his gender conformity or gender deviance.

Quintilian

Quintilian's views on voice-training are intensely ambivalent; his views on vocal propriety are shot through with gender consciousness. What he does like is manly; what he does not like is effeminate. Metaphors of

---

[43] *Non oratio eius aeque soluta est quam ipse discinctus?* (*Letters* 114.4).

[44] *Iracundi hominis iracunda oratio est, commoti nimis incitata, delicati tenera et fluxa* (ibid. 114.20).

[45] Ibid. 114.14. Cf. ibid. 56.2 and Juvenal 11.157.

[46] *dum vocem, cuius rectum cursum natura et optimum et simplicissimum fecit, in flexus modulationis inertissimae torquent.* (Seneca, "On the Brevity of Life," 12.3–4).

masculinity express his preferences in speech. We must turn to the poets of antiquity, he says, for that manliness of style (*virilitas*) that the language of the present day has lost.[47] Similarly, he compares an inappropriate match of style and content to a reversal of sex roles. "It is as if men deformed themselves by wearing necklaces, pearls, and long flowing robes, which are feminine adornments, or as if triumphal garments (than which nothing more distinguished can be imagined) should sit becomingly on women!"[48] In his discussion of preparatory studies for boys, he is quite concerned that they should learn to read poetry aloud in the proper way. Above all, their reading must be manly (*virilis*), dignified (*gravis*), but—ambivalence again—not without a certain charm (*cum suavitate quadam*). Of course, poetry should sound different from prose, "but [he zigzags] this should not justify dissolving into singsong or effeminate modulations, as so many people do."[49]

The preservation of manliness requires certain precautions. Adolescence is a tender time and, in Quintilian's view, the boy's body is vulnerable because it is moist. Tumescent with the fluids of new growth, the adolescent who uses his voice improperly may damage it.[50] If a boy must declaim an exclamatory passage loudly, he should be sure to use a chest voice rather than strain his voice with head tones.[51] There is a danger that any expressive or dramatic use of the voice may bring the young rhetorician uncomfortably close to the less respectable performing arts, and since dignity is an essential component of Roman manliness, blurring these boundaries presents a hazard to the development of proper gender identity. In passages of poetry requiring the impersonation of character through direct speech (*prosopopoeia*), the student should avoid sounding like an actor, although, as Quintilian concedes, a certain amount of vocal inflection is required at least to indicate that the poet is no longer speaking in his own person.[52] We may surmise, from Quintilian's later strictures against "singing" during passages of prosopopeia in declamations,[53] that it was precisely the tendency of such passages to become dramatic monologues that enticed declaimers to borrow unsuitable arts from the stage.

Quintilian's awareness that "it is by raising, lowering, and inflecting the voice that the orator stirs the emotions of his audience"[54] leaves him in the

---

[47] *Inst.* 1.8.9.

[48] Ibid. 11.1.3: *Ut monilibus et margaritis ac veste longa, quae sunt ornamenta feminarum, deformentur viri, nec habitus triumphalis, quo nihil excogitari potest augustius, feminas deceat.*

[49] Ibid. 1.8.2: *non tamen in canticum dissoluta nec plasmata, ut nunc a plerisque fit, effeminata.*

[50] Ibid. 11.3.28.

[51] Ibid. 1.11.8: *Curabit . . . ut, quotiens exclamandum erit, lateris conatus sit ille non capitis.*

[52] Ibid. 1.8.3: *Nec prosopopoeias, ut quibusdam placet, ad comicum morem pronuntiari velim; esse tamen flexum quendam, quo distinguantur ab iis, in quibus poeta persona sua utetur.*

[53] Ibid. 11.1.56.

[54] Ibid. 1.10.25: *Atqui in orando quoque intentio vocis, remissio, flexus pertinet ad movendos audientium adfectus.*

grip of conflicting impulses about the prospective orator's musical training. He supports his claim that musical training is of value to the orator by
citing the famous example of Gaius Gracchus and his pitch pipe, and he
seeks to soothe the doubts of philistines ("persons of a thicker Muse") with
the example of Chiron and Achilles.[55] But he hastens to add that the sort of
music he is recommending is *not* "that effeminate sort now found upon the
stage, emasculated by deviant melodies, which has in no small part excised
what manly vigor we still possess."[56]

Real men should sing the praises of the brave. They should learn the
principles of music, not the practice of the psaltry. Such stringed instru-
ments are "not even suitable for chaste girls." A general knowledge of
music is enough: "I would not have him compose music himself nor learn
to read musical notation . . . nor be a finished actor in elocution nor a
dancer in his gesture."[57]

The question of the extent to which a proper orator should avail himself
of the methods of professionals arises with actors as well as musicians.[58]
According to Quintilian, the future orator should apply to the actor for
knowledge of general principles (*pronuntiandi scientiam*), not specific techniques. "For I do not wish the boy whom we are training to be an orator to
be broken (*frangi*) by the thinness of a woman's voice or to tremble with
the tremor of old age."[59] The implication is that young boys will compromise their developing masculinity if they learn, like actors, to imitate the
voices of women or effete old men. Of course they will also compromise
their dignity if they learn to imitate drunkards and slaves, but Quintilian
mentions women and old men first because they present a more serious
problem of social differentiation: how can the *puer*, whose voice is still
high-pitched and thin, make himself sound different from those whose
femininity or decrepitude is the antithesis of the manhood he is in training
to achieve? We may suspect that these matters of deportment took on a
special urgency in upper-class Roman society, not merely for reasons of
social snobbery, but because the task of achieving a masculine gender
identity appears to be particularly difficult for children who spend their
earliest years without much contact with their fathers. Boys in this situation tend to identify with their father's position: his masculine role, pre-

---

[55] Ibid. 1.10.28–30.

[56] Ibid. 1.10.31: *Non hanc a me praecepi, quae nunc in scenis effeminata et impudicis modis fracta
non ex parte minima, si quid in nobis virilis roboris manebat, excidit.*

[57] Ibid. 1.12.14.

[58] Roman orators familiar with Greek models would remember how Demosthenes dis-
paraged Aeschines, who had been a tragic actor, for his φωνασκία (*On the Crown* 280, 308;
On the False Embassy 255, 336).

[59] *Inst.* 1.11.1: *Non enim puerum, quem in hoc instituimus, aut feminae vocis exilitate frangi volo
aut seniliter tremere.*

rogatives, and status, rather than with his personality. Such children often come to define their masculinity "largely in negative terms, as that which is not feminine or involved with women. . . . [The child] does this by repressing whatever he takes to be feminine inside himself, and . . . by denigrating and devaluing whatever he considers to be feminine in the outside world."[60]

Without crudely asserting that child psychology is a trans-historical constant, and bearing in mind that the process of developing a gender identity is in many ways culturally specific, we can use modern theories of gender development to inform our speculation about the importance of masculine mannerisms in voice and movement to upper-class Roman boys who needed to set themselves apart from the feminine and servile models of their early childhood. At the age of seven, when the sons of farmers and artisans would be beginning to assist their fathers in productive work, the boy destined for the forum would begin the tedious years of preparation necessary to obtain the proficiency in public speaking that was the prerogative and responsibility of his sex and social class. The voice changes of puberty must have served as welcome confirmation that a long apprenticeship was bearing fruit.

The task that Quintilian has set himself, then, is nothing less than that of turning boys into men. In this context there are no trivial decisions; every choice is freighted with significance. The future orator must gesticulate, for example, but it is not enough to worry about how he does so; it is also critical to establish *from whom* he should seem to have learned his gestures. Just as one should exercise caution in using theatrical techniques with the voice, so one "should not look to actors for every gesture and movement."[61] The trick is to learn from actors without seeming to have done so. "For if the orator has any art in these matters, its chief object is to seem to be no art at all."[62] We might think here of Hortensius, whose delivery was so graceful that famous actors imitated *him*.[63]

Quintilian's attitude exemplifies a certain Roman squeamishness toward Greek culture and the arts in general. His caution about the role of dance and gymnastics in education is typical. He concedes that some training in movement is essential, "so that the arms may be extended in the proper manner, that the gestures of the hands be free from all rusticity and inelegance, that the posture seem not unconventional, that the feet betray no inexperience, and that the head and eyes not wander out of alignment

---

[60] N. Chodorow, "Family Structure and Feminine Personality," in *Women, Culture, and Society*, ed. M. Rosaldo and L. Lamphere (Stanford, 1974), 49–51.

[61] *Inst.* 1.11.3. Cf. 11.3.181: *Non enim comoedum esse, sed oratorem volo.*

[62] Ibid. 1.11.3.

[63] *Ludicrae artis peritissimos viros illo causas agente, in corona frequenter adstitisse, ut foro peritos gestus in scaenam referrent*, Valerius Maximus 8.10.2.

with the rest of the body."[64] To support his contention that a little deliberate training is an acceptable way to develop these desirable qualities of masculine deportment, Quintilian cites a long list of respectable Greek authorities, from the Homeric heroes to Chrysippus, recalling the war dances of the Spartans and the priestly dances of the ancient Romans, and concluding with Cicero's somewhat grudging endorsement: "Let the orator carry himself with a vigorous and manly posture of the upper body that derives not from actors and the stage but from the army or even the wrestling-grounds."[65] Yet Quintilian is quick to point out that he would prefer young Romans to stop their dance exercises before they reach adolescence; indeed, they should not spend too much time on them even during childhood:

> For I do not want the gestures of the orator to be composed in imitation of a dancer's gestures, but rather that such boyish exercises continue to exert a certain influence, and that something of the grace that we acquired from practicing them should attend us in later life without our having any awareness of the fact (*unde nos . . . furtim decor ille discentibus traditus prosequatur*).[66]

The juxtaposition *furtim decor* epitomizes Quintilian's gingerly embrace of artistic techniques in the service of oratory. His insistence that technique should not seem studied is the result of an uncomfortable paradox: if others are supposed to judge a person's manliness from his deportment, that deportment must appear to be innate, not studied, lest the gender identity it represents be revealed as a social construct.

When he comes to discuss the style of delivery that is to result from of all these preparatory studies, Quintilian catalogs various offensive mannerisms of the voice. Worst of them all is the "singing" style: "I would more willingly tolerate any of these shortcomings than that which is now most popular in courts and schools alike, the habit of *singing*. Whether it is more useless or disgusting I cannot bring myself to decide. For what less becomes an orator than modulations that recall the stage—or even the indecencies of a drunken revel?"[67] He admits that such displays find a ready audience with those "who, among their other vices, will be led anywhere by their passion to hear sounds that soothe their ears."[68] The implication that fondness for the sung style is an outgrowth of moral depravity is a more general form of Quintilian's attempt to discredit such practices by associating them with effeminacy. "And if such singing is to be accepted at

[64] *Inst.* 1.11.16.
[65] Ibid. 1.11.18, quoting *De oratore* 3.59.220.
[66] Ibid. 1.11.19.
[67] Ibid. 11.3.57. Compare his description of exaggerated delivery in 4.2.39: *et vocem flectunt et cervicem reponunt.*
[68] Ibid. 11.3.60.

all, there is no reason why we should not assist such modulations of the voice with lyres and flutes—or even with cymbals, for heaven's sake, since they are more appropriate to the deformity in question."[69] Since the only men who sang in public to the accompaniment of cymbals were the eunuch priests of *Magna Mater*, Quintilian's image is designed to evoke effeminacy.

A similar passage in Book Nine makes a more explicit connection between musical accompaniment and effeminacy: "I would rather have the rhythm of my prose be harsh and rough than effeminate and nerveless, as it is in so many writers, particularly those of today, lilting along lewdly as if to the beat of castanets."[70] Quintilian alleges that "singing" one's speeches is easier than delivering them properly. A weak voice forces an orator "to drop his voice, change its pitch, and refresh his hoarse throat and weary lungs with a hideous singing (*deformi cantico*)."[71] Despite his awareness of these pitfalls, Quintilian concedes that *something* like singing has its place in oratory. Buttressing himself with a quotation from Cicero, he gives his tentative blessing to some forms of *flexus* and *cantus*, provided, of course, that they remain discreet (*obscurior*).[72]

In recommending that the orator polish his delivery with the tools of art, Quintilian has to be cautious. We see what he is up against when we read:

> Yet there are still some who think that the unpolished sort of delivery, in which the speaker follows the impulses of his mind, is more powerful and the only sort of delivery worthy of a man (*actionem iudicent fortiorem et solam viris dignam*). But in general these are none other than the people who disapprove of all training (*cura*), art, and polish in speaking and decry whatever is produced by study on the grounds that it is affected and unnatural, or who affect to imitate antiquity in their choice of words and in the archaic roughness of their pronunciation (*Inst.* 11.3.10).

This sort of rough-hewn purism may never have claimed large numbers of adherents but would have exerted its influence as an ideal, poised against the alleged excesses of highly polished, singsong rhetoric in a battle of the extremes that put the middle on the defensive.

Quintilian asserts that the good qualities of the voice are damaged by neglect and improved by *cura*. But what sort of *cura* is acceptable for an

---

[69] Ibid. 11.3.59.

[70] Ibid. 9.4.142: *Duram potius atque asperam compositionem malim esse quam effeminatam et enervem, qualis apud multos et cotidie magis lascivissimis syntonorum modis saltat.* The translation of *syntonorum* as "castanets" is conjectural.

[71] Ibid. 11.3.60; 11.3.13.

[72] Ibid. 11.3.60. Cf. Cicero, *Orator* 18.57.

orator? Quintilian's strategy is to start out dissociating himself from professional vocalists like the *phonasci*.[73] But he immediately backtracks to
qualify his stance: orators and voice trainers do have much in common.
Both aspire to the physical stamina (*firmitas corporis*) "that is necessary lest
our voice taper off to the exiguous tones of eunuchs, women, and in-
valids."[74] Exercise of a man's voice gains legitimacy if it serves to differentiate him from these canonically imperfect members of the species. The
health practices that both Quintilian and the *phonasci* endorse for preserving the manliness of the voice are these: walking, massage, sexual absti-
nence, and the sort of efficient digestion that comes from a frugal diet.[75]
Quintilian does not go so far as to recommend infibulation, which seems
to have been widely practiced by citharodes and actors,[76] though he shares
their belief that sexual activity, by weakening the body, harms the voice.[77]

But when it comes to particular methods of caring for the voice, the
orator and the voice trainer must differ. The *phonascus* can build his schedule around regular walks, but the orator is too busy.[78] The *phonascus* can
practice scales before each performance (*praeparare ab imis sonis vocem ad
summos*) and rest his voice whenever he needs, but the orator must sometimes speak at several trials in succession and cannot realistically aspire to
peak performance at all times. The two should not follow the same dietary
regimen, since they are not aiming to produce the same qualities of sound.
For while the *phonascus* aims to produce a voice that is soft and gentle and
tries to soften even his highest notes, the orator desires a voice that is
strong and enduring and must often speak with rugged vehemence. Besides, an orator has to stay up nights in study, inhaling smokey fumes, and
has to endure his daytime duties in a sweat-soaked toga without the re-
freshment of fresh clothing and massage.[79] Thus Quintilian presents the
regimes of the orator and of other voice professionals as differing not so
much in kind as in degree: the former has to accustom himself to more
physical hardship than does the latter and cannot indulge in as many
restorative practices as he might like. Notice that Quintilian here does not
condemn scale practice as a mode of vocal exercise but simply notes that
the active orator will not have time to warm up his voice with scales before

---

[73] Ibid. 11.3.19: *Sed cura non eadem oratoribus quae phonascis convenit.*

[74] *ne ad spadonum et mulierum et aegrorum exilitatem vox nostra tenuetur.*

[75] *Ambulatio, unctio, veneris abstinentia, facilis ciborum digestio, id est frugalitas.*

[76] Aristotle, *Hist. anim.* 581a9ff.; Martial 7.82; 11.75; Juvenal 6.73. Cf. E. J. Dingwall,
Male Infibulation (London, 1925).

[77] Celsus says that infibulation is done sometimes to preserve the voice and sometimes to
preserve health: *interdum vocis, interdum valetudinis causa* (*De Medicina* 7.25.2).

[78] *Inst.* 11.3.22.

[79] Ibid. 11.3.22–23.

every case. He takes it for granted that the exercises and health rituals of the *phonasci* actually do embellish the voice. But he also takes it for granted that the melodious quality of a voice so embellished ill becomes the masculine dignity of the true orator: "Wherefore let us not enervate the voice with delicate indulgences nor allow it to become accustomed to those conditions that it might want."[80] He compares voices too delicately trained and polished to good-looking bodies accustomed to exercise with oil in the gymnasium: despite the robustness they display in athletic contests, they wilt under the rigors of a military campaign. The true orator, by implication, is a real Roman soldier who can out-perform any number of attenuated Greeks. *He* will not desert his client to spare his voice the ill effects of speaking in inclement weather.[81] Quintilian then hastens to qualify these brave words with exceptions that defer to the medical wisdom of the time: no one in his right mind will declaim when suffering from indigestion, immediately after eating or vomiting, or when intoxicated.

The best form of vocal exercise for an orator is the recitation of a passage learned by heart, since it is difficult to give proper attention to the voice while we struggle to improvise.[82] Quintilian implies that the passage is to be in prose, unlike the doctor Antyllus, who recommended poetry. It should vary enough in tone and in substance to give us practice in speaking at different levels of intensity:

> The best form of exercise for a voice that has reached maturity is that which most resembles the orator's business: the practice of speaking daily just as we plead in the courts. For thus do we not only strengthen our voice and our lungs, but we also compose for ourselves a way of moving the body that is both generally becoming and appropriate to our speech (*Inst.* 11.3.29).

Exercise of this sort need not feel decadent nor look too much like exercise. It will produce the sort of voice that Quintilian considers ideal, neither harsh nor effeminate: "neither dull, rough, heavy, hard, stiff, and thick; nor thin, hollow, sharp, feeble, soft, and effeminate."[83] Expressed positively, this ideal becomes a voice that is "easy, strong, rich, flexible, sturdy, sweet, durable, clear, pure, and penetrating."[84] The orator will use neither the lowest nor the highest notes of his instrument, avoiding the muffled fullness of the low tones and the high register's "extreme thinness

---

[80] Ibid. 11.3.24.

[81] Ibid. 11.3.26–27.

[82] Ibid. 11.3.25.

[83] Ibid. 11.3.32: *non subsurda, rudis, immanis, dura, rigida, praepinguis, aut tenuis, inanis, acerba, pusilla, mollis, effeminata.*

[84] Ibid. 11.3.40: *vox facilis, magna, beata, flexibilis, firma, dulcis, durabilis, clara, pura, secans aera et auribus sedens.*

and excessive clarity (since it is a falsetto), which cannot be modulated in delivery nor sustain the strain for long."[85] The goal of Quintilian's training is a voice that is penetrating without being shrill, flexible without being lilting, polished not to a high gloss but to a satin finish that appears to be the patina of nature rather than of art.

"Burlesquing the Mysteries of Rhetoric": Vocal Deportment and the Greek Declaimer

The noble Romans who composed treatises on rhetoric wrote with solemn urgency about matters of decorum because they remembered the glory days of political oratory in the Republic and still felt the imperial responsibilities that weighed upon them as a class. Their Greek contemporaries did not write the same way. The individualistic performance culture of the Greek cities, in which rhetorical "stars" competed for students and applause, does not appear to have called forth the same sort of magisterial didacticism that fueled the rhetorical criticism of senatorial Romans. Greek rhetoricians, no matter how socially distinguished or professionally successful, lacked an equally compelling sense of an audience of social equals awaiting their educational directives. They do not appear to have conceived of themselves as collectively responsible for a whole cadre of young men who must be uniformly schooled so that their adult behavior will preserve the good order of society.[86] The Greeks who wrote rhetorical treatises in the early Empire do not present themselves as busy men of affairs, taking time out from political activity to write, but as professional teachers; and they do not address themselves to general issues of rhetorical deportment but choose technical subjects, like *stasis*-theory, through which to assert their individual claims to professional authority.[87]

This is not to say that Greek rhetoricians and their audiences admired technical excellence in rhetoric without also making moral judgments

[85] *Et ille praetenuis et immodicae claritatis, cum est ultra verum, tum neque pronuntiatione flecti neque diutius ferre intentionem potest* (Ibid. 11.3.41).

[86] By the fourth century, however, when the traditional rhetorical culture of the Greek cities was under pressure from Christianity and young men were pursuing Latin legal training as a route into imperial service, we find Libanius defending rhetorical education as the collective responsibility of the local governing elites. See also pp. 162–65 below.

[87] On Hermogenes and other Greek writers on rhetoric under the Empire, see the survey of G. Kennedy, *Rhetoric in the Roman World* (Princeton, 1972), 614–641. The complex views of Dionysius of Halicarnassus are beyond the scope of this study. He evidently considered crowd-pleasing "Asianist" rhetoric in the Greek cities a political as well as an esthetic disaster (a "harlot" trying to wreck the home of a chaste "Attic" wife), to be corrected by the Roman overlords (*On the Ancient Orators* 1.3.1; 1.1.2–5). See E. Gabba, "Political and Cultural Aspects of the Classicistic Revival in the Augustan Age," *CA* 1 (1982), 43–65.

about the speaker and the gender-appropriateness of his performance style. They made moral judgments aplenty. The best place to find these is not in technical treatises but in works of invective and satire. However varied the actual range of performance styles in this period, popular consciousness of stylistic differences was conditioned by polarized paradigms that we might term "effeminate" and "hyper-masculine" rhetoric. In the remainder of this chapter, I explore these stereotyped paradigms of rhetorical style as they operate in two very different Greek works of the second century: Aelius Aristides' invective "Against Those Who Burlesque the Mysteries of Rhetoric" and Lucian's satire "A Teacher of Rhetoric." The conflation of style with mores in these works reveals to modern readers the fundamental role that rhetoric played in the construction of masculine identity.

Ancient rhetorical performances normally took place in an agonistic context. "Against Those Who Burlesque the Mysteries" was no exception. It is one of the few extant sophistic display-pieces whose performance context we can reconstruct in some detail,[88] because the performer kept a journal, which still survives, chronicling the heaven-sent dreams that inspired both his literary activities and his elaborate health regimens. Aristides was a recluse who found extempore performance difficult. He relished fame, however, just as much as did any of his contemporaries. Visions of triumphant public appearances haunted his dreams. Occasionally the god of healing took pity on him and sent him instructions about when and where to perform. In January of the year 170, Aristides dreamed that he had to go to the Council Chamber, one of the premier spots in Smyrna for rhetorical display, *after having eaten a full meal*. He obeyed this summons promptly. (To appreciate his courage, we need only remember how reluctant a valetudinarian would normally be to disperse corrupted humors through his system by declaiming on a full stomach). As a distinguished out-of-town visitor during the provincial games, he expected to take precedence over the local teachers. They had other ideas. There was a confrontation: Aristides had to yield his claim to "an amazingly thick-skinned individual" who was one of the regulars. Aristides cooled his heels until noon. Perhaps he sat in the audience and availed himself of the traditional repertoire of gestures by which sophists attending one another's declamations might signal boredom and contempt. At last his rival relinquished the floor, and Aristides rose—to excoriate the effeminate rhetoric of sophists who aim only to please the crowd.[89]

---

[88] *Or.* 34. Book Four of the *Sacred Tales*, *Or.* 51.38–41, gives the circumstances. My translations from Aristides are in various places indebted to those of Charles Behr, *P. Aelius Aristides, The Complete Works*, vol. 2 (Leiden, 1981).

[89] A. Boulanger attributes Aristides' indignation to egotism: "He is really pleading for himself, and it is really his own superiority that he is arguing for in general terms" (*Aelius*

Touché! The audience loved it. Aristides describes even their approbation in agonistic terms: "The spectators were in rivalry not to be left behind by what was said." He stood to leave; they would not let him go but ordered him to stay and to take problems from the floor and contend a second time. As their enthusiasm became more violent, he capitulated and confessed to them the divine providence by which he was physically prepared to continue full-strength till sundown (as indeed he did).

Capitulation as triumph. Persuasion as violence. There is both an erotic and a military dimension to this drama of self-assertion. Indeed, Aristides frankly concedes that the goal of oratory is mastery of the audience.[90] Thus, despite his generally puritan attitude in sexual matters, he is willing to compare oratory to erotic magic because of its power to compel the listener (26). Aristides' military metaphors reveal strict notions about propriety in rhetorical performance. The good orator is a good soldier. Like a well-trained hoplite, he holds his place in line.[91] He should use weapons fashioned of the best materials (20–21); his speeches are compared to siege engines that can capture cities whether or not the defending soldiers understand how they are constructed (33).

What Aristides objects to is not the goal of mastery, but the use of corrupt techniques to achieve it. The title of his address, "Against Those Who Burlesque the Mysteries," suggests that he considers oratory to be a mystery cult. The same language appears in a Stoic sermon of Epictetus, where he attacks "those who casually take up sophistic lecturing."[92] Epictetus claims that such people vulgarize (*exorcheīn*) the mysteries by lecturing with the wrong dress, voice, and hairstyle. Aristides really brings out the root meaning of *exorcheīn*. To him, oratory is a mystery whose secrets the bad orators have vulgarized by transvestite dancing. (Making fun of mystery cults by burlesquing them in drag may have been a more common feature of men's private drinking parties than we think, though all we hear about are the most famous scandals: Alcibiades in Athens and Clodius in Rome).[93] Aristides compares good orators to Olympic athletes and by implication attacks the "enervated and intoxicated behavior" of their de-

---

Aristide [Paris, 1923], 270). Egoist indeed he was, by our standards, but to reduce his rhetorical prejudices (or his hypochondria) to the level of individual obsession is to evade the historical question, What was it about Aristides' cultural environment that enabled these preoccupations to take the form they did?

[90] κρατεῖν τῶν ἀκουόντων, *Or.* 34.33. (Further references to this oration will be by paragraph number in parentheses in the text.)

[91] τὴν τάξιν φυλάττοντες (22), τὴν τάξιν μὴ λιπεῖν (16), μένειν ἐν τῇ τάξει (61). This military image also appears in *Or.* 33.13 and 45.13.

[92] Arrian, *Diss.* 3.21, esp. sections 13 and 16.

[93] On "play at becoming other" as an element in the classical Greek *kōmos*, see F. Frontisi-Ducroux and F. Lissarrague, "From Ambiguity To Ambivalence: A Dionysiac Excursion Through the 'Anacreontic' Vases" in *Before Sexuality*, esp. 228–32.

praved rivals, who "twist about like dancing girls" (23). Far from being
suitable for manly orators, such lascivious gyrations would disgrace even
the legendary Queen Omphale, who made Heracles do women's work
(60). By singing and dancing and ingratiating themselves with their audience, "those who burlesque the mysteries" have forfeited title to any male
role at all. Instead of holding to their place in the military ranks, these
perverts "rank themselves among the music girls."[94] They contort themselves like go-go dancers! (23). To do such things while delivering a political speech or competitive display-piece is to risk gender metamorphosis:
like the mythical Kainis in reverse, those who camp it up like this could
change from men into women. And they can hardly have the face to
deliver philosophical orations on self-control and manly fortitude: it
would be like Sardanapallos singing battle-hymns while plying the loom
(61)![95]

Bad orators do not confine their vulgarities to the realm of gesture; they
also indulge in indecent vocal acrobatics. Aristides describes with relish
how a rival's display of recitative degenerated into a symphony of catcalls.
To make himself attractive to the audience, this fellow actually sang,
modulating his voice, while he added the same final clause at the end of
each sentence, like a refrain. The audience caught on quickly and began to
chant the catch phrase—ahead of schedule, so the chorus leader looked the
fool chiming in *after* his chorus. The audience kept adding improvised
insults to the refrain until the polyphony of the poor sophist and his
tormenters made a humiliating spectacle (47). Aristides was obviously
delighted by the catastrophic failure of his rival's experiment with singing
oratory, but his was a minority opinion. More often the "singing style"
was used with great success by sophists like Hadrian of Tyre, whose
rhythmic vocal flourishes enabled him to compete effectively with dancers
and other lowbrow entertainers.[96] We may suspect that blurring the
boundaries between rhetoric and popular entertainment was a type of
"burlesque" that particularly ruffled Aristides.

Vulgarity is not really the issue: it is the decorum of manhood that is at
stake. Aristides actually compares such "singing rhetors" to impenitent
androgynes: "They are behaving like some *androgynos*, or like a eunuch
who does not blame his physical disability on fate but claims that he
became that way through Providence!"[97] This certainly could be one of
Favorinus' paradoxical boasts. It is easy to imagine him, when congratu-

[94] εἰς ψαλτρίας τάττησθε (56).
[95] Sardanapallos was the king who lost Assyria by pursuing a feminine life-style: he wove,
wore women's clothes, depilated his body, and studied to change his voice (Diodorus Siculus
2.23).
[96] Philostratus, *Lives* 589.
[97] προνοίᾳ (48).

lated on the flexibility and range of his marvelous voice, responding wittily that his talents were the gift of Providence.

Two possible trains of thought may be responsible for Aristides' pattern
of association here. The subject of "singing orators" may have put him in
mind of Favorinus as one of the most notorious exponents of this style in a
slightly earlier generation.[98] Favorinus may even have been—perish the
thought—the unsuccessful performer that Aristides describes. But on a
deeper level, there may also be operating an unconscious association between "bad" oratory and imperfect masculinity. Aristides had been, after
all, a pupil of Polemo.[99] Aristides likens bad orators to men who maim
themselves or even allow themselves to be castrated for the pleasure of
others.[100] To allow one's body to be used for another's pleasure is of course
the one thing that an adult male citizen who expects to play a respectable
role in public life absolutely must not do.[101] The shocking paradox of the
bad orators' transformation is that they *choose* to become effeminate.[102]

For Aristides, rhetorical style must be mapped appropriately onto the
age and gender grid. "But can this style be appropriate for younger men? It
will make them seem like whores. To grown men? No, by definition. To
old men? Unseasonable shame! Who's left? Only women, and of these the
most depraved" (61). For Aristides, this confusion of boundaries has cosmic consequences.

> And indeed I do not give advice just on behalf of oratory, but on behalf of all
> decorum and good order—and on the question of whether it is necessary to
> remain within the limits of law, or whether anyone can pursue pleasure at whim.
> If my side wins, law and order win also, which hold together and protect not
> just cities but all earth and heaven itself (63).

When orators attempt to ingratiate themselves with the audience by
indulging it with disgraceful pleasures, they foster an unhealthy relationship that Aristides describes in the language of erotic pursuit: they may
claim that the masses pursue them (*erān*), but in fact they are engaged
inappropriately in sexual pursuit of their audience (*autoi toutōn erōntes*).
Indeed, the people in the audience should pursue the orator, not because he
tries to please them, but because the power of his oratory compels their
desire. This independent stance legitimates the true orator's manly free-

---

[98] Favorinus died at least six years before Aristides delivered this oration (A. Barigazzi,
Favorino di Arelate 11).

[99] *Suidas* s.v. Aristides, Gregory Nazianzen.

[100] εἰς τὴν ἑτέρων ἡδονήν, *Or.* 34.12–13.

[101] On the cultural logic by which passive homosexual behavior disqualified citizens from
political life in classical Athens, see D. Halperin, *One Hundred Years of Homosexuality* (New
York/London 1990), 88–99, and J. Winkler, *The Constraints of Desire* (New York/London,
1990), 45–64 = *Before Sexuality*, 171–204.

[102] αἱροῦνται μαλακίζεσθαι (16).

dom of speech: "I do nothing to please," Aristides claims, "and I fail to please in nothing" (43). Elsewhere he describes his audience as his "desperate lovers" (*duserōtes*), who ought to cultivate *him* and haunt *his* doors, "the way those who desire to marry sit at the doorways of girls" (33.24,14). Thus, according to Aristides, the correct relationship that should obtain between an orator and his audience is like the relationship between a sequestered virgin or chaste boy and their admirers. These secluded objects of desire do nothing consciously to enhance the force of the attraction they emit. In just such a way, the orator's words, unadorned by ingratiating gestures, ought to have the power to enforce desire. So much for the orator's relationship to his audience. It is in his relationship to Rhetoric, however, that Aristides feels the orator should play the role of active lover. He defines this relationship in another passionate oration: "To Those Who Criticize Him Because He Does Not Declaim."[103] There he attempts to blame his difficulties with *ex tempore* performance on his audience (or rather, on those who ought to him but prefer baths, whores, and banquets). Apparently by some sort of projection, the deeply disturbing sense of personal cowardice provoked by his failure to perform has become externalized as the effeminacy of his audience. The disappointed fans who blame him for failing to appear are like *wives* who blame their own shortcomings on their husbands (16). In an elaborate figure, Aristides defines his isolation as a lover: to some the company of boys is sweet; to others, the baths. Some prefer to drink wine, others are turned on by horses and dogs. But for me, rhetoric is everything: *logoi* have taken the place of children, of parents, work, and recreation. As an eager lover, I haunt Rhetoric's door.[104]

A pathetic spectacle, at best, to modern readers, Aelius Aristides prostrate before the doors of Rhetoric would earn from Lucian nothing but contempt. But it is remarkable how similar the gender stereotypes deployed in Lucian's satire are to those used by the entirely humorless Aristides. In the *Teacher of Rhetoric*, Lucian also imagines Rhetoric as a bride, to be wooed and won by the successful speaker.[105] Lucian presents a choice of

---

[103] *Or.* 33, an epistolary oration justifying the infrequency of his public appearances.

[104] Ibid. 33.19–20. Aristides' journal records a dream in which he declines to participate in a procession in honor of Eros but stays inside to discuss rhetoric, even rejecting a young boy who is offered to him there as a student (Ibid. 51.57–59).

[105] Gendered personifications of careers appear elsewhere in Lucian. In an autobiographical parody he presents himself as a young Heracles, at a crossroads between two careers. Sculpture and Paideia appear as two ladies vying to get their hands on him. The former is described as markedly masculine in appearance (ἀνδρική, ἀνδρώδης), so by implication Paideia, distinctly better-looking, is the more "feminine" of the two (*Dream* 6). In Lucian's *Twice Accused* 28, Rhetoric appears as his jilted *wife*, whom he has abandoned in favor of a sexual relationship with Philosophy, a hirsute older man. This habit of thinking about careers in gendered terms was not peculiar to Lucian: Artemidorus' dream handbook shows that people expected the vicissitudes of a man's professional life to be symbolically foreshadowed by sexual activity in his dreams.

access-routes to her aspiring suitors: on the one hand, a steep and narrow path that portends a tedious and sweaty climb; on the other, an easy promenade through fragrant meadows, pleasantly shaded and conveniently brief. As guide and guardian of the steep and narrow path, we will find "a strong, rather tough-looking fellow, who has a manly step, a deep tan, and a masculine, vigilant look."[106] This sinewy paragon recommends a rhetorical training program whose ascetic elements would appeal to the invalid Aristides: abstension from wine, sleepless nights of hard work expended in imitation of the ancients. Lucian understood the importance of these classical texts as paradigms of manhood. He compares them explicitly to early-fifth-century sculptures of the male body: "wasp-waisted, sinewy, hard, meticulously definite in their contours."[107] He bids us, however, to "dismiss this hairy specimen of excessive virility,"[108] so that we may turn our attention to the depilated alternative.

The guide of the easy road to rhetoric is all effeminate charm. His hips sway as he walks, his neck is limp, his glance distinctly feminine, his voice honey-sweet. He reeks of perfume, scratches his head with his fingertip, and carefully preens his thinning hair.[109] Tossing back his curls, the exponent of the primrose path (let us call him the Exquisite) smiles faintly (his perfectly polished customary smile) and with his voice affects the ingratiating smoothness of the practiced whore. A manly appearance is, after all, uncouth, ill-befitting an orator of alluring refinement.[110] By precept as well as by example, he presents a program for maximum rhetorical success with minimum effort.

First, toss aside all moral inhibitions. Arm yourself with the loudest voice you can muster. Use an absolutely uninhibited singing delivery (15). "And whenever you sense an opportunity for recitative, intone everything you say and turn it into a song" (19). You must jiggle your rear as you walk. Translucent clothing and feminine sandals will enhance the impression (15). Why bother with tedious memorization of the classics? A few clichés and some affected pronunciation is all you need to give your speech that old-time Attic flavor; an armamentarium of archaic periphrases and mind-boggling neologisms will stun your audience into stupefied amazement (16–17). And after all, it is always possible to wriggle out of difficult

---

[106] καρτερός τις ἀνήρ, ὑπόσκληρος, ἀνδρώδης τὸ βάδισμα, πολὺν τὸν ἥλιον ἐπὶ τῷ σώματι δεικνύων, ἀρρενωπὸς τὸ βλέμμα, ἐγρηγορώς . . . *Teacher* 9.

[107] *Teacher* 9, trans. A. M. Harmon (*Lucian*, vol. 4 [Loeb Classical Library, London and Cambridge, Mass., 1925]).

[108] δασύς . . . καὶ περὶ τοῦ μετρίου ἀνδρικός (10).

[109] εὑρήσεις . . . πάγκαλον ἄνδρα, διασεσαλευμένον τὸ βάδισμα, ἐπικεκλασμένον τὸν αὐχένα, γυναικεῖον τὸ βλέμμα, μελιχρὸν τὸ φώνημα, μύρων ἀποπνέοντα, τῷ δακτύλῳ ἄκρῳ τὴν κεφαλὴν κνώμενον, ὀλίγας μὲν ἔτι, οὔλας δὲ καὶ ὑακινθίνας τὰς τρίχας εὐθετίζοντα (11).

[110] Αὐτοθαΐδα . . . τινὰ μιμησάμενος τῷ προσηνεῖ τοῦ φθέγματος· ἄγροικον γὰρ τὸ ἀρρενωπὸν καὶ οὐ πρὸς ἁβροῦ καὶ ἐρασμίου ῥήτορος (12).

declamation topics by disparaging them thus: "Not one of 'em fit for a real man."[111] Clearly, the implication is that declamations on difficult topics are expected to be a test of manly excellence.

In keeping with the agonistic ethos of ancient rhetorical performance, the Exquisite also offers carefully circumstantial advice about how to be rude at someone else's declamation (22). These helpful suggestions quite precisely mirror Plutarch's strictures about how *not* to be rude at a public lecture.[112] Where Lucian recommends laughing at all the speakers (22), Plutarch enjoins us to maintain a sedate countenance even when the performance is a fiasco (45C). While Lucian's Exquisite counsels us to withhold gestures of assent and take care to appear dissatisfied (22), Plutarch deprecates the practice of affecting gravity and withholding praise (44AB). And where Lucian advises that we criticize a successful lecture for being derivative, Plutarch urges us to commend a weak lecture for its allusions to tradition, if nothing else (44E). From this congruity of opposites, we may be sure that the techniques of harrassment Lucian recommends were commonly employed by temporarily inactive performers and members of the audience at large as a recognized means of self-assertion.

The Exquisite is also at pains to advise the aspiring sophist on how to conduct himself socially in ways that will enhance his professional notoriety. Drinking, dicing, and lechery are highly recommended, especially lechery: "You should boast of adultery, whether truly or not; make no secret of it, but exhibit *billets-doux* from your frail ones (real or invented). Try to pass for a pretty fellow, much in favor with the ladies; the report will be professionally useful to you, your influence with the fair sex being attributed to your rhetorical eminence, which has penetrated even to the women's quarters."[113] It is a good idea to develop a reputation for pathic pleasures also, "and for further impact, don't be ashamed to be seen to be pursued by other men, even if you're bearded or already bald" (23). Delightfully spurious logic supports this advice: since women surpass men in verbosity and verbal abuse, so you too will surpass everyone in these arts if you play the feminine sexual role (*ta homoia paschois*). Depilation ("at least where it counts") is essential for success, and the Exquisite concludes his recipe for rhetorical success with a sizzling disquisition on the variety of uses an orator may make of his tongue.

When we step back, it is not hard to see that Aristides and Lucian are playing off a common set of stereotypes. While the athletic "Guide of the

---

[111] οὐδὲν ὅλως ἀδρῶδες αὐτῶν (18).

[112] *On Listening to Lectures*, *Mor.* 44, 45 CD. Libanius, *Or.* 3.11–14 describes more possibilities.

[113] *Teacher* 23, trans. adapted from H. W. and W. G. Fowler, *The Works of Lucian of Samosata* (Oxford, 1905).

Steep and Narrow Path" of Lucian might not care to emulate the valetudinarianism and extreme sexual continence of Aristides, they share a
conception of rhetorical training that requires rigorous manly hard work
and would find themselves united in their opposition to the mellifluous
vocal acrobatics and the effeminate gyrations of the more "depilated" sort
of rhetoric. The "effeminate" techniques deplored by Aristides are, of
course, just what Lucian's successful Professor recommends. Both authors assume that a hyper-manly style is more respectable, but both concede that an "effeminate" style is more successful. How this dissonance
was resolved in practice is difficult to say. But the coexistence of these
stereotypes may indicate areas of contradiction and unease in the ideology
of rhetorical performance as a zero-sum game. Can one vanquish one's
rivals in a manly fashion without making oneself appealing to one's audience in a feminine way? Is a military assault on the sensibilities of one's
listeners appropriate or even possible? Are refinement and manliness fundamentally incompatible? That was the challenge embodied by the practitioners of "depilated" rhetoric.

As we shall see in the next chapter, Favorinus could be made to look like
a prototypical example of that despised and fascinating category. It appears
that Aristides considered him to be one of those who "burlesque the
mysteries," and, though there is no evidence to indicate that the *Teacher of
Rhetoric* is directed specifically at him, Lucian's portrait of the effeminate
sophist who takes the easy road to success does recall various elements of
the style of Favorinus. He was, after all, notorious for the bewitching
power of his high-pitched voice, deployed with maximum effect in the
"odes" that he sang as a coda to his performances: "He charmed his audience with the resonance of his voice, the expressiveness of his glance, and
the rhythm of his speech. He enchanted them also with the epilogue of his
speeches, which they called 'the ode,' but I call showing off, since it is sung
after the argument has been proved.[114]

Since effects like these were observed to mesmerize even the illiterate, it
was from here, if we are to believe his detractors, but a small step to the
black arts. Polemo sought to portray Favorinus as a charlatan of the agora
who gave practical demonstrations of erotic magic.[115] Like Lucian's decadent Exquisite, Favorinus anointed his tresses with great care (this again
according to Polemo); he appears to have followed another of the Exqui-

---

[114] ἀλλὰ κἀκείνους |sc. ὅσοι τῆς Ἑλλήνων φωνῆς ἀξύνετοι ἦσαν] ἔθελγε τῇ τε ἠχῇ τοῦ
φθέγματος καὶ τῷ σημαίνοντι τοῦ βλέμματος καὶ τῷ ῥυθμῷ τῆς γλώττης. ἔθελγε δὲ αὐτοὺς
τοῦ λόγου καὶ τὸ ἐπὶ πᾶσιν, ὃ ἐκεῖνοι μὲν ᾠδὴν ἐκάλουν, ἐγὼ δὲ φιλοτιμίαν, ἐπειδὴ τοῖς
ἀποδεδειγμένοις ἐφυμνεῖται (*Lives* 491–92). Dio Chrysostom and Hadrian of Tyre were
credited with a similar power to attract those who knew no Greek (*Lives* 488, 589).

[115] *Phys.* 1.162F. For a general discussion of magic and rhetoric, see J. de Romilly, *Magic
and Rhetoric in Ancient Greece* (Cambridge, Mass., 1975).

site's precepts by making no secret of his scandalous affair with a married woman (*Lives* 489). It is worth noting, however, that no source, however hostile, makes the accusation that Favorinus preferred exclusively to play an effeminate role in sexual relationships with other men. A preference for such a role is part of the standard armamentarium of invective against practitioners of refined grooming and *bel canto* rhetoric, but the worst that Polemo seems to have said of his rival is that "he both did and suffered everything that is disgraceful."[116] This phrase might mean that Favorinus' libidinous disposition caused him to indulge in oral sex with male or female partners, or that he sometimes allowed himself to be penetrated by males and at other times returned the favor, but in either case it is clear that not even Polemo was able to accuse him of the consistent effeminacy that was the hallmark of the *cinaedus*. Favorinus' public identity was not in the keeping of a single stereotype; he was more than the sum of his parts.

[116] *Anon. Lat.* 40,2.58F, in a passage that the author attributes to Polemo: *hunc dicit impatientia libidinum quae turpia sunt omnia passum esse et egisse quae passus est.*

Chapter Six

MANHOOD ACHIEVED THROUGH SPEECH: A EUNUCH-PHILOSOPHER'S SELF-FASHIONING

W E NOW RETURN to Favorinus to look at him from three perspectives, bearing in mind that all formulations of his identity are in some sense fictions: Favorinus the eunuch philosopher as seen in satire, Favorinus the philosopher as remembered by his Roman friends, and Favorinus the philosopher in exile as he presents himself.

The problem of distinguishing philosophical sophists from eloquent philosophers in this period is largely the product of a head-on collision between the inclusive ideal of well-rounded learning typical of ancient aristocrats, and the modern scholar's passion for taxonomy. The characteristic polymathy of the Second Sophistic intensified the traditional rhetoric of rivalry between philosophy and oratory, even as the two disciplines became progressively indistinguishable in practice.[1] Favorinus' claim to the title of philosopher was not impaired in the eyes of his contemporaries by his reputation as a virtuoso public speaker. Philostratus categorizes Favorinus as "a philosopher whose eloquence proclaimed him among the sophists," comparing him to Dio of Prusa.[2] As for the title of sophist, Philostratus observed that having quarreled with one was enough to have earned Favorinus that appellation, too.[3] *Suidas* characterizes him as "a polymath in all areas of learning . . . full of philosophy, who applied himself more to rhetoric." Polemo, at least in his surviving writings, ignored but did not challenge his rival's claim to be a philosopher.[4]

It is easier to grant Favorinus the title than to figure out what it means.

---

[1] J. Hahn, *Der Philosoph und die Gesellschaft: Selbstverständnis, öffentliches Auftreten und populäre Erwartungen in der hohen Kaiserzeit* (Stuttgart, 1989), 88.

[2] *Lives* 489, cf. 479, 484.

[3] Ibid. 491.

[4] We know nothing about the speeches he composed "Against Favorinus," except that they earned the censure of his teacher Timocrates, himself a philosopher-sophist (*Lives* 536). In the *Physiognomy* Polemo concedes Favorinus' mastery of Greek, in virtue of which "he was called a sophist" (*Phys.* 1. 162–63F).

Clearly, in Favorinus' case at least, to be a philosopher was to be a poly-math. The content of his conversations and lectures extended over a wide range of philosophical subjects. He addressed questions of natural philoso-phy, holding forth at dinner parties on the names and quarters of the winds, distracting Fronto from the pangs of gout with disquisitions on the shades of colors and their terminology.[5] He tackled questions of logic and epistemology, demolished Stoic claims for the reliability of sense-perception with skeptical zest, and composed a treatise on the Pyrrhonian tropes.[6] He lectured frequently on ethics, including points of Roman law and social conduct.[7] He wrote philosophical biography (he is frequently quoted as a source by Diogenes Laertius)[8] and moralizing literary criticism ("On the Philosophy of Homer").[9] But being a philosopher was some-thing more than just talking about philosophy; it was a way of life. In the eyes of his contemporaries, the philosopher embodied a life-style or *bios* whose outlines were defined by a remarkably stable set of social expecta-tions.[10] Did Favorinus fit into this paradigm, or should he be considered an exception to it? Was his own philosophical persona anything more than the sum of his displays on philosophical themes? He actually wrote a treatise, "On the Life-styles of the Philosophers,"[11] which, were it still extant, might reveal which traits he considered truly worthy of the breed. In its absence, we must build from other sources a tessellated picture of Favor-inus's philosophical persona.

FAVORINUS THE EUNUCH-PHILOSOPHER IN SATIRE

A chair of Peripatetic philosophy has fallen open at Athens. The candidates in contention are exchanging abuse by the cart-load, ten thousand drach-mae a year as the prize. "This was the Helen for which they fought in single combat," the narrator proclaims.[12] Lucian's scenario is ideal for a send-up of academic greed and philosophical pretensions. It also reveals the tena-

---

[5] *Attic Nights* 2.22; 2.26.

[6] Ibid. 11.5.5; *Lives* 491. See Galen's attack on Favorinus' epistemological writings in his "On the Best Teaching" 1–5 (K1.40ff. = A. Barigazzi, *Favorino di Avelate Opere* [Florence, 1966], fr. 28).

[7] *Attic Nights* 14.2; 20.1; 2.12.5.

[8] E. Maass actually claimed that Favorinus was Diogenes' main source (*Philologische Unter-suchungen* 3, 1880, 1–141). An angry refutation by Wilamowitz was published in the same volume. See now J. Mejer, *Diogenes Laertius and His Hellenistic Background, Hermes Einzelschriften* 40 (1978), 8–9, 30–32: fifty references to Favorinus, but the search for a "main source" is misconceived.

[9] Barigazzi, fr. 22.

[10] J. Hahn (above, n.1).

[11] *Suidas* s.v. Favorinus; see Barigazzi, fr. 23, cf. 71, 76.

[12] Lucian, *The Eunuch* 3.

cious roots of Greek intellectual life in the contest system. The wrangling philosophers are described as participants in the funeral games of the deceased (4). They contend, like the aspiring orators in the *Teacher of Rhetoric*, for a female prize, whose allure is measured in the competitive display of male excellence that she can mobilize. Mock-heroic images superimpose themselves on images drawn from the other traditionally agonistic venues of Greek cultural life. The contest is described as a trial, a legal proceeding in which the protagonists are to be judged by the most eminent men of the city (2). Their Homeric duel (*monomachia*) is also a classical democratic test of suitability for office (*dokimasia*) and a Hellenistic/Roman epideictic display, in which the thesis proposed for competitive argument is this: "Should a eunuch be approved to teach philosophy to the young?" (8).

Here is manly competition with a twist. One of the two finalists is reputed to be a eunuch. This is Bagoas, whose very name connotes the luxury and effeminacy of Persian slaves. His rival is the notoriously disputatious Diocles. The preliminary contest has been indecisive: in a display of Aristotelian doctrine, neither gained the upper hand (4). Passing from pedantry to character assassination, Diocles begins to make an issue of his rival's physique and life-style. Lucian's interlocutor endorses this move toward *ad hominem* argument, on the grounds that a philosopher should be judged more by his *bios* than by his doctrines.

The essence of Diocles' argument is that eunuchs are unclean. They are unlucky to look upon and should be excluded not only from philosophy but also from shrines and holy-water fonts and all places of public assembly *because they confuse categories*. They are neither man nor woman, but "composites, hybrids, monstrosities outside the pale of human nature."[13] Unable to control his cowardly blushes, sweating visibly and at a loss for words, Bagoas at length responds, in feeble feminine tones, that it is unfair to exclude eunuchs from philosophy when even women have taken part in it (7). His list of examples includes Aspasia, Diotima—and Favorinus, "a certain Academic from the Pelasgians who shortly before our time was famous among the Greeks." So the aspiring eunuch-sophist introduces Favorinus as the climax of a catalog of *women*, thereby undercutting the *a fortiori* structure of his own argument. Diocles, though conceding Favorinus' popularity with the crowd, says that he should be excluded, too. Diocles insists that philosophers must have presence (*schēma*), a good physical endowment (*sōmatos eumoiria*), and a big beard. Bagoas retorts, "If philosophers are to be judged by their beards, then the billy goat should be preferred to them all!"[14]

---

[13] Ibid. 6: οὔτε ἄνδρα οὔτε γυναῖκα εἶναι τὸν εὐνοῦχον λέγοντος, ἀλλά τι σύνθετον καὶ μικτὸν καὶ τερατῶδες, ἔξω τῆς ἀνθρωπείας φύσεως.

[14] Ibid. 9, cf. *Demonax* 13.

Matters are at an impasse until a bystander breaks in with an unexpected revelation: were Bagoas to strip, you would find him, despite his beardless cheeks and effeminate voice, "all man" (10). He was, in fact, once caught in the act of adultery but got off by taking refuge in his reputation as a eunuch: the judges took one look at him and refused to believe him capable of the crime. This disclosure, borrowed quite obviously from Favorinus' biography,[15] puts Bagoas in a bind: he could welcome the allegation as clinching evidence of his manhood, but in so doing he would have to abandon the "cover" that had protected him from the male aggression that was the normal consequence of such crimes. Indeed, his position is remarkably similar to that of the soldier-*cinaedus* in one of Phaedrus' fables, who robs his commander's baggage train but escapes punishment for his crime because the general cannot believe him capable of it. Despite his effeminate appearance, this *cinaedus* is actually a prodigious warrior. He redeems his reputation by decapitating an enemy champion in single combat, at which point the general exclaims, while awarding him the crown of victory, "I'll be damned if it wasn't you who stole my baggage the other night!"[16]

While Lucian spoofs, but does not seriously challenge, his culture's assumptions about virility and philosophy, the Phaedrus fable is a more disturbing text, since it explicitly sets up a dissonance between the expectations generated by the cinaedic appearance of the thieving soldier and his actual performance on the battlefield. This fact cannot be unrelated to the social status of the story's author. As a freedman, Phaedrus could not hope to emulate the manly dignity of aristocratic generals but created instead a folk-hero of dubious virility who nonetheless manages, like the slave-hero of the *Life of Aesop*, to upstage or outwit his conventionally masculine master. Both Lucian's and Phaedrus' stories suggest, however, that some males might deliberately opt out of the competition that governed public interaction among "real" men by adopting an effeminate persona in which voice, gait, and mannerisms all proclaimed *nolo contendere*. But this was supposed to be a permanent adaptation, not a tactic to be employed and discarded as the convenience of the moment might dictate. The man who adopted an effeminate pose for self-protection only to reassert his claim to full membership in the male community by an unexpected deed of derring-do would have to reckon with the vindictive indignation of his fellows.

---

[15] *Lives* 489. In a rhetorical handbook we find the following declamatory exercise: a man who finds a eunuch mounting his wife slays him as an adulterer but is put on trial for murder, presumably on the grounds that by his own admission his victim was incapable of the alleged crime (Hermogenes, ed. Rabe pp. 59–60). For a real-life instance of effeminacy shielding a guilty individual from punishment, see Tacitus, *Annals* 11.36. Only a real man can commit a political crime.

[16] Phaedrus, *Fabulae*, Appendix 8.

Lucian takes the agonistic element of masculine competition latent in Greek intellectual culture and exaggerates it into a comic spectacle of philosophers struggling to demonstrate a crudely sexual virility: "Bagoas . . . is in training, playing the manly part (*andrizetai*) . . . keeping the matter in hand" (13). The satire reduces to absurdity the claims of philosophy to perfect the molding of men. As the narrator says regarding the future education of his infant son, "I might well pray that he has not his brain, nor his tongue, but his private parts in shape to practice philosophy."

While Lucian's *Eunuch* freely plagiarizes Favorinus' biography to create the comic character of Bagoas, his *Demonax* purports to record various run-ins between a Cynic sage and the historical Favorinus. Demonax has been criticizing Favorinus' lectures behind his back, singling out for special condemnation the enervated quality of his recitatives.[17] He gives three grounds of complaint, each of which reveals some assumptions about speech. He calls Favorinus' vocal mannerisms low-born (*agennes*). This criticism implies that speech should be an indicator of social standing and perhaps implies also that crowd-pleasing sound effects reveal the speaker to be insufficiently attentive to the more refined standards of his peers. He also calls Favorinus' practice womanlike (*gynaikeion*). The assumption behind this criticism is that speech is gendered independently of the speaker's anatomical sex, and perhaps also that seeking to please is somehow inherently feminine behavior. Last, Demonax has been saying that Favorinus' speech is completely inappropriate to philosophy (*philosophiā hēkista prepon*). Here the assumption is that philosophy is governed by special restrictions; it is a gendered form of discourse, and that gender must be male.

When these remarks were reported to Favorinus, he had several options. He could have contented himself with a retort uttered in the circle of his friends, upon whom he could rely to circulate it, the way Polemo addressed his witticisms about Favorinus to Timocrates, trusting that they would reach their target indirectly.[18] But in this case, as Lucian tells the story, he sought out his attacker and confronted him face to face: "Who are you to mock my speeches?" Perhaps Favorinus is implying that Demonax, master of the cynic one-liner, could not produce sustained, rhetorically elaborated arguments comparable to his own productions and that therefore he should not presume to judge them. Demonax answered, "Who am I? A man whose ears are not easily deceived." That is, your rhetorical prowess is so much snake oil, from the point of view of the real philosopher. Favorinus picks up on this, as his retort shows: "What qualifications

---

[17] τῶν ἐν αὐταῖς ⟨ὁμιλίαις⟩ μελῶν τὸ ἐπικεκλασμένον, *Demonax* 12.
[18] *Lives* 541.

have *you*, Demonax, to leave school and commence philosophy?"[19] Favorinus implies that Demonax has not completed his basic training in *paideia*, let alone the rhetorical apprenticeship that ought to precede a young man's studies in philosophy. Favorinus may have had his finger on a weak spot here: Cynics were always open to the charge of being uneducated.[20] But in this case, Favorinus' decision to continue harping on Demonax's lack of advanced educational qualifications turns out to be a tactical blunder, since it gives his opponent the opportunity to clinch the debate with a brutally succinct claim to the one credential that Favorinus, for all his training, could never duplicate. What qualifications does Demonax say he has to practice philosophy? "Balls" (*orcheis*).

As embedded in its narrative context, Demonax's victory is a foregone conclusion, since Lucian's biography has been designed to showcase his wit. But if there is any kernel of historical truth in the situation, it is worth noting that Favorinus obviously expected to win. The sort of victory he was aiming for may be conjectured from the story of a more successful confrontation recorded in Gellius. While waiting to pay their morning salute to the emperor, Favorinus and his friends are forced to listen to a pretentious grammarian discoursing on the gender of a Latin word. Favorinus quietly asks him for a definition of the word in terms of genus and species, a request that so unnerves the grammarian that he abjectly disclaims any pretensions to higher learning: "I have never studied philosophy nor sought to learn it."[21] A remarkable feature of this debate is the opportunity Favorinus offers his opponent to give him a vicious set-down, though the poor grammarian is apparently too stunned to take advantage of it. For while lecturing his victim on the distinction between giving a definition and giving examples, Favorinus says, "If I were to ask you now to tell me and more or less define in words what a 'man' is, you would not, I imagine, answer that you and I are men."[22] We can only imagine what Demonax would have made of *that*.

The second squaring-off between Demonax and Favorinus, as Lucian presents it, focuses again on Demonax's credentials as a "school-less" (or unschooled) philosopher. Favorinus took the initiative by asking him which sect he preferred, obviously intending to refute whatever claim Demonax advanced. Demonax finessed with Socratic irony, "Who told you I was a philosopher?" and laughingly turned to leave. But Favorinus wasn't about to let him go like that and asked him why he was laughing.

---

[19] τίνα δὲ καὶ ἐφόδια ἔχων, ὦ Δημῶναξ, ἐκ παιδείας εἰς φιλοσοφίαν ἥκεις; *Demonax* 12, trans. A. M. Harmon, Loeb Classical Library, *Lucian*, vol. 1 (London and Cambridge, Mass., 1913).

[20] As Lucian's defensiveness about Demonax's education shows (*Demonax* 4).

[21] *Attic Nights* 4.1.13.

[22] Ibid. 4.1.12.

"It seemed ridiculous to me," said Demonax, "that you should think that you can judge philosophers by their beards when you yourself have none."[23] Just as in their former encounter, Demonax has managed to shift the ground of the discussion from his educational qualifications as a judge of rhetoric and philosophy to Favorinus' physical qualifications as a male.

Although other anecdotes show Demonax making sport of effeminate deportment,[24] the special interest of these remarks to Favorinus lies in the way they reveal the intense *physicality* of the Cynic's conception of the philosopher's role. We see this elsewhere in Lucian's biography, when evidence for Demonax's physical fitness is presented side by side with his educational qualifications: "He also trained his body and cultivated toughness" (4). Physical hardiness had been a contributing element in the philosophical persona ever since Socrates impressed his contemporaries with his powers of endurance. Favorinus was an Academic and espoused a different conception of the philosopher's role: more rhetorical, less ascetic, and in many ways more aristocratic. He simply did not compete with the Cynics in displays of physical toughness and bravado but sought to embody the claim that *paideia* and the rhetorical skill that was its proper fruit were the essential prerequisites for philosophy. Many cultivated gentlemen, as we shall see in the next section, preferred his paradigm to that of Demonax; it could not have been as obvious to them as it is to us that, thanks to Christianity, Demonax's ascetic virility would eventually become the dominant paradigm of human excellence in the Greco-Roman world.

Even if the verbal duels in Demonax's biography are entirely fictional, they would still reveal the pattern of expectations about philosophy and virility that the historical Favorinus had to reckon with. But is is not entirely out of the question that they did in fact take place. After all, in a world where hearsay was the mass media, quotable quips were tickets to a kind of immortality.[25] Some of these could become material for a biography. Though not every prominent sage found his Boswell, Favorinus was

---

[23] *Demonax* 13. This bon mot reverses the usual premises of Roman satire on these matters, in which the satirist's target, whose beard is a vital part of his self-presentation as a philosopher, is revealed to be a pathic by his depilated rear end. Compare Martial 9.47, on the hirsute philosopher whose philosophy is sodomy, and Juvenal 2, an attack on *cinaedi Socratici*.

[24] *Demonax* 15:18:50.

[25] A philosopher-sophist would think of his bons mots as generating *chreiai* for students to practice declaiming about. Compare Theon, who gives many examples attributed to Diogenes the Cynic: *Progymnasmata* 3.1–14, (pp. 186–229 in the edition of James Butts, "The *Progymnasmata* of Theon: A New Text with Translation and Commentary," Diss. Claremont Graduate School, 1987).

fortunate to have a young provincial in his entourage who recorded numerous displays of his erudition and *savoir-faire*.[26]

FAVORINUS THE PHILOSOPHER AS REMEMBERED BY HIS ROMAN FRIENDS

It is a busy business day in Rome. The consul is hard at work judging cases from the tribunal. His friend Favorinus, a Greek philosopher at leisure, is waiting for him to finish; they will stroll over to the baths together, perhaps, when the day's legal work is done. To pass the time, Favorinus transacts some business of his own. While walking with his followers about Trajan's Forum, he makes the gilded equestrian statues adorning the roof of the colonnade his point of departure for a display of literary learning. Aulus Gellius, one of the company, records how the discussion proceeded.[27] Pointing to the inscription beneath the statuary, EX MANUBIIS, Favorinus asks the assembled company what they think it means. The first to volunteer his opinion is a man with a reputation for learning. *Ex manubiis*, he says, means "from the spoils" (*ex praeda*), and adds a painfully obvious etymological explanation: it is booty captured by hand (*manu*). "Even though," Favorinus begins his reply, "I have devoted my efforts primarily and almost exclusively to Greek learning and language, I am nonetheless not so inattentive to the Latin language (which I study in piecemeal and impromptu fashion) that I am unaware of that commonplace interpretation of *manubiae* that equates it with *praeda*."

Readers attuned to the nuances of scholarly competition in Gellius will have known this was coming. Favorinus' interlocutor (identified not as an individual but as the possessor of a reputation) has been too eager to answer, and worse, he has framed his answer in the wrong terms, relying on the practices of common speech (*usus*) and etymology (*ratio*), the province of grammarians, rather than *auctoritas*, the authority of literary tradition that is the province of gentlemen scholars.[28] We watch Favorinus preparing to strike: he disclaims full expertise in Latin, a graceful dip of the knee to the ideal of modesty among equals that his interlocutor neglects.

---

[26] Aulus Gellius, *Attic Nights* 16.3.1: *Cum Favorino Romae dies plerumque totos eramus tenebatque animos nostros homo ille fandi dulcissimus atque eum, quoquo iret, quasi ex lingua prorsum eius capti prosequebamur; ita sermonibus usquequaque amoenissimis demulcebat.*

[27] *Attic Nights* 13.25. It is simply not possible to determine whether Gellius' anecdotes are historical truth or verisimilar fiction.

[28] Here I owe a fundamental debt to two unpublished essays of Robert Kaster: "Competition and Restraint: The Classicism of Aulus Gellius," ©1981; and "The Ethics of Archaism in Aulus Gellius," ©1986.

He frames this disclaimer, however, in carefully chosen archaic Latin words.[29] Having skewered his interlocutor's definition as commonplace (*vulgarius*), Favorinus continues, "But I wonder whether M. Tullius, a man most careful in his choice of words, joined *manubiae* and *praeda* in a pointless and inelegant repetition [in his speech on the agrarian law], if indeed those two words mean the same thing and do not differ in any way."

At this point Favorinus shows off his prodigious memory by quoting Cicero's very words. By bringing the authority of Cicero to bear on the question in this way, Favorinus has placed his unfortunate opponent in a bind. He implies, Either you're saying Cicero is an ass, or you are one yourself. In an archaizing literary culture where diligence in the pursuit of *le mot juste* is valued as a moral virtue, to imply that Ciceronian usage is frigid or inept is worse than a lapse of good taste. Is Cicero then guilty of the pleonastic excesses of Aeschylus? Favorinus asks (citing from memory five relevant lines from the *Frogs* of Aristophanes). The interlocutor has no choice but to demur. Favorinus, however, is only gathering steam. Examples of ornamental pleonasm quoted from memory pour from his mouth in profusion: Cicero again, two examples; Homer, six; Cicero, one more time. Yet all this erudition functions merely as foil. Cicero's conjunction of *manubiae* and *praeda* is *not* an example of ornamental pleonasm after all, we learn in paragraph twenty-five. The words mean different things, "according to books on antiquities and early Latin." *Praeda* refers to the actual objects carried off as booty, but *manubiae* are the monies realized from their sale by the quaestor of the Roman people. Some writers, he concludes, may carelessly or negligently have used *manubiae* and *praeda* interchangeably, but Cicero knew what he was doing.

Watching the spoils of imperial conquest transmuted into the weapons of an elegant form of civil dueling, the people in the audience must have enjoyed being on the right side of invisible boundaries reaffirmed, relieved no doubt that it was not their own half-baked learning that provoked the debate. Favorinus' claim not to be an expert in Latin merely enhances the public shame of his interlocutor, presumably a native speaker, as we see from his treatment of the boastful grammarian who was unable to define his word by genus and species. On that occasion he observed (after defining the word himself with reference to the juridical writings of Scaevola), "These things, although I had devoted myself to philosophy, I did not neglect to learn, since it is no less disgraceful for Roman citizens who speak Latin to refer to something by the wrong word than to call a man by the

---

[29] For the conscientious archaist's credo, compare Fronto on the sheer effort that the discovery and correct deployment of unusual words requires, and the dangers that lurk for the half-learned (*Letters to Marcus* 4.3.2).

wrong name."[30] The assimilation of scholarly error to social gaffe in this admonition is particularly striking.

There was, after all, no clear distinction made by Roman aristocrats in this period between social and intellectual *savoir faire*. Literary knowledge was a form of symbolic capital to be displayed, and unwritten rules governed the competitive contexts in which this display took place. Vignettes from Gellius can suggest something of the flavor of these occasions, without providing a full typology. In an archaizing literary culture, the primary form of intellectual inquiry was solitary reading of the ancients, if we discount the invisible presence of the literate slaves who read aloud or took down extracts at dictation.[31] In its secondary stages, intellectual inquiry took the form of social entertainment. Favorinus gave dinner parties for his intimates at which historical selections or passages from the poets were read aloud by a slave, sometimes in Greek, sometimes in Latin, while the guests were at table.[32] An etymological treatise from Cicero's day might provide the host with an opportunity to make a quick correction,[33] or a rare word from Latin poetry might provoke the assembled company to ask for a longer disquisition.[34] Although Favorinus gave daily public lectures on suggested themes,[35] the display of learning in private social gatherings took place under special constraints. Favorinus himself acknowledges these when he remarks to his guests, "And since I have drunk a fair bit, I would have babbled on about the meanings of all these words, had I not already said a great deal while all the rest of you remained silent, as if I were giving a rhetorical display. For to deliver a monologue at a dinner party is neither ethically correct nor socially agreeable."[36]

Besides taking advantage of the display opportunities afforded by public forums and private dinner parties, Favorinus also made what might be termed philosophical housecalls. Fronto is laid up with gout; Favorinus goes to visit him with Gellius in tow. A number of learned men are also present, and a discussion ensues.[37] We glimpse him on another occasion at

---

[30] *Attic Nights* 4.1.18.

[31] Gellius' preface discusses his method of research and his conception of its intended audience: busy men who have no time to acquire *honesta eruditio* but wish to spare themselves the embarrassment of boorish ignorance. On the compositional methods of Diogenes Laertius, compare J. Mejer, *Diogenes Laertius and His Hellenistic Background*, Hermes Einzelschriften 40 (1978), 16–29.

[32] *Attic Nights* 2.22.1.

[33] Ibid. 3.19.

[34] Ibid. 2.22.2.

[35] Galen, *On Prognosis* 5 (K 14.627 = *CMG* 5.8.1).

[36] *neque honestum est . . . neque commodum* (*Attic Nights* 2.22.26). For a philosopher who makes himself disagreeable to his guests by "behaving as if he were in a lecture hall instead of at a convivial gathering," see the Greek *Aesopica*, ed. B. E. Perry (Urbana, Ill., 1952), 68.

[37] *Attic Nights* 2.26.

the bedside of an ailing friend, lecturing the assembled physicians on the digestive theories of Erasistratos![38] This is exactly the sort of behavior that Plutarch has in mind when he warns the sickbed visitor "not to chatter officiously in sophist-fashion about blockages and influxes and methodist clichés, incidentally showing off one's knowledge of medical terminology and treatises."[39] A blessed event provides the occasion for another house-call. A senatorial Roman, one of those who listened to Favorinus' lectures and followed him around, has just had his first son.[40] Favorinus immediately leads a troop of the other students over to pay a call. Inquiring politely after the medical details of the birth, Favorinus is told that the young mother, exhausted, has fallen asleep. "I have no doubt," he remarks, "she will nourish her son with her own milk." The girl's mother retorts that her daughter is to be spared the trouble. In accordance with common practice, they will employ wet nurses instead. With her retort, Favorinus has conjured up a springboard for an impromptu rhetorical display.[41]

His sermon on breastfeeding starts out as teleological ethics: "I beg you, madam, let her be wholly and entirely the mother of her own child. . . . Or do you perhaps also think that Nature gave women nipples as a sort of beauty spot, not for feeding their children but to ornament their chests?" Favorinus compares a refusal to breastfeed with abortions undertaken for the sake of feminine vanity. Then, his actual interlocutor as effectively silenced as her daughter (whose absence makes her more object than subject in this conversation), the philosopher varies his pace by introducing the objection of an imaginary interlocutor: as long as the child is nourished, it makes no difference whose milk does the job. From here Favorinus launches into a display piece of natural philosophy: "Is the blood which is now in the breasts not the same as it was in the womb, merely because it has become white from abundant air and warmth?" These arguments about the purposes of Nature serve, as so often happens, to reinforce the prejudices of culture: just as trees transplanted to inferior soil fail to thrive, so the inbred nobility of the aristocratic newborn's body and soul, "formed from gifted seeds," can be corrupted by the "alien and degenerate nourishment of another's milk."[42] Slave, servile, or foreign, unprincipled, ugly, sluttish, and drunk—he sketches a quick portrait of the typical wet nurse and demands, "Shall we then allow this child of ours to be infected with some dangerous contagion and to draw into its mind

---

[38] Ibid. 16.3. The best sketch of the intellectual milieu of the aristocratic Roman sickbed remains Galen's memoir *On Prognosis* (above, n.35).

[39] *Mor.* 129D.

[40] *Attic Nights* 12.1.1.

[41] He spoke in Greek (ibid. 12.1.24).

[42] Ibid. 12.1.17.

and body a spirit (*spiritus*) derived from a body and mind of inferior quality?" So thoroughly is Favorinus absorbed in the role of aristocratic family confidant that he exhibits here no sense that he himself might be considered a foreigner, a physically inferior specimen whose origins lay in some "alien and barbarous nation."[43] His lurid picture of contagion spreading from the nursemaid's breasts draws upon his contemporaries' complex beliefs about aristocratic identity: it is an amalgam of psychophysical components that must continuously be fostered by appropriate environmental influences and health practices. To be formed from first-class seeds (*bene ingeniatis primordiis inchoatum*) is a necessary, but not a sufficient, condition for the full development of the child's *nobilitas*. As Plutarch says, when he explains why a wet nurse must be Greek in manners and character, "For just as the limbs of babies' bodies must be molded starting from birth, so that they may grow straight and unwarped, so right from the beginning it is appropriate to work on the orderly formation of children's manners and character."[44]

Ringing the changes of drawing-room display-rhetoric, Favorinus turns to literary criticism to support his argument. While adducing the relevant passages of the poets, as every gentleman should know how to do, he works in a little lesson on how Virgil has improved upon Homer. Patroclus' outburst to Achilles, "Horseman Peleus was never thy sire . . . but the grey sea and the flinty rocks," has been improved by Virgil, who added to the charge of inhuman birth the charge of wild and savage nurture: "And Hyrcanean tigers gave thee suck." Favorinus' art here consists of locating the ancient authority for his argument about the importance of nurture precisely in a passage that will delight his audience for other reasons, since comparisons of Homer and Virgil, especially to the latter's advantage, were a favorite parlor game of Roman intellectuals.

Favorinus closes with cautionary remarks about how failure to breast-feed affects the development of maternal love. He even compares infants turned over to alien nurses to those exposed at birth. Potential counter-examples to this affecting picture of ruptured family ties are obliterated with a philosophical distinction: the love that appears to subsist between parents and the children whom they have given to others to nurse is not natural but conventional, based not on true knowledge but on opinion.[45]

[43] Ibid. 12.1.17.

[44] *Mor.* 3E. For ῥυθμίζω used of infant massage compare Soranus, *Gynecology* 1.83 and Rufus as quoted in Oribasius, *Incerta* 20. Wet-nurses for Plutarch were only a second choice; like Musonius Rufus and Favorinus, he played the role of philosophical advocate of maternal breastfeeding (*Mor.* 3C; Musonius, ed. Lutz, "Musonius, the Roman Socrates," YCS 10 [1947], 42). Soranus urged Romans to employ Greek wet-nurses. Their influence on the infant's language development seems to have been his chief concern, though he also thought Greek women more nurturing than Roman: *Gyn.* 2.19.15; 2.44.1–2.

[45] *Attic Nights* 12.1.23.

A conspicuous feature of this visit is the way Favorinus avails himself of the philosopher's freedom to censure the behavior of others while standing himself somehow outside the fray. His discussion of breastfeeding introduces questions about the relationship of nature to nurture and the relationship of physical to moral defects that might be thought embarrassing to him personally, but Favorinus' identification with his role is so complete that somehow the question is never raised. One last vignette from Gellius will illustrate how Favorinus' fully achieved public persona could sustain his weight while he skated over thin ice.

It is early spring, and we find ourselves strolling with Favorinus in the tepid sunshine of the courtyard of the Titian baths. He has noticed a friend carrying around a copy of Sallust's *Catiline* and asks him to read from it as they walk. "Avarice, . . . steeped as it were in noxious poisons, renders effeminate both the manly body and the manly soul." Turning to Gellius, the philosopher asks, "How is it that avarice renders the *body* effeminate? For I more or less understand how the manly soul is thus affected, but I have not yet discovered how it feminizes a man's body also."[46] Gellius, nonplussed, at length replies that he had been about to ask the very same question. A bolder student, with an assumed air of experience, breaks in to say that Valerius Probus once pronounced Sallust's "body and soul" a poetic circumlocution for "man." As usual, the overeager poseur has revealed not his knowledge but his ignorance; Favorinus denies both that Sallust ever used such a trope and that Valerius ever attributed it to him. A man of learning happens to be walking the same promenade. He does not offer his opinion until Favorinus asks for it, and then he suggests that an avaricious man, intent on sedentary indoor pursuits, neglects "manly labor" and lacks enthusiasm for physical training. His answer certainly presupposes a concept of manliness as something that will dwindle without exercise. Favorinus' retort pushes a little harder at the possibility that the state of the body may not accurately reflect the state of the soul: "How are we to explain the fact that it is possible to find many men who are avaricious but still robust and vigorous?" The learned stranger replies that such men must have other interests, but Favorinus remains unconvinced. "Either what you have said is plausible, or Sallust, through hatred of avarice, laid against it an unfairly heavy charge." Favorinus' resorting to the Academics' notorious suspension of judgment only reminds us of how many other issues are here left unresolved. Is effeminacy the result of nature or nurture? And what really is the relationship between physical and moral defects?

Not all the exchanges recorded in Gellius are as amicable as this one, but people were evidently able to disagree with Favorinus without challenging his claim to be a philosopher or making an issue of his physical defect. The

[46] Ibid. 3.1.3.

irascible grammarian Domitius, responding to a civil question from Favorinus about the correct usage of a Latin word, erupts with a categorical attack on philosophers who occupy themselves with words and definitions. Indeed, they impinge upon his territory to the neglect of their proper role. "For I, a grammarian, pursue the study of life and manners while you philosophers are nothing but funereal gibberish, as Cato would say, since you go about collecting glossaries and little word-lists— disgusting stuff, as trivial and foolish as the voices of female hacks hired to sing dirges."[47] However savage this criticism of philosophers' linguistic affectations as funereal and therefore feminine, it is by no means an *ad hominem* attack on Favorinus. Similarly Galen, when defending Epictetus from Favorinus' snobbish disparagement or attacking his radical skepticism, may accuse Favorinus of philosophical incoherence or impugn his Attic style but never attributes these deficiencies to his physical imperfection.[48]

Favorinus then, when observed in action among his Roman friends, appears at ease in the role of philosopher, a role subject to certain stereotyped expectations, which presupposed a deliberate stylization of identity. Taking title to the philosophical persona with an imperturbable authority, and adopting the sententiousness and frank speech, if not the shaggy grooming, of the traditional role, Favorinus was able to carry off many contentious social encounters that might otherwise have exposed him to personal ridicule. But Favorinus was also a sophist, a role that encouraged the stylization of eccentricity. Hence the slogan with which he summed up his identity in three paradoxes: It was as a sophist that he boasted to be a Gaul who spoke Greek. Certainly it was not as a philosopher that he boasted to be a eunuch prosecuted for adultery. To claim to have quarreled with an emperor and lived to tell the tale is to claim both a philosopher's courage and a sophist's arrogance.

Like Polemo with his exotic chariot and specialized hunting-dogs, Favorinus also used props in his play of self-presentation. His favorite slave, whom he bequeathed to Herodes Atticus, was, like himself, a barbarian with a physical defect. He was an Indian, strikingly black-skinned, and his attempts to speak Greek made him appear to have a speech impediment. Like his master, he made a virtue of his defect and delighted the two erudite friends when they drank together by sprinkling his Indian dialect with Attic words stammered out among the barbarisms.[49] This mascot

---

[47] Ibid. 18.7.3.

[48] Favorinus had written a dialogue in which he did not attack Epictetus *in propria persona* but delegated the task to an imaginary *slave* of Plutarch's. Galen seems to take exception to Favorinus' skepticism because it subverts the hierarchy of teacher-student, expert-layman relationships. Galen, *On the Best Teaching*, K1.41 = Barigazzi, fr. 28, cf. 30.

[49] *Lives* 490. Similar taste must have dictated one of Herodes' gifts to Favorinus' pupil Alexander: two lisping children from the Attic deme of Kollytos (ibid. 574).

must have made a piquant contrast to Herodes' pet "Heracles," a wild man born near Marathon who wrestled with animals and spoke perfect Attic Greek.[50] A prodigy like this obviously appealed to Herodes and his friends because he embodied a connection between their Atticism, the product of elaborate literary culture, and a sort of pure, primitive, and manly *Ur-Atticism* that, as they liked to think, existed in nature.

A friendship with Herodes Atticus was not just a friendship; it was, to use the the the language of Madison Avenue, a statement. The same goes for a feud with Polemo. Both relationships were cultivated. When we step back to try to reconcile the positive with the negative portrayals of Favorinus left to us by divers sources, the contrast defeats all attempts at synthesis until we apply Favorinus' own dictum, "It is more disgraceful to be praised feebly and coldly than to be harshly attacked."[51] For, as he explains, people tend to discount the criticism of someone who obviously hates you, but the person who praises you faintly appears to be a friend who is doing his best but can find nothing better to say. As we saw in the case of Favorinus' statue, attacks could be rhetorically useful because they provided a speaker with an opportunity to say things about himself that would otherwise be condemned as self-praise. We now consider how Favorinus' exile (real or imagined) provided him with opportunities for self-defense and self-definition.

FAVORINUS AS EXILE

The awkward fact is that we cannot be certain whether Favorinus was ever exiled at all.[52] Favorinus' surviving works, except for the papyrus to be discussed below, do not allude to a period of exile, and neither does his admiring friend Aulus Gellius. His critics, Polemo and Lucian, are also silent. The biographer Philostratus was either ignorant or devious. He observes blandly, "When a dispute came up between him and the emperor Hadrian, he came to no harm."[53] Is it permissible understatement to say, of a man exiled by an autocrat, that he "came to no harm" because he escaped with his life? Philostratus certainly had the darker possibilities on his mind:

---

[50] *Lives* 552–54. He dressed in wolf skins; his bristly eyebrows met above his piercing eyes; and like some sort of holy man, he was endowed with a supernatural "nose" for spiritual impurity that could detect in a ritual bowl of milk the polluting touch of the woman who prepared it.

[51] *Attic Nights* 19.3.

[52] Barigazzi takes it for a fact, but Bowersock points out difficulties (*Greek Sophists in the Roman Empire*, 36). S. Swain, "Favorinus and Hadrian," *ZPE* 79 (1989), 150–58, is skeptical but inconclusive.

[53] οὐδὲν ἔπαθεν, *Lives* 489.

he commends Hadrian in this passage for disagreeing on equal terms with someone whom he could have executed. Did his desire to draw a moral here, combined with a characteristically "protective attitude toward his subjects,"[54] make him screen the disgrace of Favorinus from posterity? After all, only a page before, he had told us that Dio of Prusa was not really an exile, although Dio himself frequently and ostentatiously tells us that he was.[55] If we had more orations of Favorinus, would we find him boasting of his exile too? We cannot be sure, but their situations were not entirely alike: to have suffered like Dio under a bad emperor was almost a guarantee of philosophical authenticity; falling out with a noted philhellene conferred less distinction.

Yet trouble with the emperor was definitely part of Favorinus' public image: it was one of the three paradoxes of his life that he had "quarreled with the emperor and lived."[56] What did they quarrel about? Hadrian criticized Favorinus on a point of vocabulary; Favorinus declined to pursue the dispute with the master of thirty legions.[57] Then there is Favorinus' attempt to gain immunity as a philosopher from the burdensome duties of a high priesthood in Gaul.[58] The emperor was not impressed, and Favorinus backed down just in time, explaining that he had been advised to serve his country by his philosophical teacher, the great Dio of Prusa, who took the trouble to visit him in a dream. This socially graceful explanation retracted his claim to a philosophical immunity while reasserting his claim to a philosophical pedigree. Yet to claim apparitional intimacy with a famous philosopher is not quite the same thing as to cleave to the philosopher's role oneself, and it should be pointed out that by electing to behave with the deference of a courtier, Favorinus was abandoning an opportunity to behave with the fearless frankness of a philosopher. To appreciate the contrast, we have only to compare the popular story of Secundus, the so-called silent philosopher, who stood by his principles and intrepidly defied Hadrian's commands.[59]

In Philostratus's version of the immunity incident, there is nothing overtly menacing about Hadrian's behavior. He hastens to assure us that "the Emperor had been acting for his own amusement: he used to pay attention to sophists and philosophers as a diversion from imperial

[54] C. P. Jones, "The Reliability of Philostratus," *Approaches to the Second Sophistic*, ed. G. W. Bowersock (Philadelphia, 1974), 14.

[55] *Lives* 488; Dio Chrysostom 13.1; 19.1; 36.1; 45.1; C. P. Jones, *The Roman World of Dio Chrysostom* (Cambridge, 1978), 45–55. J. L. Moles, "The Career and Conversion of Dio Chrysostom," *JHS* 98 (1978), 79–100, appreciates his exile's mythic dimensions.

[56] *Lives* 489.

[57] *Historia Augusta: Life of Hadrian* 15.12–13.

[58] *Lives* 490; Dio Chrysostom 69.3.

[59] *Secundus the Silent Philosopher*, ed. B. E. Perry, *American Philological Association Monographs* 22, 1964.

cares."⁶⁰ By contrast, Philostratus continues, the affair seemed so serious to the Athenian magistrates that they took Favorinus' statue down "as if he were an out-and-out enemy of the emperor." Favorinus handled this insult by remarking that Socrates would have been better off if the Athenians had merely destroyed his statue. This retort shows how the ability to commandeer for oneself a paradigm from myth or history might be useful in controlling public perceptions of the vicissitudes of one's career.

Historically, it is hard to see why the immunity incident should have provoked such a strong reaction on the part of the Athenian magistrates. Perhaps their sudden sensitivity to Hadrian's taste anticipated his forthcoming visit to Athens: the Temple of Olympian Zeus was to be dedicated in 130 or 131, with Favorinus' arch-enemy Polemo as official orator. The historian Dio takes a darker view of Hadrian and says without qualification that he tried to destroy Favorinus by promoting his rivals.⁶¹ He also claims that Hadrian quarreled with Favorinus and Dionysius of Miletus but had to spare them because he could find no pretext to put them to death, while in the case of Apollodorus, the architect who criticized his plans for the temple of Venus and Roma, he began by exiling and ended up executing him.⁶² As for Favorinus, there was also the scandal of his trial for adultery: the aggrieved husband was of consular rank.⁶³ Perhaps Hadrian had the adultery charge in mind when he refused to grant Favorinus a liturgical immunity "on the grounds that he was not a philosopher."⁶⁴ Given the inconsistent narratives of Philostratus and Dio, however, and the inconsistent behavior of Hadrian himself, the complete story of Favorinus' quarrels with the emperor will never be told.

On the basis of the surviving evidence, no one could have predicted that in 1931 a Vatican papyrus would turn up in which Favorinus discourses philosophically about his own exile.⁶⁵ Because the information that survives outside the text is insufficient to prove its historicity, we are left with

⁶⁰ *Lives* 490.
⁶¹ Dio Cassius, *Roman History* (epitome) 69.3.
⁶² Ibid. 69.4. S. Swain, "Favorinus and Hadrian," 151, suggests that Hadrian probably quarreled with all three at about the same time, near the beginning of his reign. Philostratus mentions no quarrel between Dionysius and Hadrian; indeed, Hadrian made that sophist a procurator as well as a member of the Museum (*Lives* 524).
⁶³ *Lives* 489.
⁶⁴ ὡς μὴ φιλοσοφοῦντι, ibid. 490.
⁶⁵ M. Norsa and G. Vitelli in *Studi e Testi* 53 (1931); text with editor's supplements in Barigazzi, pp. 375–409. The authorship of the papyrus is secure: Stobaeus quotes from it twice under the lemma Φαβωρίνου. The title Περὶ Φυγῆς is only a conjecture, since neither on the papyrus nor in Stobaeus has a title been preserved. Favorinus' speech has been copied on the verso of a recycled papyrus containing administrative documents from Marmarica dating from the end of the reign of Commodus (d. 192). One column is missing at the beginning and probably somewhat more at the end. Susan Stephens has generously checked the readings of the papyrus for me at several points.

the problem of whether the document can authenticate itself. Severed by the accidents of time from the historical context of its composition, Favorinus' exile speech, whether fact or fiction, has come to resemble the words of the bronze maiden marking Midas' tomb in the *Corinthian Oration*: a self-authenticating monument that exists as words alone, any objective correlative having disappeared. Whatever details we may cite to prove its "truth" as a record of lived experience (references to the speaker's deceased parents and beloved sister, for example, or specific allusions to Chios as his place of exile),[66] all these might have been invented to lend verisimilitude to a fictionalized declamation-cum-diatribe in which a philosopher who has never been exiled practices what he would say if he were. If we argue that Favorinus' exile speech *must* be historical because no orator trying to impersonate a philosopher true-to-genre would be likely to mention something as trivial as the existence of his sister, then we must cope with the passage in which the speaker expresses confidence in future progeny: could this possibly be the eunuch from Gaul speaking *in propria persona*, or has the "real" Favorinus, speaking in the persona of a philosopher, simply allowed himself to get carried away?

All these interpretive choices depend on the assumption that there was such a person as the "real" Favorinus. Better to follow the instructions of the Wizard of Oz: "Pay no attention to the man behind the curtain!" As long as Favorinus' exile lacks genuinely independent corroboration or disproof, it exists only as a construct of his own words and his own self-generated mythology. Given that this mythology was created by a performing artist whose self-fashioning was perpetually in progress, it is naive to ask the real Favorinus to please stand up. If Helen never went to Troy, and Ovid never went to Tomi,[67] then maybe Favorinus never went to Chios. Where does that leave us? Inside the world created by the text.

Exile, real or imagined, presented Favorinus with a rhetorical opportunity. Here we explore what use he made of it. For this purpose it is not necessary to sort out Stoic from Cynic platitudes or chase elusive citations to their source. The focus is on the speech as a work of the imagination. Despite its fragmentary condition, it is possible to examine how Favorinus created multiple personae for himself, invisible interlocutors for those selves to talk to, and even at times made the audience play a role in his fictions. These are the same techniques he used in the defense of his statue

[66] References to family (cited by papyrus column and line number): col. 11.21–25; to Chios: col. 14.39–42, cf. 25.36–37; 26.14,26.
[67] As argued on meteorological grounds by A. D. Fitton Brown, "The Unreality of Ovid's Tomitian Exile," *Liverpool Classical Monthly* 10.2 (1985), 18–22, with appropriate reference to the fictionalized love-affairs pursued on paper by elegiac poets in general and the adoption of legendary personae in the *Heroides* by Ovid in particular.

in the *Corinthian Oration*. Here, as there, he accomplished much of his role-playing through brief allusions to the literary tradition that was his heritage in common with his audience. No elaborate explanations were necessary; he could change the scene with a very light touch.

As in the *Corinthian Oration*, a recent insult to the speaker's reputation brings him a peculiar rhetorical advantage. Strong cultural pressures to use rhetoric as a vehicle for self-assertion sometimes collided with strong cultural inhibitions against self-praise. Rhetorical handbooks discussed how to handle the problem;[68] Favorinus' friend Plutarch tackled it head-on with a treatise on inoffensive self-praise,[69] in which he observed, "Not only those on trial and in danger, but also those in misfortune, may brag and boast more appropriately than may those in good fortune." Plutarch makes an analogy between speech and posture as vehicles of self-presentation: just as a fighter is applauded for standing tall and may carry himself in a way that would be considered ridiculous in a person sauntering down the street, "so a man brought low by fortune, when he draws himself up to his full height as a competitor, 'like a boxer, hand to hand,' and uses his boasting to change from a humbled and pitiable condition to a state of exultation and pride, does not seem to us offensively aggressive, but great and invincible."[70]

Yet even in a speech of apology, there lurked opportunities for offensive self-assertion. Dio Chrysostom, for example, discusses his exile in a speech of self-justification to his native city but cuts himself short with the comment that people will think he is not really grieving, just boasting.[71] The trick is to capture the good will of one's audience by striking the right balance between self-assertion and vulnerability. Favorinus alludes to this dilemma in the first extant words of the exile speech, where he says that someone might suspect that he has composed his speech out of boastfulness (*alazoneia*). Evidently, like Dio, he felt that speaking about his own exile required some sort of prophylactic gesture. Favorinus declines to discuss why he has been exiled but compares himself to the sages of the past who have maintained their philosophical composure under similarly trying circumstances. One might think that by refusing to refute the charges against him he has renounced the opportunity to structure his

---

[68] Two second-century examples are Alexander's *Topics for Rhetors* (Spengel, *Rhetores Graeci* [Leipzig, 1856], vol. 3, p. 4) and the rhetorical handbook attributed to Aelius Aristides (Spengel, vol. 2, p. 506).

[69] Περὶ τοῦ ἑαυτοῦ ἐπαινεῖν ἀνεπιφθόνως, *Mor.* 539–57. On the links of this treatise to the rhetorical tradition, see L. Radermacher, "Studien zur Geschichte der griechischen Rhetorik, II: Plutarchs Schrift *de ipso citra invidiam laudando*," *Rh. Mus.* 52 (1897), 419–24.

[70] "On Inoffensive Self-Praise," *Mor.* 541B.

[71] ἀλαζονεύεσθαι, *Or.* 45.2. Aristides, in his *Concerning a Remark in Passing*, often says with savage irony that his self-defense will be construed as boasting.

speech as a self-defense and hence has forfeited the opportunity to include material that in other contexts might be condemned as self-praise. (To quote Plutarch again, "One may praise oneself without inspiring resentment if one is defending oneself against slander or a legal charge.")[72] But it will become apparent that Favorinus has indeed preserved for himself the posture of self-defense by constructing an imaginary scenario in which he as paradigmatic exile is under attack by all the things he has loved and lost. Then it becomes his job as philosopher-orator to defend the beleaguered exile: that is, it becomes his job in one role to defend himself in another, exactly as he did in the *Corinthian Oration*.[73] The first few columns of the papyrus can be seen as a warm-up for the main scenario, in that they explore more generally the issues of paradigms and role-playing.

In the *Corinthian Oration* Favorinus described himself as equipped by the gods to be a paradigm for Greeks, Romans, and Celts. In the exile speech Favorinus promises to supply more than mere words of exhortation to other exiles: he will offer himself as a paradigm.[74] Plutarch comments on this tactic when he discusses the possibility of praising oneself in order to exhort others and inspire them with emulation and ambition. He thought it was legitimate for Nestor in the *Iliad* to recount his own triumphs because he did so to inspire Patroclus and rouse reluctant champions for single combat against Hector.[75] In Plutarch's view, "protreptic that contains both word and action and offers a personal example to be emulated (*paradeigma*) is full of life; it rouses and spurs on the hearer . . . and gives him hope that what is in question can be attained and is not impossible."[76] Speeches of philosophical exhortation traditionally turned for their paradigms to Homer, the tragedians, and the legendary sages of the past. Favorinus' programmatic announcement that he will also use his own experience as a paradigm foreshadows the fact that when he does invoke some of the traditional paradigmatic figures, he will use them in an idiosyncratic and appropriative way.

Favorinus goes on to claim that his work will endure like a dedicated monument and will remain useful to others.[77] This echo of Thucydides' claim to usefulness and immortality is followed by an echo of Thucydi-

---

[72] *Mor.* 540C.

[73] See Chapter One. Favorinus' epideictic speech *On Fortune* is also structured as a defense ([Dio Chrysostom] 64); see page 12 above.

[74] οὐ λόγῳ μόνον, ἀλλὰ καὶ τῷ οἰκείῳ παραδείγματι προτρέπων (col. 1.42–44).

[75] *Mor.* 544D. In *Or.* 57 Dio Chrysostom spends some ten pages defending Nestor from the charge of boasting in what turns out after all to be a speech in defense of *himself.*

[76] *Mor.* 544D–E. Aristides' speech of self-defense "Concerning a Remark in Passing" echoes Plutarch and uses some of the same examples (*Or.* 28.35,104,141).

[77] ἀνακείσεται δὲ ἥδε ἡ γραφὴ κτῆμα καὶ ἄλλῳ ποτέ αὖθις (col. 1.46–47), cf. Thuc. κτῆμα ἐς αἰεὶ . . . ξύγκειται, 1.22.

dean syntax: an immense series of articular infinitives spells out how readers of his treatise should make proper use of the examples it contains. The next section develops an analogy between life and the stage, but in a direction slightly different from the one it usually takes in works of popular philosophy: Favorinus does not urge that we act with dignity in whatever role heaven has assigned.[78] Instead, he uses the analogy to demonstrate the fundamental unity of the actor's self behind the many roles he plays, whose constant shifts betray their triviality. Should we humans, who adapt so readily to the widest range of theatrical roles, complain of the part assigned us by the Playwright of the Universe?[79] People who have fallen into exile from positions of power should see that they have "changed the costume and mask of a role *but remain themselves inside,* just like . . . [there is a hole in the text just when it seems about to give us an image of what abides behind the mask] . . . changing into all kinds of shapes according to the parts they play."[80]

Here Favorinus appears to advocate an attitude of fundamental irony toward all the parts one plays. Favorinus may have been unusually self-conscious about role-playing, but every veteran of sophistic training had extensive practice speaking in the voice of another—this was, after all, the essence of declamation—and those who aspired to the status of philosopher were acutely conscious of the need to harmonize their self-presentation with the great paradigms of the philosophic pantheon. Dio Chrysostom, for example, frequently adopted the personae of great figures of the past in his orations and showed a particular fondness for presenting himself in the guise of Diogenes, Socrates, or Odysseus.[81] Favorinus follows his generalized discussion of role-playing with the specific examples of Diogenes, Heracles, and Odysseus.

He claims that these men actually gained in reputation because of their exile. What Favorinus chooses to emphasize is Odysseus' paradoxical quality: the hero is not as he first appears. Before he went to Troy, he seemed no different from the other local kings; in his reluctance to go to Troy, he seemed like a coward; even at Troy, his fighting skill seemed nothing special, but he revealed his true manhood in the trials of shipwreck, hunger, filthy clothes, and the indignity of submission to a woman's will (col. 4.3–4).

With a brisk "Now *I,*" Favorinus turns the spotlight from Odysseus to himself. Just as in the *Corinthian Oration* he created out of thin air an imaginary trial scenario under whose terms the rest of the speech was to

---

[78] Cf. Epictetus, Synesius, and Teles (Barigazzi, p. 415).

[79] τῷ . . . τοῦ κόσμου ποιητῇ θεῷ, col. 2. 48–50. Lucian recounts a vision of human roles as stage costumes, only in his version Fortune arbitrarily plays impresario (*Menippos* 16).

[80] Col. 3.7–12. Barigazzi suggests restorations, but there is very little to build on.

[81] Moles cites numerous examples (above, n.55), 96–100.

take place, so here too he sets up his own stage. This time we are at Olympia. As the athletes enter the stadium, their friends and family cheer them on, reminding them that these are the games for which they have expended so much time, toil, and perspiration. Favorinus joins the chorus of advice, splitting himself into the personae of advisor and advisee. "I seem to myself to be exhorting and reminding myself of this (I speaking to myself in the present situation just like someone else to another): that these are the very disasters and reversals of fate for which you have been practicing and training your soul since childhood." (col. 4.34–39) From here he starts to speak in the persona of his second self, which, in the role of advisor, addresses his original self (the advisee) as "you." Saved by this expedient from the offensiveness of full-strength self-praise (*periautologia*), he allows his "second self" to rehearse his acquaintance, through education, with the exemplary accomplishments of the past, his personal association with the worthies of the present, and his wide travels, in both Hellenic and barbarian regions.

Favorinus' "mighty opponents" are all the factors that threaten to destroy the exile's peace of mind: longing for his native land, for parents and friends, for wealth and honors, and finally for freedom. The imagery, once decorously Olympic, is now brutally gladiatorial: the opponents do not wait their turn but attack the exile's soul pell-mell (col. 5.35f.). The crowd cheers them on from above. This is not the stage of Dionysus, we are told, where he wins who makes the most men laugh or cry. This is the stage of Heracles, the stadium of Virtue. In a sonorous flourish the master of ceremonies announces that we are watching a contest that has nothing to do with words: *ergōn ou logōn ho agōn*.

Nothing to do with words? With this paradox Favorinus' speech appears to dismantle itself in favor of the imaginary world it has itself created. But the speaker's delight in paradox is not merely playful. The sophist's "word" *is* his "work" and has all the seriousness of the warrior's task, as it should in a society where rhetoric is the form of heroic combat open to the public figure. Then Favorinus practically dismantles his audience by implying that its reaction has no bearing on the success of his speech: "One must despise clapping and hissing, praise and ridicule and all that kind of noise, and, placing one's hopes in oneself alone, tough it out with soul stripped naked under the blazing sun and the thirsty dust." (col. 6.5–10)

Playing the herald of his own games, Favorinus calls forth the first opponent, longing for one's native land. The device of announcing his next "opponent," which he re-invokes with every change of topic, enables him to present the exile's temptations as a series of items in a sustained descriptive catalog of challengers and responses, a sort of philosophical analogue to the catalog of opposing champions in the *Seven Against Thebes*. Favorinus begins his discussion of longing for one's native land by quoting Polyneices, who recalls:

> The gymnasia where I was reared, and Dirce's waters,
> From all these I was driven unjustly away, to live
> In a strange city, where sorrow's river
> wells up from my eyes.[82]

Though Favorinus has announced that he is going to ignore the crowd, he still needs an addressee for his remarks. So he commandeers Polyneices as an interlocutor (col. 6.25–26). There is no clear indication of when this apostrophe to Polyneices ends, because apostrophe to Polyneices can substitute for apostrophe to the audience. This tactic allows the speaker to maintain the good will of his actual audience while enlivening his talk with passages of invective scolding an imaginary addressee.[83]

Thus at times Favorinus engages literary characters in dialogue; at other times he appropriates their words in monologue. When recounting his own experience of travel abroad, he incorporates first-person quotations from Homer and Sophocles seamlessly into his first-person narrative, making the words of Odysseus and Theseus his own. He says:

> But for me, who before my enforced exile have passed most of my life in diverse parts of land and sea and in dealings abroad with foreign men,

> "Work was never absorbing,
> Nor domestic life, that raises glorious children,
> But oared ships have always been my delight,
> And battles and polished spearpoints and arrows."
> (col. 11.8–15-*Od.* 14.222–25)

Favorinus is impersonating Odysseus the impersonator, the Odysseus of the Cretan Tales. He continues,

> It is not an appropriate time to deplore my present absence from home, like someone who experiences an excess of longing for the land of his birth,

> "As I know myself, as one brought up abroad,
> Just like . . . "

> Theseus in Sophocles,

> "I wrestled like no other man
> With mortal perils far from home."
> (*Oedipus at Colonus*, 562–64)

When Favorinus appropriates the heroes of the past, he does not so much adopt their personae as make them do his will. Dio Chrysostom also

---

[82] Euripides, *Phoenician Women*, 367–70.

[83] Plutarch subjects the same passage of Euripides to schoolmasterly exegesis without any use of apostrophe or personification (*On Exile*, 16). Musonius takes a livelier approach, combining apostrophe to Euripides with comments addressed to a contemporary interlocutor (*That Exile Is Not an Evil*, pp. 72–74 Lutz).

uses literary exempla when discussing his experience of exile, but he quotes without impersonating: "And then I recalled Odysseus, who" (*Or.* 13.4), or "And again I recalled how Electra asks" (*Or.* 13.5). Dio prefers to speak in the persona of Socrates, and, because he claims to have been appointed to his philosophical mission by the God at Delphi, he has been accused of "plagiarizing Socrates' biography."[84] To say this is to apply anachronistic notions of sincerity and authenticity to a stylized traditional medium. In the culture of Dio and Favorinus, to be an exile *as Odysseus*, to be a philosopher *as Socrates*, is to be more, not less, oneself.

A personal paradigm can confer citizenship in the culture of *paideia*, independently of the speaker's particular social and geographical ties. Yet Favorinus is not willing to settle for this generalized citizenship alone. Claiming to have been settled in his place of exile by God himself, Favorinus redefines the traditional terminology of citizenship to secure for himself a place in the citizen body of his place of exile. "For it is neither laws nor the metic-tax that makes men citizens or strangers, but their attitude of mind (*gnōmē*). And taking courage from this, I enroll myself, not with documents, but with good will, as a citizen of this town."[85] His sponsor? Zeus Patroos himself. One might expect a philosopher discoursing about his exile to introduce the Stoic notion of world citizenship, but it is not quite the same thing to say that all men are fellow-citizens as it is to say, as Favorinus does, that I am such a man as can make myself a citizen of any city. The boldness with which Favorinus redefines citizenship in this passage and appropriates for his own purposes Stoic platitudes is in keeping with his bold use of personae and his appropriative use of quotation.

A good example of the latter appears in the next round of imaginary combat, where the exiled orator, after doing away with "loss of homeland," tackles his second opponent, "loss of friends." One's friends at least can travel: the Argonauts, the Greeks at Troy, Pylades, and Theseus all undertook immense journeys for friendship's sake (col. 13.31ff.). Would Theseus hesitate to cross over to Chios,[86] who crossed over to Hades to accompany his friend? Will *my* friend allow *me* to languish *etc.*? It would not be quite right to speak of a "transition from myth to reality" here. Favorinus has, it is true, changed the subject from Theseus to himself, but at the same moment he creates an entirely imaginary friend, his own heroic twin. This "friend" exists as a foil for self-dramatization in various postures of abandonment: "Will he think fit that I live, in grief for him, a life of misery and pain, just like another man did once when, bereft of friends,

[84] Moles (above, n.55), 100.

[85] Col. 11.47–12.10. He does not use the middle voice but the active: ἐμαυτὸν . . . ἐγγράφω.

[86] It is on the basis of this reference that the original editors of the papyrus suggested that Favorinus had been relegated to Chios.

'He would look out, weeping, on the barren sea'" (col. 14.44–48, incorporating *Od.* 5.84,158). "Might my friend refuse to come? Then to hell with him!" Favorinus is no longer Odysseus in mourning, but Oedipus, angrily rejecting Creon's offer of hospitality:

> Be off!
> Let us live here in peace. For even as we are
> We would not be badly off, so long as we remain content.
>
> (*Oedipus at Colonus* 797–99)

Despite its moments of drama, however, this section ends flatly, with Favorinus criticizing and rewriting assorted proverbs on friendship so that they better prove his point.

The next challenger with which the beleaguered exile must contend is the loss of wealth and honors. Here Favorinus quotes Jocasta, rebuking her son for his ambition.[87] Favorinus administers an additional scolding to the resentful exile: "Why do you boast, you wretch, so full of self-conceit?" But as the pitch of his invective rises, we begin to suspect that the speaker is aiming beyond his professed target to us, the audience:[88]

> By the Gods, are you not ashamed to boast of external garments and dyes, and to have a large and beautiful bronze statue (*eikōn*) of your body in the Prytaneion, while you carry about inside a shameful and skimpy likeness of your soul? . . . Will you not put aside and take off these symbols and show yourself naked to us as you are—rather, not even naked, but clothed in poverty instead of purple, and crowned with freedom from office (*anarchia*) rather than with office and official insignia? (col. 18.17f.)

This imagery of honor as clothing has its proximate source in an anecdote about the "Eastern Ethiopians" (col. 17.43ff.). As Favorinus tells it, the king of that land, when he wishes to honor someone, gives him one of his own garments to wear, and people flock about to do him obeisance as long as he wears it. But once the king reclaims that garment, no one will give the erstwhile honoree the time of day.

To talk of wealth and honors as garments is to say that they are interchangeable, quintessentially removable, and totally separate from the self. To strip off old garments is to make room for the new: an exhortation such as Favorinus' to replace purple with poverty could come from a Christian sermon, although the imagery can be traced back to Plato who spoke of

---

[87] Col. 18.2–9; Euripides, *Phoenician Women*, 531–35. In Euripides the son in question is actually Eteocles, but Favorinus calls him Polyneices, perhaps because he has already introduced Polyneices as a member of his imaginary cast of characters.

[88] Philosophy is supposed to sting: Plutarch compares a lecture of philosophical admonition to a biting drug that should burn the soul with shame ("On Listening to Lectures," *Mor.* 46D).

wearing virtue instead of clothes.[89] In both pagan mystery initiations and Christian baptism, the initiate's "change of state" could be symbolized by the casting off of old garments and their replacement by new ones.[90] Yet sometimes the symbolic significance of nudity lies less in the new identity one puts on after the removal of one's old clothes, than in the revelation of the original identity underneath. Like an athlete, one strips down to one's true self. It is in this sense that we should understand the appearance of Odysseus in the next section.

"Don't you see what Odysseus was like when he was wearing ugly rags upon his body, so that for this reason, among others, the suitors marveled at him: 'What thighs shows the old man from underneath his rags!' "[91] The abrupt "Don't you see?" grabs the listener/reader by the collar and places him squarely inside the imaginary scene. Polyneices, the ostensible target of the previous chapter's harangue, has entirely dropped from view; Favorinus is talking to us, presenting Odysseus to us as if we were the suitors gaping at his massive thighs.

This image of heroic epiphany appealed to many philosophers. Dio was reputed to have stopped a mutiny in the Roman army when he shed the tattered clothing of a philosopher-in-exile, leapt naked onto an altar, and began, "Thus Odysseus of the many counsels stripped him of his rags."[92] Favorinus appropriates this traditional image by rewriting the quotation, substituting moral qualities for physical ones: "They admire his thighs, but I admire something else: 'What pluck and courage shows the old man underneath his rags,' vagabond though he is and more destitute than Iros" (col. 19.14–18). Favorinus continues with a conversation that is not to be found anywhere in Homer at all:

> And Odysseus seems to me, in all these twists of fate, to be constantly saying to God, "If it is your will, O Zeus, that I rule over the Ithakans, then that is also my desire. . . . Is it your will that I be shipwrecked? Then that is also my desire. But I will be more pious in shipwreck than Ajax. Is it your will that I endure hunger? Then I will endure hunger also, but with more self-control than my companions.

This sort of dialogue with God was a feature of the diatribe,[93] though a Cynic philosopher would normally speak *in propria persona*. Here Favorinus conjures up Odysseus as a paradigm of moral fortitude, evoking him

[89] This is how female guardians are supposed to deal with nudity, *Rep.* 457a.
[90] J. Z. Smith, "The Garments of Shame," in *Map Is Not Territory* (Leiden, 1978), 1–23.
[91] Col. 19.10–14, quoting *Od.* 18.74.
[92] *Od.* 22.1 in Philostratus, *Lives* 488 (trans. W. C. Wright, *Philostratus and Eunapius* [Loeb Classical Library] London and Cambridge, Mass., 1921]). Dio himself is the most likely source of this story.
[93] Compare Epictetus, *Diss.* 2.16.42; 4.1.89ff.

with a well-known hexameter and a pastiche of Homeric phrases, but makes him speak, in the first person, words of his own choosing. Thus it remains ambiguous whether Favorinus has become Odysseus or Odysseus has become Favorinus.

In the last sentence of this dialogue, Favorinus moves from his own words back to Homer's, concluding his homemade Odyssean diatribe as he began it, with a quotation of genuine Homeric hexameters: "Should you bid me, I will even sail again; if it seems best to you, 'Until I come to men who do not know the sea/ And do not eat their food with salt'" (*Od.* 23.269–70). This transition decreases the intensity of imaginative effort required of the audience. Favorinus-Odysseus, interlocutor of Zeus, by quoting Homer's well-known words, ceases to follow Favorinus' script, and the compound image resolves into its component parts as Favorinus appropriates the first person and relegates Odysseus to the third: "Thus spoke the man from Ithaka" (col. 19.39f.).

Favorinus' account of his battle with Freedom, his last adversary, is incomplete; but just before the papyrus breaks off, it preserves an evocative image. "Freedom" advances against him, armed with the argument that he will have neither independence nor liberty of movement, shut away on a single island, deprived of free pasture, "like the wild beasts raised in a Persian garden, that Cyrus said were scrawny, mangy, and stripped of their strength; while those on the plains were sleek, because they were unconfined and free" (col. 25.38–42). Favorinus is referring to an incident in Xenophon's *Education of Cyrus* in which the young prince, having been allowed at last to hunt outside the royal park, exultantly proclaims to his friends the superiority of wild game over the limp, tame specimens that he used to pursue inside the park. "Confined in a small space, they become thin and mangy; some of them are lame, others missing body parts (*kolobos*)."[94] Cyrus goes on to describe the manly competitive behavior of the wild boar who live in freedom: "They charge at close quarters the way brave men do [in battle]." As a philosopher, Favorinus must of course disagree with Cyrus. He claims freedom is an inward quality. Like citizenship, it is something that exists as a mental construct (*en tē gnōmē*). Hence no form of imprisonment can constrain the soul of a good man. But can this moralizing reinterpretation of Cyrus' comment entirely conceal Favorinus' image of himself as a physically incomplete specimen, a wild beast forced to be tame?

No wonder he was so quick to withdraw his gaze from Odysseus's great thighs to his inner qualities: by the second century, that magnificent age of intellectual hypochondriacs, Greek culture had lost the ease of equation between physical and moral condition that the archaic age had taken for

[94] *Education of Cyrus* 1.4.11.

granted. To reveal his true self, it was no longer enough to shed his rags; the truly superior man might have to shed his body too. The shimmer of instability that Favorinus' shifts of persona cast over his prose mirrors in microcosm the ambiguous configuration of his body and adumbrates the spiritual configuration of an age that was experiencing deep shifts in its models of personal identity. Favorinus used his anomalies as opportunities for self-creation. Born in a bilingual enclave in the western empire, he developed a mastery of literary Greek that brought him an impressive following in the East and made of himself a social and intellectual success in the capital. Born sexually ambiguous, he claimed the anomaly as a divine dispensation and developed a falsetto that could spellbind even the uneducated. Afflicted with the persistent enmity of Polemo, he used the quarrel to enhance his reputation, throwing himself wholeheartedly into something that resembles the symbiotic feuding of divas on the modern opera stage. If indeed he was exiled by the emperor, he used his loss of worldly rank to enhance his status as a philosopher and made of his trials an opportunity for rhetorical self-display. His identity was self-fashioned, though to a large extent of traditional materials. To assume and then assimilate personae was to become oneself. It is in this sense that we can apply to Favorinus a paradox coined by the arch-poseur of another age: "Man is least himself," wrote Oscar Wilde, "when he talks in his own person. Give him a mask and he will tell you the truth."[95]

[95] "The Critic as Artist: A Dialogue, Part II," in *The Artist as Critic*, ed. R. Ellman (Chicago, 1968), 389.

CONCLUSION

A MONG THE EDUCATED upper classes of the empire, a masculine identity was an achieved state. It took years of training to perfect one's public demeanor. This training involved both voice and body, both rhetoric and deportment. We have looked at this process by comparing two rival rhetoricians, their biographies, and specific case studies of their work. Some of the issues at stake in these studies—the tension between hyper-masculine and "effeminate" deportment, and the role of the voice in self-presentation—led our attention outward from Polemo and Favorinus to the matrix of their struggle: a complex web of cultural expectations about how the individual embodies manliness and how society "reads" the signs of this embodiment.

Manliness was not a birthright. It was something that had to be won. Perhaps physical strength once had been the definitive criterion of masculine excellence on the semi-legendary playing fields of Ilion and Latium, but by Hellenistic and Roman times the sedentary elite of the ancient city had turned away from warfare and gymnastics as definitive agonistic activities, firmly redrawing the defining lines of competitive space so as to exclude those without wealth, education, or leisure. Political and legal rivalries filled varying proportions of the leisured gentleman's time, depending on the size and relative independence of his native city; competitive displays of wealth (mostly liturgical extravagance in the Greek cities, mostly private extravagance at Rome) consumed varying proportions of his capital—but the form of competitive masculine activity that proved most electrifying as a spectator sport was rhetoric. For the audience, its appeal was the spectacle of peak performance under dangerous conditions, with the risk falling exclusively on the performers while they, as the spectators, punished failure with ridicule. Indeed, a rhetorical performance, whether triumph or fiasco, was in some sense a collaboration between speaker and audience, and the educated audience relished being the ultimate arbiter of success.

For those who performed, mastering the crowd was an achievement made sweeter by the absence of the factors that usually facilitated an aristocrat's domination over others. Rhetorical skill, in contrast to wealth and social position, could be developed only by individual effort, and thus the outcome of rhetorical competition was never entirely a foregone conclusion. This is how Tacitus has a successful rhetorician from Gaul describe the joy of performance:

> What greater enjoyment can there be for the spirit of a freeborn gentleman, born fit for pleasures of a higher kind, than to see his house filled daily with crowds of the most distinguished men, and to know that he owes this not to his wealth, his need for heirs, or his official position, whatever it might be, but to himself?

> What a supreme delight it is to gather yourself to your feet, and to take your stand before a hushed audience that has eyes for you alone! And the growing crowd streams round about the speaker, and takes on any mood in which he may care to wrap himself, as with a cloak!

> Then it is that I feel I am rising above the level of a tribune, a praetor, or even a consul, and that I possess an asset which, unless it comes unbidden, can neither be conferred by letters-patent nor follow in the train of popular favor.[1]

Although a skillful speaker may have perceived his success as a vindication of nothing more than his own ability, for this culture as a whole the image of an individual performer dominating his audience by individual talent functioned as a potent myth. Like the myth of the heroic entrepreneur in American society, it validated a larger system of class dominance by presenting it in purely personal terms as the inevitable triumph of innate *virtus*.

Because rhetorical skill was considered a definitive test of masculine excellence, issues of rhetorical style and self-presentation easily became gendered. We find issues of power debated as if they were issues of gender. Gender is, after all, a primary source of the metaphorical language with which power relationships are articulated, in our own time as in antiquity.[2] In the high-stakes game of self-presentation among articulate upper-class males, ways had to be found to define losers as well as winners. There had to be a hierarchy within the population of eligible competitors, a language in which comparative assessments could be made. This environment fostered the practice of skewering one's opponents for their effeminate style. It was a polemic that had nothing to do with women, who had no place whatever in this performance culture. So absent indeed were real women that the "other," an apparently essential component in the process of self-fashioning,[3] had to be called into being within an entirely masculine con-

---

[1] *Dialogue on Oratory* 6–7, trans. adapted from that of W. Peterson (Loeb Classical Library [Cambridge, Mass., 1958]).

[2] See P. Bourdieu, *The Logic of Practice* (Stanford, 1990), 71–72.

[3] Stephen Greenblatt, *Renaissance Self-Fashioning* (Chicago, 1980), 9. With the partial exception of Favorinus, second-century sophists, and the gentlemen for whom they furnished paradigms, differ from the subjects of Greenblatt's study chiefly in that they *did* possess "family tradition or hierarchical status that . . . rooted personal identity in the iden-

text. Thus polarized distinctions (smooth/hirsute, high voice/low voice, pantherlike/leonine) that purport to characterize the gulf between men and women instead divided the male sex into legitimate and illegitimate players. For individuals, these stereotypes facilitated a process by which the self became exteriorized through certain highly stylized forms of self-display.

But using male effeminacy as a conceptual category in debates about rhetorical performance brought primal prejudices into play. In almost every culture known to anthropologists, the proper separation of male and female is felt to be essential to the preservation of the cosmic order. Like the abominations of Leviticus, male effeminacy confuses categories and was readily stigmatized as unclean.[4] When a second-century person turned back to his house to begin his day again because he happened to have seen a eunuch, a cut priest, or a monkey upon setting out,[5] he did so for good reason. These were all near-miss men, "composites, hybrids, monstrosities outside the pale of human nature."[6] The invective that Polemo and Demonax aimed at Favorinus focused on his physical status as a defective male. When we examine what seemed wrong to them about a eunuch's practicing rhetoric or philosophy, the burden of their objection seems to be that if these arts represent the highest achievement of civilized man, then they must not be contaminated by practitioners who are imperfect examples of the species. While Favorinus' physical peculiarities were indeed unique, the categories used to attack him were not.

When we savor the intensity of critical contempt that the "effeminate" style provoked, we may well wonder why so many dared to adopt it. Obviously it was possible to silence critics by "bringing down the house," but the knowledge that one's rivals were waiting to seize on any lapse or blunder must have had a chilling effect. There would have been a temptation to insulate oneself from censure by adopting a rigidly "correct," hyper-masculine, performance style. Had everyone done this, there would soon have been no game left to play. This did not happen, I believe,

---

tity of a clan or caste" and thus diverge much less than his middle-class Renaissance men in their choice of what Greenblatt calls "authority." Although physicians and philosophers might dispute the authority claims of rival sects, the Attic Ten remained a stable pantheon and no one seriously challenged the authority of the glorious past they represented.

[4] On Leviticus and related matters, see Mary Douglas, *Purity and Danger* (London and Boston, 1966), esp. chaps. 1–3.

[5] Lucian, *The False Critic* 17.

[6] Lucian, *The Eunuch* 6: οὔτε ἄνδρα οὔτε γυναῖκα εἶναι τὸν εὐνοῦχον λέγοντος, ἀλλά τι σύνθετον καὶ μικτὸν καὶ τερατῶδες, ἔξω τῆς ἀνθρωπείας φύσεως. Eunuchs are "an ambiguous sort of creature (ἀμφίβολόν τι ζῷον) like the crow, which cannot be reckoned with either the doves or the ravens" (8). Compare Pseudo-Lucian, *Erotes* 21, which terms eunuchs ἀμφίβολον αἴνιγμα διπλῆς φύσεως.

because there were subtle temptations pulling the other way. There was something manly, after all, about taking risks—even the risk of being called effeminate. And there may also have been a temptation to appropriate characteristics of "the other" as a way of gaining power from outside the traditionally acceptable sources. Locked into a very narrow form of competition where they strained to set themselves apart from the very men whose approbation they sought, some participants evidently chose to distinguish themselves by adopting mannerisms of self-presentation—languid gestures, a high-pitched voice, or mincing walk—that served, in their culture, as stylized signifiers of the feminine.

Why this more androgynous style of self-presentation was so effective with audiences, I will not dare to speculate. But its successful deployment left rivals with a stark choice: condemn or imitate.

The way that Favorinus used the possibilities available to him was both conventional and creative. We could view his aspirations to superstardom in rhetoric in Marxist terms, as a form of false consciousness, or in Romantic terms, as a heroic triumph of the individual spirit over the constraints of anatomy and society. But I would prefer to see Favorinus' audacious self-fashioning as the conceptual equivalent to the exception that proves the rule: the fact that he could aspire to fill the roles of sophist and philosopher without the necessary anatomical prerequisites (as Lucian would put it), and the fact that he succeeded, provide convincing evidence that in his culture gender roles were constructed by the interplay of individual effort and social expectations; a male could not claim title to them by the mere fact of biological sex.

Stepping back a bit, we may wonder whether the intensely nuanced preoccupation with gender definition in our sources may hide an issue too big to be seen, and that is social class. Wasn't the development and display of *paideia* as much an instrument of class delineation as it was an arena for masculine competition within the elite? Perhaps it was only within the immense security of the *Pax Romana* that local aristocrats could afford to challenge each other's masculinity, while they remained absolutely sure of their collective dominance.

To see better how individualistic displays of masculine excellence could be implicated in larger issues of social dominance and the display of symbolic capital by the curial class as a whole, we can go forward in time to a moment when the whole system is fraying around the edges—to the late fourth century. Theodosius' closure of the pagan temples is just a few years away.

Little dreaming of the catastrophic extinction of traditional practice that is just around the corner, Antioch's chief sophist is preoccupied by an insidious ecological shift. Spring after spring the old professor has watched the migration of young men abroad—young men who ought to be in his lecture room, whose fathers were his pupils. He grinds his teeth to see the civic leaders of his native town escort their sons to the harbor to set sail for Rome or Beirut. And for what? To study law or perfect their Latin while currying favor with senators and imperial officials in hopes of obtaining a government appointment—an appointment that would allow them to leave, and thus destroy, their native class.[7]

Libanius (himself immune from the financial obligations of a town-councillor, thanks to his profession) was not above invoking the repressive machinery of the Theodosian state to staunch this hemorrhage of local talent. In an open letter to the emperor he urged legislation to confine the sons of council members to the educational path trodden by their forefathers, "for whom it was ambition enough to serve their native city by means of the Greek language."[8]

Yet it is clear that the young men who *did* stay in Antioch to study with Libanius were not acquitting themselves very well either. He berates them in an open letter, "To Those Who Do Not Speak."[9] Somehow the stress required to produce this invective-cum-self-justification has crystallized a number of his implicit beliefs about the social function of rhetoric. Let us turn our attention to them now.

Libanius is enraged to see his recent pupils take silent parts in city government. He contrasts them ruthlessly with his pupils from years past "who [now] hold power because they *speak*."[10] To him, the essence of educated speech is power. He reminds his students that this power gives one leverage against other ranks in society. He points out that the eloquent man can intimidate the low-level imperial functionary whom the silent man must fear. He can fill a fellow-citizen with unease by a mere glance; he can get away with violence—assault another man in anger, detain him against his will, strip off his clothes, or worse.[11]

With men of one's own rank, he who fails to speak yields first place to his more articulate peers. Not to speak is to *lose*. Libanius makes this explicit when he criticizes the young men's obsession with the charioteers'

---

[7] Libanius, *Or.* 48.22–29; *Or.* 49.27; *Or.* 1.214; *Or.* 2.43–44. On the rise of Latin and legal studies, see J.H.W.G. Liebeschuetz, *Antioch* (Oxford, 1972) 233ff.

[8] Libanius, *Or.* 49. 29 (388 A.D.).

[9] *Or.* 35, Πρὸς τοὺς οὐ λέγοντας. This speech, traditionally ascribed to 388, cannot be precisely dated. A French translation is available in A. J. Festugière, *Antioche Païenne et Chrétienne* (Paris, 1959), 484–91.

[10] ἔχουσιν ἐκ τοῦ λέγειν τὸ κρατεῖν, *Or.* 35.12.

[11] οἴ [those who are both willing and able to speak in public] φοβεῖν δύνανται τοὺς τῶν ἀρχόντων ὑπηρέτας, οὓς ὑμεῖς δεδοίκατε. καὶ ἔστιν αὐτοῖς ῥᾴδιον λυπῆσαι βλέμματι, λυπῆσαι ῥήματι, λυπῆσαι χειρί, λαβέσθαι μετ' ὀργῆς, στῆσαι καὶ μὴ βουλόμενον, ἀποδῦσαι καὶ πού τι καὶ πλέον, ibid. 8.

victories in the hippodrome. They have lost sight of the fact that, because of their own silence in courts, they have no victories of their own. "So great has become your habit of losing," he says scornfully.[12] Not only are his former pupils unable to hold their own among their social equals; they lose ground before their social inferiors. "No doubt the manual laborer will readily feel bashful in your presence, no doubt he will hasten to perform your commands, no doubt he'll look to *you* for help with a troublesome problem when you need other people to speak on your behalf!"[13]

Indeed, without differences in speech it becomes difficult to tell man from master. Libanius therefore exhorts his pupils, "Use your tongues to make yourselves superior to your slaves, for now you are superior only by chance."[14] In other words, rhetorical skill is what makes relations of social dominance seem more than just contingent. To drive home his point about the role of educated speech in legitimating arbitrary status differences, he asks his pupils to imagine the following scenario: "If anyone came upon you with your slaves, all naked and chatting informally together, if he didn't know anything else about you, I don't think that he would think it just that one group has power over the other."[15] The old teacher's remedy is simple:

> Move closer to the classic orators; purify your language. . . . After dinner, if you have no guests, don't waste your time in disputation with your slave over the track-records of various charioteers. Call for a book, and go to bed after honing your tongue. When the nights lengthen, chant [vocal exercises] at cockcrow. When you go to the marketplace, declaim again, if business permits, and don't be ashamed to be seen learning something from a book (*Or.* 35.18).

The world of the hippodrome promotes mimesis of lower-class behavior, while the daily exercise of *paideia* maintains status boundaries. The hippodrome clearly was a favorite haunt of Libanius' students, where the vicarious thrills of competition were enhanced by explicit violence, gang rivalry, and betting. What bothered Libanius was to see the flower of curial youth looking for the *habitus* in all the wrong places. Instead of clinging to their books, they venerate bookmakers and circus hacks. "*These* are the men you praise, emulate, imitate; you would rather resemble them than your fathers!"[16]

Antioch was famous for the eloquence of its ruling class, and Libanius

[12] τοσαύτη τις ἡ τοῦ νικᾶσθαι γέγονεν ὑμῖν συνήθεια, ibid. 14.

[13] Ibid. 7.

[14] γένεσθε κατὰ τὰς γλώττας τῶν οἰκετῶν βελτίους· ὡς νῦν γε τύχῃ μόνον ἐστὲ βελτίους, ibid. 15.

[15] οὐκ ἄν μοι νομίσαι δοκεῖ δίκαιον εἶναι τοὺς ἑτέρους τῶν ἑτέρων κρατεῖν, ibid. 15.

[16] τούτους τοίνυν ὑμεῖς μακαρίζετε, ζηλοῦτε, μιμεῖσθε· τούτοις ἐοικέναι βούλεσθε μᾶλλον ἢ τοῖς πατράσι, ibid. 13.

claims that his renegade students have squandered their cultural capital by refusing to show themselves *heirs* of the town council's reputation for eloquence.[17] Note the economic metaphor: they are failing to claim an inheritance. Libanius can see the glory built up by so many generations of collective effort crumbling like neglected city walls.[18] He is also disturbed by the way his ex-pupils' refusal to engage in public speaking has endangered the symbolic chemistry of the liturgical system. Without formal rhetoric to catalyze the conversion of economic capital into symbolic capital, the illusion of voluntary beneficence is spoiled, and with it the symbolic surplus value that the illusion used to generate. He points out that the town councillors who practice public speaking gain the sort of reputation that really commands respect (*aidōs*) from their inferiors; the silent young council-members of today do not achieve these intangible benefits. *Their* liturgical expenditures, he says, are attributed to legal compulsion. When society is not given the opportunity to admire the spiritual excellence of the town councillor as he might display it in speaking, the material functions he performs as a liturgist are made to look obligatory, a mere tax. "They are not unaware of the liturgies that you perform and have performed in the past, but because they are unable to admire your souls, they attribute your liturgies to legal and material compulsion."[19]

Libanius, at the end of the fourth century, saw things with the terrible clarity of a man who fears that he will not be able to pass on intact the essence of his own culture. He blamed his students, but the situation was not entirely their fault. Many things had changed since the glory days of the second century. The arduous *paideia* that greased the wheels of urban life had lost value as economic pressures contracted the glorious voluntariness of traditional city government. By 390 it was rational for young men to seek the greener pastures of imperial service that offered liturgical immunities and, increasingly, protection from corporal punishment but did not require the Attic of Demosthenes. The increasing objectification of status distinctions among the propertied (the clarissimate, for example, and the division of the curial class into major and minor landowners) had pulled the rug out from under intra-elite rhetorical competition. But the past is never more present than when our connection to it seems at risk. Thus the jeremiad of a disappointed teacher precisely spells out the relationship between speech and power in an ancient and infinitely precious tradition that was slipping away.

---

[17] Ibid. 9. The economic metaphor appears again in section 13: ἀλλ᾽ ἐκείνοις μὲν ἐφυλά-χθη τὸ κτηθέν, ὑμῖν δὲ διερρύη.

[18] Ibid. 9.

[19] οὐκ ἀγνοοῦντες μὲν ὑμῶν ἃ καὶ λειτουργεῖτε καὶ λελειτουργήκατε, τῷ νόμῳ δὲ καὶ ταῖς ἀνάγκαις ταῦτα λογιζόμενοι, τὰς ψυχὰς δὲ ὑμῶν οὐκ ἔχοντες θαυμάσαι, ibid. 8.

Libanius did not use gendered invective. John Chrysostom did. We have only to recall his stinging rebuke of those ascetics who mar their manhood by cohabiting with virgins (see Chapter Four above). Perhaps it was the temporal security provided by the church that permitted ecclesiastics to carry on rhetorical traditions that secular wordsmiths, closing ranks against bureaucrats and barbarians, felt they could no longer afford. But deep-seated beliefs remained about deportment as a system of signs that reveal both one's self-control and one's fitness to rule others. Half a millenium after Libanius, we find the Patriarch of Constantinople admonishing the Khan of the Bulgars:

> Now don't neglect the appearance and movement of your body as something trivial. For the optimal order and disposition of these factors would seem to be not the least part of practical wisdom. . . . Wherefore it is necessary to aim at good order and gravity in the expression of your face, the dressing of your hair, and the arrangement of your clothing, avoiding the extremes of both dandyism and neglect, both of which are unseemly and inappropriate for a prince. An orderly gait befits a prince also; he should not disfigure his deportment in the direction of looseness and effeminacy nor affect as a novelty a disturbed, uneven step. In general, every single motion should be arranged in orderly fashion.[20]

The *habitus* dies hard!

Where do Favorinus and Polemo stand in the long evolution between Hellenistic and late antique culture? Against the background of the *longue durée*, do they appear to be throwbacks, pioneers, or quintessential men of their time? We could define the long high noon of Hellenistic civilization[21] as the age when the city, with its own cults and feuds and self-consciously cultivated history, constituted both the ideal audience and the ultimate judge of worth for all those who aspired to preeminence in the "performing arts" of politics and rhetoric. Late antiquity begins when these status seekers start to draw on extra-social sources of validation, bypassing the approval of their peers to a hitherto unparalleled extent, a scenario that fostered the eccentric behavior of larger-than-life personalities in the fourth century, the age of Antony, Athanasius, Constantine, and Julian.

---

[20] Photius, Letter 8.334, *PG* 102, 665–68. This reference I owe to Peter Brown, whose *Persuasion and Power in Late Antiquity* (Madison, 1992) follows the themes of *paideia* and power into later times.

[21] "[Hellenistic civilization] is not autumnal, tormented with nostalgic regrets for a vanished spring. On the contrary, it looks upon itself as firmly established in the unchanging present, in the full blaze of a hot summer sun." H.I. Marrou, *A History of Education in Antiquity* (New York, 1956), 161. The Hellenistic age did not know it was Hellenistic: it thought it was still classical.

In the second century, by and large, the city still held center stage. In the urban enclaves of the Roman Empire, liturgists commemorated their generosity with public inscriptions, and sophists like Polemo and Favorinus grappled for the approbation of their peers. Yet, if we probe beneath the conventional familiarity of this picture, signs of change are already beginning to appear. Polemo strikes us as the epitome of the conventional second-century gentleman: impeccably situated by birth within a local aristocracy, firmly grounded by exhaustive training within the performance conventions of an ancient rhetorical tradition, and thoroughly steeped in the immemorial prejudices of the physiognomic art. Yet in his reworking of that very stylized system of prejudices, there is something new, something that looks forward to that vast cultural shift now called late antiquity. Polemo's self-presentation as a man of almost occult insight, whose physiognomical diagnoses draw on a type of clairvoyance that remains inaccessible to even his most diligent student, is perhaps something new. The persona he projects shares some characteristics with the late-antique holy man—we think of Plotinus, who could recover stolen necklaces just by looking over the suspects with his penetrating gaze—particularly in its claim to specialized prophetic knowledge not grounded in cult.

Favorinus was not rooted in the social environment of his birthplace. He presented himself as a paradigm of self-transformation. Though his native language may well have been Greek, he chose to present himself as "the Gaul who spoke Greek," an embodied paradox of triumphant *paideia*.

Favorinus did not derive his self-definition from the place, geographical or social, into which he had been born. Unlike Polemo, he struck no local coins, preferred to perform no civic liturgies, and claimed no descent from local kings. He was not born into his place, but reborn or initiated into it. His *paideia* (as he appears to have presented it) was not the natural or inevitable outgrowth of his social, geographical, or biological circumstances. Rather, those circumstances existed only to be transcended enroute to *paideia*. It is in keeping with the transcendental nature of this process that Favorinus' rhetoric represented it by means of visions and epiphanies. Polemo's dedication of a statue to Demosthenes in commemoration of his visionary contact with one of *paideia's* chief divinities represents a cultural instinct at once more localized and more concrete than that which prompted Favorinus' claim to have levitated his own invisible statue by the power of words alone. Like contemporary devotees of diasporic Hellenistic divinities, Favorinus did not even belong to his cult's "original ethnic group" (not being, anatomically, fully male), and we can observe how, in his Exile speech, "projecting [his] diasporic existence into the cosmos, he discovered himself to be in exile from his true home" and "found . . . true freedom in stripping off his body which belonged to this world." Favorinus' *paideia*, like diasporic religion, was "utopian in the strictest sense of the word, a religion of 'nowhere,' of transcendence."[22] Thus Favorinus' position in his culture is diasporic rather than native, and utopian rather than localized. Would it also be right to see his self-creation as rebellious rather than celebratory? Certainly late-twentieth-century sensitivity to dissonance, anomie, and sexist repression invites us to romanticize him in this way. But Favorinus was the sort of radical whose innovation consists of taking traditional premises to their logical extreme. His bravura performances never faltered in their control of language; and their hypnotic power, enhanced by a wider range of voice and gesture than many of his competitors permitted themselves, sprang from total mastery over a traditional medium. "*Paideia* really has the transformative power that has been claimed for it over the ages" (so ran the subtext of every performance); "see how thoroughly it has been able to transform *me*."[23] And so the paradox emerges that Favorinus was more deeply conventional than his conservative rival, because his identity was entirely the product of art. To find poignancy in that wild beast who cut such a magnificent figure in *paideia*'s Persian garden would do but scant justice to the boundless optimism of his self-transforming exercise and the equally boundless vitality of traditional culture in his age.

---

[22] Jonathan Z. Smith, *Map Is Not Territory: Studies in the History of Religions* (Leiden, 1978) = Jacob Neusner, ed., *Studies in Judaism in Late Antiquity*, vol. 23, p. xiv, cf. 186 and passim.

[23] Compare his claim in the Corinthian oration to have been designed by the gods expressly as a paradigm to show the Greeks that fame can be a product of *paideia* as much as of birth: ἵνα ἔχωσιν οἱ ἐπιχώριοι τῆς Ἑλλάδος παράδειγμα ὡς οὐδὲν τὸ παιδευθῆναι τοῦ φῦναι πρὸς τὸ δοκεῖν διαφέρει (27).

A NOTE ON FINDING SOURCES
IN TRANSLATION

M ANY OF THE ANCIENT TEXTS cited in this book may be read in English in the bilingual editions of the Loeb Classical Library of Harvard University Press. Favorinus' *Corinthian Oration* and *On Fortune* may be found as Orations 37 and 64 in the Loeb edition of Dio Chrysostom. I do not know of any translations of the Exile speech. Polemo's works are likewise untranslated. As for the rest of the physiognomical corpus, the treatise attributed to Aristotle is available in a Loeb edition (*Aristotle, Minor Works*, trans. W. S. Hett [Cambridge and London: Harvard University Press, 1936]); the anonymous Latin treatise is available in a French translation by J. André (see Bibliography).

Firmicus Maternus' *Mathēsis* is available in a translation I have not seen by J. R. Bram under the title *Ancient Astrology* (Park Ridge, New Jersey, 1975). The dream book of Artemidorus has been translated by R. J. White, *The Interpretation of Dreams: Oneirocritica by Artemidorus* (Park Ridge, New Jersey, 1975). It is also available in a well-annotated French edition by A. J. Festugière, *Artémidore: La clef des songes* (Paris, 1975). Magical papyri are available in the translation of H. D. Betz (see Bibliography).

The medical authors excerpted in Oribasius may be read in the French translation of U. C. Bussemaker and C. Daremberg, *Collection Médicale* (including the *Libri Incerti*), 6 vols. (Paris, 1851–76). Galen's autobiography, *On Prognosis*, is translated into English by V. Nutton (*CMG* 5.8.1, Berlin, 1979). For translations of other works, see Green, May, and Walzer in the Bibliography. *Small Ball Workout* must be read in Greek. For Soranus and Caelius Aurelianus, see Temkin and Drabkin in the Bibliography.

John Chrysostom's diatribe against the cohabitation of men and women may be found in E. A. Clark, *Jerome, Chrysostom, and Friends: Essays and Translations* (New York and Toronto, 1979). Clement of Alexandria's manual of etiquette for wealthy Christians is available in English as *Christ the Educator*, trans. S. P. Wood in the series *Fathers of the Church* (New York, 1954).

Latin rhetorical writers may all be found in Loeb editions, as will the Greeks Epictetus, Lucian, Philostratus, and Plutarch. For Aelius Aristides and Musonius Rufus, see Behr and Lutz in the Bibliography. Suetonius *On Insults* still awaits a translator.

SELECT BIBLIOGRAPHY

Anderson, G. *Philostratus*. London, 1986.

André, J. *Anonyme Latin: Traité de Physiognomonie*. Paris, 1981.

Baldwin, B. *Studies in Lucian*. Toronto, 1973.

Barigazzi, A. *Favorino di Arelate Opere*. Florence, 1966.

Behr, C. P. *Aelius Aristides, The Complete Works*. Vol. 2. Leiden, 1981.

Betz, H. D. *The Greek Magical Papyri in Translation*. Chicago, 1986.

Bonner, S. F. *Roman Declamation in the Late Republic and the Early Empire*. Liverpool, 1949.

———. *Education in Ancient Rome*. Berkeley, 1977.

Boulanger, A. *Aelius Aristide*. Paris, 1923.

Bourdieu, P. *Outline of a Theory of Practice*. Cambridge, 1977.

———. *The Logic of Practice*. Stanford, 1990.

Bowersock, G. W. *Augustus and the Greek World*. Oxford, 1965.

———. *Greek Sophists in the Roman Empire*. Oxford, 1969.

———, ed. *Approaches to the Second Sophistic*. University Park, Pa., 1974.

Bowie, E. L. "The Greeks and Their Past in the Second Sophistic." *Past and Present* 46 (1970), 3–41 (= *Studies in Ancient Society*. Ed. M. I. Finley. London and Boston, 1974, 166–209).

———. "The Importance of Sophists." *YCS* 27 (1982), 29–50.

Branham, R. B. *Unruly Eloquence: Lucian and the Comedy of Traditions*. Cambridge, Mass., 1989.

Cadoux, C. J. *Ancient Smyrna*. Oxford, 1938.

Chodorow, N. "Family Structure and Feminine Personality." In *Women, Culture, and Society*. Ed. M. Rosaldo and L. Lamphere. Stanford, 1974, 43–66.

Cumont, F. *L'Égypte des Astrologues*. Brussels, 1937.

Douglas, M. *Purity and Danger: an Analysis of the Concepts of Pollution and Taboo*. London and Boston, 1966.

Dover, K. J. *Aristophanes, Clouds*. Oxford, 1968.

———. *Greek Homosexuality*. Cambridge, Mass., 1978.

Drabkin, I. E. *Caelius Aurelianus: On Acute Diseases and On Chronic Diseases*. Chicago, 1950.

du Boulay, J. "Lies, Mockery, and Family Integrity." In *Mediterranean Family Structure*. Ed. J. G. Peristiany. Cambridge, England, 1976, 389–406.

Evans, E. C. *Physiognomics in the Ancient World = Transactions of the American Philosophical Society* 59 (1969).

Fairweather, J. *Seneca the Elder*. Cambridge, 1981.

Fantham, E. "Imitation and Decline: Rhetorical Theory and Practice in the First Century After Christ." *CP* 73 (1978), 102–16.

———. "Quintilian on Performance: Traditional and Personal Elements in *Institutio* 11.3." *Phoenix* 36 (1982), 243–62.

Festugière, A. J. *Antioche Païenne et Chrétienne*. Paris, 1959.

———. *La Clef des Songes*. Paris, 1975.

Förster, R., ed. *Scriptores Physiognomonici Graeci et Latini*. Leipzig, 1893. 2 vols.

Foucault, M. *The Care of the Self, a History of Sexuality*. Vol. 3. Trans. Robert Hurley. New York, 1986.

Friedl, E. *Vasilika, a Village in Modern Greece*. New York, 1962.

Gabba, E. "The Classicistic Revival in the Augustan Age." *CA* 1 (1981), 43–65.

Garnsey, P., and R. Saller. *The Roman Empire: Economy, Society, Culture*. London and Berkeley, 1987.

Gilmore, D. *Manhood in the Making: Cultural Concepts of Masculinity*. New Haven, 1990.

Glucker, J. *Antiochus and the Late Academy*. Göttingen, 1978 (*Hypomnemata*, Heft 56).

Goffman, E. *The Presentation of Self in Everyday Life*. Garden City, N.Y., 1959.

———. *Interaction Ritual: Essays on Face-to-Face Behavior*. Garden City, N.Y., 1967.

Goggin, M. "Rhythm in the Prose of Favorinus." *YCS* 12 (1951), 149–201.

Gouldner, A. *Enter Plato: Classical Greece and the Origins of Social Theory*. New York, 1965.

Green, R. M. *Galen's Hygiene*. Springfield, 1951.

Greenblatt, S. *Renaissance Self-Fashioning*. Chicago, 1980.

———. "Fiction and Friction." In *Reconstructing Individualism: Autonomy, Individuality, and the Self in Western Thought*. Ed. T. C. Heller, M. Sosna, and D. E. Wellbery. Stanford, 1986, 30–52.

Hahn, J. *Der Philosoph und die Gesellschaft*. Stuttgart, 1989.

Halperin, D. M. *One Hundred Years of Homosexuality and Other Essays on Greek Love*. New York and London, 1990.

Herdt, G. *Guardians of the Flutes: Idioms of Masculinity*. New York, 1981.

———. ed. *Rituals of Manhood: Male Initiation in Papua New Guinea*. Berkeley, 1982.

Herzfeld, M. *The Poetics of Manhood: Contest and Identity in a Cretan Mountain Village*. Princeton, 1985.

Holford-Strevens, H. *Aulus Gellius*. Chapel Hill, 1988.

Hopkins, K. "Elite Mobility in the Roman Empire." In *Studies in Ancient Society*. Ed. M. I. Finley. London and Boston, 1974, 103–20.

Jones, C. P. *Plutarch and Rome*. Oxford, 1971.

———. *The Roman World of Dio Chrysostom*. Cambridge, Mass., 1978.

———. "Prosopographical Notes on the Second Sophistic." *GRBS* 21 (1981), 374–77.

———. *Culture and Society in Lucian*. Cambridge, Mass., 1986.

Judge, E. "The Early Christians as a Scholastic Community: Part II." *Journal of Religious History* (Sydney, 1961), 125–37.

———. "Paul's Boasting in Relation to Contemporary Professional Practice." *Australian Biblical Review* 16 (1968), 37–50.

Jüttner, H. *De Polemonis Vita Operibus Arte*. Breslau, 1898. Reprint Olms: Hildesheim, 1967.

Kaster, R. "Competition and Restraint: The Classicism of Aulus Gellius." ©1981.

———. "The Ethics of Archaism in Aulus Gellius." ©1986.

Kennedy, G. *The Art of Rhetoric in the Roman World*. Princeton, 1972.

Laqueur, T. "Orgasm, Generation, and the Politics of Reproductive Biology." *Representations* 14 (1986), 1–41.

———. *Making Sex: Body and Gender from the Greeks to Freud.* Cambridge, Mass., 1990.

Lloyd, G.E.R. *Science, Folklore, and Ideology.* Cambridge, 1983.

Lonie, I. M. *The Hippocratic Treatises "On Generation," "On the Nature of the Child," "Diseases IV."* Berlin, 1981.

Lutz, C. "Musonius Rufus, The Roman Socrates." *YCS* 10 (1947), 3–147.

MacC. Armstrong, A. "The Methods of the Greek Physiognomists." *Greece and Rome* 5 (1958), 52–56.

MacMullen, R. "Roman Attitudes to Greek Love." *Historia* 31 (1982), 484–502.

———. "What Difference Did Christianity Make?" *Historia* 35 (1986), 322–43.

Magie, D. *Roman Rule in Asia Minor.* Princeton, 1950.

Marrou, H. I. *Clément d'Alexandrie: Le Pédagogue. Sources chrétiennes* 70. Paris, 1960.

———. *A History of Education in Antiquity.* Madison, 1982.

Mason, H. "Favorinus' Disorder: Reifenstein's Syndrome in Antiquity?" *Janus* 66 (1979), 1–13.

May, M. T. *Galen on the Usefulness of the Parts of the Body.* Ithaca, 1968.

Mejer, J. *Diogenes Laertius and His Hellenistic Background. Hermes Einzelschriften* 40. Weisbaden, 1978.

Mensching, E. *Favorin von Arelate.* Berlin, 1963.

Mesk, J. "Die Beispiele in Polemons Physiognomonik." *Weiner Studien* 50 (1932), 51–67.

Moles, J. L. "The Career and Conversion of Dio Chrysostom," *JHS* 98 (1978), 79–100.

Norsa, M., and G. Vitelli. *Il Papiro Vaticano 11.1:* Φαβωρίνου περὶ φυγῆς. *Studi e testi* 53. Rome, 1931.

Onians, R. B. *The Origins of European Thought About the Body, the Mind, the Soul, the World, Time, and Fate.* Cambridge, England, 1951.

Ortner, S., and H. Whitehead. *Sexual Meanings: The Cultural Construction of Gender and Sexuality.* Cambridge, 1981.

Preus, A. "Galen's Criticism of Aristotle's Conception Theory." *Journal of the History of Biology* 10 (1977), 65–85.

Price, S. *Rituals and Power: The Roman Imperial Cult in Asia Minor.* Cambridge, England, 1984.

Reardon, B. *Courants littéraires grecs des IIe et IIIe siècles après J.-C.* Paris, 1971.

Richlin, A. *The Garden of Priapus.* New Haven, 1983. Rev. ed. New York, 1992.

———. "Not Before Homosexuality: The Materiality of the *Cinaedus* and the Roman Law against Love between Men." *Journal of the History of Sexuality* 3 (1993), 523–73.

Rivet, A. *Gallia Narbonensis.* London, 1988.

Rousselle, A. *Porneia.* Paris, 1983. English trans. Oxford, 1988.

———. "Parole et inspiration: Le Travail de la voix dans le monde romain." *History and Philosophy of the Life Sciences* (Pubblicazioni della Stazione Zoologica di Napoli, Section 2) 5 (1983), 129–57.

Russell, D. A. *Plutarch.* London, 1972.

———. *Greek Declamation.* Cambridge, England, 1983.

Schöne, H. "ΠΕΡΙ ΥΓΙΕΙΝΗΣ ΑΝΑΦΩΝΗΣΕΩΣ." *Hermes* 65 (1930), 94.

Schrijvers, P. H. *Eine Medizinische Erklärung der Männlichen Homosexualität aus der Antike*. Amsterdam, 1985.

Scott, J. W. "Gender: A Useful Category of Historical Analysis." *American Historical Review* 91 (1986), 1053–75.

Smith, J. Z. *Map Is Not Territory*. Leiden, 1978. = Jacob Neusner, ed. *Studies in Judaism in Late Antiquity*. Vol. 23.

Swain, S. "Favorinus and Hadrian." *ZPE* 79 (1989), 150–58.

Temkin, O. *Soranus' Gynecology*. Baltimore, 1956, repr. 1991.

Van Groningen, B. A. "General Literary Tendencies in the Second Century A.D." *Mnemosyne* 18 (1965), 41–56.

Walzer, R. *Galen on Medical Experience*. Oxford, 1944.

Winkler, J. *The Constraints of Desire: The Anthropology of Sex and Gender in Ancient Greece*. New York and London, 1990.

Winterbottom, M. *Roman Declamation*. Bristol, 1980.

INDEX LOCORUM

14

GENERAL INDEX

actors, rhetoricians' attitudes toward, 105–6, 108, 112, 114–16
Adamantius, sophist and physiognomist, 31, 34, 37
Alexander of Cilicia, sophist, 75–76, 144n.49
Ambrose, bishop, 61
analogy, 97
Anderson, G., xviiin.4, xixn.8
androgynoi, 62–64, 77–79, 124; disguises of, 79–80; in Phlegon's *Mirabilia*, 39; sounds of, 82–83; voices of, 101
Antoninus Pius, 26n.33
Antinoos, Hadrian's lover, 23 and n.17
Antioch, curial class of, 162–65
Antipater, sophist, xxii
Antonine Age, xvii–xviii
Antyllus, physician, 88–89 and n.39, 96, 106
Aper, Marcus, orator from Gaul, 4, 160
Apollonius of Tyana, wonder-worker, 45n.113
Apuleius, sophist and philosopher, 8n.29, 15n.61
Arion, poet, 10
Aristeas, poet, 19 and n.73
Aristides, Aelius, sophist, xviii; as ambassador, 23; and Asclepius, 25; declaims *Against Those Who Burlesque the Mysteries of Rhetoric*, 122ff.; failure to declaim, 126; on gender in rhetoric, 122–26; hypochondria of, 122–23 and n.89; performs at Smyrna, 122–23; pupil of Polemo, 125; strategies of self-defense, 149n.71, 150n.76
aristocrats, xxi, 159; competition with peers, 159–60, 163–65; grooming and refinement of, 74–76; importance of eloquence for, xxi; intellectual life of, 140; Libanius berates, 162–65; as sole source for ancient society, 94. See also *paideia*; symbolic capital
Aristotle, 14, 29; physiognomy treatise attributed to, 29, 31–33, 35–36, 38, 133
Arles (Arelate), amenities of, 5
Artemidorus, dream-interpreter, 37
Asclepius, 26

Asianism, 107–9 and n.31. *See also* Atticism
askēsis, xiii, 101; culture of, 84–87, 110, 112; and molding of infants, 71
astrology, *cinaedi* in, 66–67
Atticism: conflict with Asianism, xix and n.6, 107–9 and n.31; less important in late fourth century, 165; in nature, 145; in sophistic rivalry, 26; shortcuts to in Lucian, 127
audience, role of, xxiii, 124, 159
Aulus Gellius, 27; as biographer of Favorinus, 136ff.; classicism and archaism in, 138 and n.28; purpose in writing, 140n.31

Baldwin, B., xviiin.4
Barigazzi, A., 8nn.30, 32
Beirut, 163
body: care of, 84, 87; reflects state of soul, 29, 143. See also *askēsis*; exercise; flesh; massage; physiognomy
body language. *See* deportment
Bompaire, J., xixn.7
Bonner, S. F., xixn.8
Boulanger, A., xixn.8, 27
Bourdieu, P., xii, xxi and n.11, xxiv and nn. 9–20 and 22, xxvin.25, 160n.2
Bowersock, G. W., xviii, 21n.3, 23n.15, 44n.112, 84n.13
Bowie, E. L., 53
boys, xxii; flesh of, 114; Quintilian on education of, 114–19
Branham, R. B., xixn.8
Brown, P., xii, 166n.20

Caelius Aurelianus, physician, 80, 93 and n.50
Caligula, emperor, xxiii, 56
castration, 6 and n.22
children. *See* boys; girls; infants
Christianity, 156, 166. *See also* Clement of Alexandria
Cicero, orator: on managing one's countenance, 57; performance style of, 107 and n.16; quoted as an authority, 139; on voice training, 105–8

188 GENERAL INDEX

cinaedi, 64–67, 74, 77, 79–81, 130; in astrology, 66–67; military, 134; synonyms for, 65; voice of, 83

class. *See* social class

Cleanthes, Stoic physiognomist, 77

Clement of Alexandria, Christian moralist, 61, 68–70; on adolescent decorum, 71–72; on depilation and effeminacy, 68–70; on women's luxury, 64–65

clothing: concealing women, 48–49, 98; cross-dressing, 100–101; and identity, 155–56

competition, xxiii, 9

Crassus, orator, 108

cross-dressing, 100–101

cultural capital. *See paideia*; symbolic capital

Cynics, 135–37; diatribes of, 156

Cyrus, Persian prince, 157

dance training, 116–17

declamation: by adults, xxii; hypothetical elements in, 21; and improvisation, xix and n.7; in medical regimens, 88ff.; "middle style" best for, 88–89 and n.40; of Polemo, 27, 37; *prosopopoeia* and role-playing in, xxii, 151; recommended by Libanius, 12, 164; rudeness during, 128; stress of, 72; terminology of, 103–4; in training of Roman orators, 104ff.; as vocal exercise, 88ff.; by women, 99. *See also* vocal exercise; voice

Demonassa, myth of, 12–13

Demonax, Cynic philosopher, 135–37, 161

Demosthenes, orator, xxii, 25, 167

depilation, 68–70, 76 and n.94, 109; as metaphor for literary style, 75 and n.90; and rhetorical stereotypes, 127, 129

deportment, xii–xiv; deceptive, 76–80; as a language, xiii; masculine ideal of, 60ff., 159; Quintilian on, 36n.82; and social class, xxvi

Dio Cassius, historian, 147

Dio Chrysostom (Dio of Prusa), sophist and philosopher, 14; compared with Favorinus, 131; exile of, 146, 149; on effeminacy, 68; on gait, 61; self-defense of, 150n.75; on snorting in Tarsus, 82–83; teacher of Favorinus, 146; use of paradigms, 151; use of personae, 150, 154, 156

Diogenes Laertius, xviiin.2, 132 and n.8, 140n.31

Dionysius of Miletus, sophist, quarrel with Polemo, 72

Dorotheus of Antioch, eunuch presbyter, 6n.23

Douglas, M., 7n.28, 161n.4

education, xxiii–xxv; elite, xii; and modeling of infants, 70–71; oral elements in, xxii; of women, 98–99. *See also* boys; girls; *paideia*; rhetoric; voice

effeminacy: concealment of, 76ff.; as a deliberate pose, 74–76, 134; and desire to please others, 65, 79, 125, 135; in gait, 63–64 and n.42, 107n.16; induced by avarice, 143; physiognomical signs of, 62ff.; as protection from punishment, 134 and n.15; in rhetoric, 84, 105ff., 127–30, 160–61; Seneca the Elder's view of, 108–11; Seneca the Younger on, 112–13; Stoic view of, 67–69; as uncontrolled pursuit of pleasure, 42. *See also androgynoi; cinaedi*

Ephesus, 22

Epictetus, Stoic philosopher, attacked by Favorinus, 144 and n.48; on effeminacy, 68–69; slides between constructionist and essentialist view of masculinity, 73

epiprepeia, 34–36

euergetism. *See* liturgies

eunuchs: bad orators compared to, 125; confuse categories, 133, 161; flesh of, 90; in Polemo's physiognomy, 46–47; as priests, 118, 161; rarity of, 6; as unclean, 133; voice of, 83, 91, 118–19. *See also* Dorotheus of Antioch; Favorinus; Lucian

exercise: effect on flesh, 85, 87, 90, 111; Galen on, 94; for girls, 95–96; gymnastic vs. military, 120; for men, 87ff., 143; passive, 87 and n.32, 93, 95, 111 and n.37, 112; reading as, 90, 92–93 and n.50; for scholars, 87, 111; singing as, 93–97. *See also* vocal exercise

Favorinus, sophist, xxiii; adultery of, 147; attacks Epictetus, 144 and n.48; attempts to avoid liturgies, 146; birth and background, 3–5; biography of, 136ff.; and breast-feeding, 141–42; not a *cinaedus*, 130; on competition, xxiii; *Corinthian Oration*, xii, 8–20, 149; daily lectures of,

MAUD W. GLEASON has degrees in classics from Harvard, Oxford, and the University of California at Berkeley. She teaches at Stanford University.

Lightning Source UK Ltd.
Milton Keynes UK
UKOW06f1529260715

255820UK00009B/157/P